Distributive Justice
and Disability

Distributive Justice

& Disability

Utilitarianism against Egalitarianism

MARK S. STEIN

Yale University Press   New Haven and London

Published with assistance from the Louis Stern Memorial
Fund and from the John K. Castle Publications Fund of Yale
University's Program in Ethics, Politics, and Economics.

Set in Minion type by Integrated Publishing Solutions.
Printed in the United States of America.

Library of Congress Cataloging-in-Publication Data

Stein, Mark S., 1958–
    Distributive justice and disability : utilitarianism against
egalitarianism / Mark S. Stein.
        p.   cm.
    Includes bibliographical references and index.
    ISBN-13: 978-0-300-10057-0 (alk. paper)
    ISBN-10: 0-300-10057-4 (alk. paper)
    1. People with disabilities—Services for. 2. Distributive justice.
I. Title.
HV1568.S698 2006
362.401—dc22
2005027744

A catalogue record for this book is available
from the British Library.

The paper in this book meets the guidelines for permanence
and durability of the Committee on Production Guidelines
for Book Longevity of the Council on Library Resources.

10 9 8 7 6 5 4 3 2 1

To Mom, and in memory of Dad

Contents

Acknowledgments

This book is a descendant of the doctoral dissertation I wrote at Yale University, Department of Political Science. I am tremendously grateful to Ian Shapiro, the Chair of my dissertation advisory committee, for his advice and support. Ian is entirely free of dogmatism, able to see the strengths and weaknesses in every approach. Without such an undogmatic advisor, I probably would not have been able to pursue my own dogmatic utilitarian course. Many thanks also to Rogers Smith and John Roemer, the other members of my advisory committee.

Thanks to the three once-anonymous readers who reviewed my manuscript on behalf of Yale University Press: Anne L. Astott, Ellen Frankel Paul, and Grant Reeher. Thanks also to Julia Driver, who did me the great favor of reviewing an entire draft of the manuscript. The book is better because of their suggested revisions; remaining mistakes are my own.

Many people have read parts of this book, in various incarnations, and have given me helpful comments, including Jim Murphy, Peter Singer, Greg Forster, Bruce Ackerman, Casiano Hacker-Cordon, Cora True-Frost, Eva Feder Kittay, Robert Cummins, Roger Gottlieb, Margaret Dancy, Udo Schuklenk, and Ruth Chadwick.

I would like to record a special thanks to the late great R. M. Hare. Many years ago, Professor Hare sent me a kind and encouraging note after reviewing a paper I had written on the use of examples in moral theory. Part of that paper survives in Chapter 2 of this book.

I am grateful to my editors at Yale University Press, John Kulka and Keith Condon, for their help and advice.

Financial support for this book was provided by the Lentz Peace Research Association and the University of Missouri– St. Louis.

Parts of this book have previously been published in article form. Chapter 4 is based in part on my article "Utilitarianism and the Disabled: Distribution of Resources," *Bioethics,* vol. 16, no. 1 (2002), pp. 1–19. Chapter 6 is based in part on my article "Rawls on Redistribution to the Disabled," *George Mason Law Review,* vol. 6 (1998), pp. 997–1012. Chapter 7 is based in part on my article "Ronald Dworkin on Redistribution to the Disabled," *Syracuse Law Review,* vol. 51 (2001), pp. 987–1014. Chapter 11 contains material from two of my articles: "The Distribution of Life-Saving Medical Resources: Equality, Life Expectancy, and Choice behind the Veil," *Social Philosophy and Policy,* vol. 19, no. 2 (Summer 2002), pp. 212–245; and "Utilitarianism and the Disabled: Distribution of Life," *Social Theory and Practice,* vol. 27, no. 4 (2001), pp. 561–578. I thank all of the aforementioned journals for permission to republish my work here. In addition, I thank their editors and referees for helpful comments.

At the beginning of my graduate school career, I had illuminating discussions on distributive justice with Amrit Singh. I believe I first conceived the argument that would become this book as a result of those discussions.

I am sure there are people I have forgotten to thank, and to them I apologize.

Distributive Justice
and Disability

I

Introduction

This book is about the contest between utilitarianism and egalitarianism. Utilitarianism, as a theory of distributive justice, tells us to help those who can most benefit, those who can gain the greatest increase in welfare. Egalitarian theories of distributive justice tell us to help those who are in some way worse off.[1] I advocate utilitarianism.

There is sometimes a convergence between utilitarianism and egalitarian theories; sometimes, those who can most benefit are those who are worse off in various ways. At other times, the theories diverge. One area in which utilitarianism often diverges from egalitarian theories is the area of disability.

I argue in this book that utilitarianism handles distributive issues involving disability better than do egalitarian theories. Egalitarianism would provide either too little help to the disabled or too much, depending on what is sought to be equalized.

An egalitarianism that seeks to equalize material resources would in general make no special provision for the disabled. Resource egalitarianism would not, in general, subsidize the medical expenses of poor people or pay for disability aids such as wheelchairs or guide dogs. Under resource egalitarianism, the disabled poor would be entitled only to the minimum income guaranteed to everyone in society; after spending that income on disability-related expenses, they would end up with a lot less than the nondisabled poor, and in some cases they would needlessly die.

On the other hand, an egalitarianism that seeks to equalize welfare would massively redistribute social resources to those severely disabled people who are considered to have the least welfare, such as, for example, young people with terminal cancer. Welfare egalitarianism would continue to lavish resources on the least-welfare disabled long after they ceased to derive much benefit from additional resources. In a welfare-egalitarian system, the nondisabled poor would be viewed purely as a means to increase the welfare of those with least welfare. The nondisabled poor would receive little, if any, help from the government, and they might even be subject to high taxes.

The common defect of egalitarian theories is that they are insensitive to relative benefit. Resource egalitarianism would distribute too little to disabled people who could benefit greatly from additional resources; welfare egalitarianism would distribute too much to disabled people who could benefit hardly at all from additional resources. By contrast, utilitarianism is completely sensitive to relative benefit. Utilitarianism seeks to place resources where they will do the most good. Only utilitarianism, or a theory with a large element of utilitarianism, can avoid both inadequate provision for the disabled and excessive redistribution to the disabled. Utilitarianism is the golden mean of distributive justice.

Because egalitarianism is insensitive to relative benefit, egalitarian theorists are driven to incorporate an element of utilitarianism into their theories: they are driven to distribute resources to those who are better off, by the lights of their own egalitarian theories, in cases where the better-off would benefit more. Sometimes this incorporation of utilitarian elements is done relatively openly, as by Amartya Sen; sometimes it is done in an obscure manner, as by Ronald Dworkin.

The foregoing assertions about egalitarianism and egalitarian theorists need to be backed up, of course. I hope to back them up, to the reader's satisfaction, through the course of this book.

I begin, in Chapter 2, by discussing some preliminary but important matters of method. Like many normative theorists, I test theories against each other through the use of examples. Many of these examples involve interpersonal comparisons of welfare. I argue in Chapter 2 that moral intuition can be confounded if the examples used to test moral intuition contain interpersonal comparisons that are merely stipulated rather than interpersonal comparisons based convincingly on the facts of the example. Thus, Robert Nozick's famous "utility monster" example evokes utilitarian intuitions and turns them, deceptively, against utilitarianism.

Though it is possible to employ such deceptive examples on behalf of utilitarianism rather than against it, I forbear to do so. When I adduce examples in which one person supposedly has more welfare than another person, or in which one person would supposedly benefit more from a scarce resource, I never stipulate that these interpersonal comparisons must be assumed by the reader as true; I always leave it to the reader to determine whether she agrees with my interpersonal comparisons, just as I leave it to the reader to determine whether she agrees with my intuitive judgment that certain distributive results are right or wrong.

In accordance with my belief that interpersonal comparisons should be convincing, I review, in Chapter 3, some empirical work on the relationship between disability and welfare. The common-sense view, reflected in the work of almost all distributive theorists, is that disability tends to reduce a person's welfare, and that the severely disabled have, on average, less welfare than the nondisabled. I generally endorse this view, with the reservation that because people have the capacity for hedonic adaptation, disability often may not reduce welfare by as much as the nondisabled observer might think.

I also briefly consider, in Chapter 3, the issue of what is a disability. There is no universally applied definition. Rather, the definition of disability varies according to the purpose of the inquiry. This book is a work of distributive theory; it is more about distributive justice than it is about disability. I use disability as a testing ground for utilitarian and egalitarian theories. In line with this approach, I take a broad view of what constitutes a disability. In my discussion, for example, cancer as well as blindness is a disability. Although my view of disability is broad, it is not idiosyncratic; I do not consider anything a disability that would not also be considered a disability by many other writers on distributive justice.

In Chapter 4, I discuss the utilitarian approach to disability and distribution. Utilitarianism seeks to maximize welfare. As disability tends to reduce welfare, measures to cure or ameliorate disability can substantially increase welfare. Therefore, utilitarianism will often endorse such measures. However, utilitarianism will not approve of aid to the disabled that would benefit them only slightly and would divert resources from alternative uses that could provide people with greater benefits.

I discuss at length, in Chapter 4, the argument, most identified with Sen, that utilitarianism would often allocate *fewer* resources to disabled people than to nondisabled people, so that the disabled would end up with fewer resources and *also* less welfare. This argument, I claim, is based on a fallacious exaggeration of the circumstances in which disabled people would benefit less from resources than would nondisabled people. In those unusual circumstances in which it is truly credible that disabled people would benefit less, I argue, it does not seem unfair to allocate fewer resources to them.

In Chapter 5, I discuss egalitarian approaches to disability and distribution. For the most part, my discussion of egalitarian theories in this chapter is thematic; I defer detailed consideration of specific egalitarian theorists until subsequent chapters.

Egalitarian theories vary along a number of dimensions. As already suggested, the key dividing line, as concerns disability and distribution, is the one between resource egalitarianism and welfare egalitarianism. I take this dichotomy from Dworkin. However, I give a somewhat different and, I believe, more natural meaning to the term "resources" than does Dworkin. Whereas Dworkin sometimes uses the term "resources" to mean material resources and sometimes uses that term to mean something else, in my discussion "resources" refers only to material resources.[2]

Like Dworkin, I use the term "welfare" broadly. In my discussion, a welfare egalitarian is one who is concerned not with resources, but with the benefit that people derive from resources, in the broadest possible sense. Sen says that he wants to equalize not welfare, but "capabilities" to achieve "functionings";[3] G. A. Cohen says that he wants to equalize not welfare, but "access to advantage."[4] I treat both Sen and Cohen as welfare egalitarians, as both are concerned with the benefits that people get from resources rather than merely with the equal distribution of resources.

As Ian Shapiro has observed, most contemporary theories of distributive justice can be described across two dimensions, according to the metric they use,[5] and the principle or function they apply to the chosen metric.[6] For utilitarianism, the metric is welfare and the function is maximization: utilitarianism seeks to maximize welfare. Welfare egalitarianism uses the same metric as utilitarianism—welfare—but a different function: welfare egalitarianism seeks to equalize welfare. Resource egalitarianism uses the same function as welfare egalitarianism—equalization—but a different metric: resource egalitarianism seeks to equalize resources.

Resource egalitarians and welfare egalitarians often raise issues of disability in their arguments with each other. The resource egalitarian contends that welfare egalitarianism, if taken seriously, could require virtually unlimited redistribution from the nondisabled to the disabled, in order to bring the disabled as close as possible to equality of welfare with the nondisabled.[7] The welfare egalitarian responds that a strict resource egalitarianism would allow disabled people no more resources than the nondisabled poor, even if the disabled would fare horribly without additional help.[8]

I conclude, in Chapter 5, that welfare egalitarians and resource egalitarians are correct in the criticisms they level against each other. Welfare egalitarianism does indeed require too much redistribution to the disabled, and resource egalitarianism does indeed require too little.

I next proceed to a detailed consideration of particular egalitarian theorists. I devote more space to resource egalitarians than to welfare egalitarians, as resource egalitarians make a greater pretense of putting forth distributive principles that rely not at all on considerations of relative benefit. In Chapters 6, 7, and 8, respectively, I discuss three of the most prominent resource egalitarians: John Rawls, Ronald Dworkin, and Bruce Ackerman. I demonstrate that these theorists must contort their theories in order to provide redistribution to the disabled. They must then contort their theories once more in order to halt redistribution to the disabled. Thus, resource-egalitarian theorists oscillate between inadequate redistribution to the disabled and excessive redistribution to the disabled. Only when resource egalitarians surreptitiously incorporate an element of utilitarianism into their theories do they reach an intermediate and satisfying position.

I devote greatest attention to Dworkin's theory. Dworkin's system of hypothetical insurance is a challenge to my contention that a pure egalitarian theory cannot achieve a position intermediate between inadequate redistribution to the disabled and excessive redistribution to the disabled. I contend that Dworkin's hypothetical insurance is actually a form of utilitarianism, akin to hypothetical-choice variants of utilitarianism offered many years ago by utilitarian economists John Harsanyi and William Vickrey. Hypothetical insurance is a rough and not entirely satisfactory way of distributing resources to the people who would most benefit from them.

In Chapter 9, I turn to the contest between utilitarianism and welfare egalitarianism. I engage with a number of theorists who adhere at least partially to welfare egalitarianism, including Sen, Cohen, Norman Daniels, and Martha Nussbaum.

No theorist even pretends to be a pure welfare egalitarian; all of the welfare-egalitarian theorists acknowledge, some more explicitly than others, that one criterion in the distribution of resources to disabled people must be the extent to which the disabled would benefit from those resources. The real contest, therefore, is between utilitarianism and a hybrid theory, often called prioritarianism, that combines elements of utilitarianism and welfare egalitarianism. As considerations of relative benefit will often be determinative in prioritarianism, as they are in utilitarianism, it is difficult to pose the choice between the two theories in a manner perspicuous to moral intuition. I offer some considerations on behalf of utilitarianism and against prioritarianism, but I cannot completely rule out prioritarianism as an appealing theory; I can only conclude that a plausible version of prioritarianism must be very close to utilitarianism.

In Chapter 10, I consider the problem of aggregation. If many small benefits sum to more than a few large benefits, is it right to help the many rather than the few? I argue that utilitarianism rarely produces wrong-seeming results in cases involving aggregation; we are rarely convinced both that the many small benefits really do sum to more than the few large benefits and that it is wrong to help the many rather than the few. I also explain, in Chapter 10, why the utilitarian commitment to aggregation allows utilitarianism to be more respectful of liberty than a pure egalitarian theory can hope to be.

In Chapter 11, I discuss the distribution of life. Utilitarianism is able to advocate substantial aid to the disabled based on the assumption that disability substantially reduces welfare: in view of this substantial reduction, some measures to cure or aid the disabled hold the promise of substantially increasing welfare. However, the assumption that disability substantially reduces welfare also suggests the possibly counterintuitive conclusion that disabled lives are less worth saving, on utilitarian grounds, than are nondisabled lives. So although utilitarianism seems to give the right answers in most distributive contexts, it may apparently produce counterintuitive results in addressing the distribution of scarce life-saving medical resources.

Peter Singer and other utilitarian bioethicists have accepted the conclusion that disabled lives are in general less worth saving than nondisabled lives. Singer et al. have proposed that disabled people should receive less consideration, in the allocation of life-saving treatment, than people who are not disabled (other than in their need for such treatment).[9] So, for example, a life-saving organ transplant should be given to an ambulatory person in preference to a paraplegic who would have the same post-transplant life expectancy, in order to maximize quality-adjusted life years.

I am troubled by the conclusion that disabled lives are less worth saving than nondisabled lives. I am not sure that utilitarianism requires us to discriminate against the disabled in the distribution of life; I offer an argument in Chapter 11 that utilitarianism does not so require. If utilitarianism does require discrimination against the disabled in the distribution of life, I am not sure that utilitarianism gives the right answer in all matters concerning the distribution of life. My advocacy of utilitarianism, then, is less confident in this area.

If the distribution of life poses problems for utilitarians, it poses even bigger problems for egalitarians. Any plausible theory in this area must take into account at least one form of relative benefit: life expectancy. In many cases, it seems right to give preference, in the distribution of life, to those who would gain the most life years. Egalitarian theories cannot do so. In addition, many versions of egalitarianism would appear to require that we discriminate in *favor* of disabled people in the allocation of life-saving medical treatment; to me, this policy would if anything be more counterintuitive than discriminating against the disabled.

While most of this book is an argument against egalitarianism, I should make it clear that I support the value of equality, in matters of distributive justice, in two ways. First, I believe that society should treat (at least) all its members with equal respect.[10] This does not distinguish me from other distributive theorists; as Sen has demonstrated, every contemporary theory of distributive justice can claim to be based on some notion of equal respect.[11]

Second, I am an economic egalitarian; I support measures to help the poor, both in my own country and in foreign countries where poverty causes enormous suffering. Economic egalitarianism is justified on utilitarian grounds because the poor can benefit so greatly from additional resources.

What I oppose is philosophical egalitarianism, or egalitarianism as a fundamental distributive principle—the principle that we should help those who are worse off, whether or not they can most benefit from our help. I claim that we should instead embrace the utilitarian principle of helping those who can most benefit, whether or not they are worse off.

II

Intuitionist Theory and Interpersonal Comparisons

Intuitionist Theory

Like many works of normative theory, this book takes an intuitionist approach.[1] I discuss situations, real and imagined, in which utilitarianism seems to me to yield just results and egalitarian theories seem to me to yield unjust results. I invite the reader to share my intuitions about the justice of certain results and further invite her to share my conclusion that these intuitions support utilitarianism. While I do not expect to convert opponents of utilitarianism into ardent utilitarians, I hope to convince at least some readers that utilitarianism is more intuitively appealing than they may have supposed.

This book is probably more intuitionistic than the work of most contemporary utilitarians. I am an intuitionist first and a utilitarian second. Over a wide range of cases, including the general distribution of resources between disabled people and nondisabled people, utilitarianism seems to me to produce just results. I am less confident of the justice of utilitarianism in other areas, including the distribution of life between disabled people and nondisabled people.

It is possible that not every reader will share all of my intuitions. In Chapter 5, I observe that whatever social minimum is established by resource egalitarianism, some people will not be able to afford expensive medical procedures that can benefit them greatly (such as dialysis or heart surgery), and others will be able to afford expensive procedures only by destituting themselves. To me, this is an argument against resource egalitarianism; it would not be an argument against resource egalitarianism to someone who felt that the disabled poor should receive no more resources than the nondisabled poor. I also suggest, in Chapter 5, that welfare egalitarianism would require excessive redistribution to those severely disabled people who are considered to have least welfare, in the form of medical research projects that are highly unlikely to succeed, and also in the form of outright income grants of millions of dollars. To me, this is an argument against welfare egalitarianism; it would not be an argument against welfare egalitarianism to someone who felt that justice requires virtually unlimited redistribution to those with the least welfare, even if the resources at issue could do much more good elsewhere. If a reader's intuitions diverged markedly from mine in one of these two ways, my normative arguments would probably be of little interest to her; perhaps she might still be interested in my analytic claim that in dealing with distribution to the disabled, egalitarians have smuggled into their theories a large unacknowledged element of utilitarianism.

Arguably, all normative theory makes some appeal to moral intuition and can have little force if the reader does not share the writer's intuitions on key points. This is certainly true of avowedly intuitionistic work. In her classic article on abortion, for example, Judith Jarvis Thomson compares the situation of a woman who wants an abortion to the situation of a kidnap victim who is involuntarily wired up to a talented violinist in order to save the violinist's life.[2] If the kidnap victim de-attaches herself from the violinist at any time within 9 months, the violinist will die.

Thomson invites us to share

1. her intuition that the person attached to the violinist should have the right to de-attach herself, even if by so doing she will kill the violinist;
2. her view that the situation of the person attached to the violinist is analogous to the situation of a woman who wants an abortion; and
3. her conclusion that women should have the legal right to have an abortion.

Suppose that one of Thomson's readers believes that the hypothetical kidnap victim attached to the violinist should *not* have the right to de-attach herself. Thomson's arguments will probably have little effect on such a reader, except perhaps to confirm the reader in her own view that abortion should not be permitted.[3]

Sometimes a reader's intuitions may converge with an author's on some points and diverge on others. I will offer many examples to support my arguments on behalf of utilitarianism. I hope that readers will share my intuitive evaluation of all those examples, but it would be foolish to expect total intuitive convergence.

Welfare and Interpersonal Comparisons

Like other discussions of disability and distributive justice, this book is filled with interpersonal comparisons of welfare (hereinafter IPCs). I will make both level IPCs and increment IPCs. A level IPC compares levels of welfare, while an increment IPC (sometimes also referred to as a "unit" IPC) compares gains and losses of welfare.[4] Suppose that A is dying of thirst, while B has a slightly dry throat. If I say that A has less welfare than B, that is a level IPC; if I say that A would benefit more from a glass of water than would B, that is an increment IPC. In this example, the person with less welfare is also the person who would benefit more from a scarce resource. That will not always be the case.

Now it is possible that someone (to whom I will refer as "Wiseacre") may doubt that a person dying of thirst has less welfare than a person whose throat is a little parched, or may doubt that a person dying of thirst would benefit more from a glass of water. I will deal with Wiseacre's skepticism later in this chapter.

There are various conceptions of welfare, and various different ways of making IPCs. Among contemporary utilitarians, the dominant conceptions of welfare, probably, are the hedonic account and the informed-preference account.[5] Under the hedonic account, positive welfare is a positive mental state or subjective experience, such as happiness or enjoyment; negative welfare is a negative mental state such as unhappiness or suffering. Bentham and Sidgwick were hedonic utilitarians.

Under the informed-preference account, positive welfare is the satisfaction of preferences, while negative welfare is the frustration of preferences. However, the only preferences that count are informed preferences. Someone may want to eat a certain fish because he thinks it will taste good, but having this preference satisfied will not increase his welfare if in fact eating the fish will make him deathly ill.

This book is not an attempt to resolve intra-utilitarian disputes. I will try to be as neutral as possible between these rival utilitarian views, but I should confess that I have considerable sympathy for the good old-fashioned hedonic account of welfare, insofar as distributive matters are concerned. The great credibility of the informed-preference account comes from its association with prudential choice. If someone has an informed preference for X, it seems a little ridiculous to say he should choose Y instead because it will make him happier. He knows Y will make him happier, but he still wants X; who are we to tell him he is wrong?

The idea of insisting on the hedonic account for prudential choice recalls the old joke about two revolutionaries in czarist Russia:

> "Come the revolution, we will all eat strawberries with cream."
> "But I don't want to eat strawberries with cream."
> "Come the revolution, you'll *have* to eat strawberries with cream!"[6]

Although the hedonic account may seem ridiculous and even offensive in the context of prudential choice, it does not seem so ridiculous in the context of interpersonal distributive judgments. Suppose there are two claimants for a scarce good. Person A has a more intense preference for the good (however that might be measured), while person B would obtain a greater increase in happiness from the good. It is not clear to me that the good should be distributed so as to maximize preference satisfaction rather than happiness.

In some distributive settings, the hedonic account and the informed-preference account may point in different directions. I will take notice of such divergences. Mainly, however, I will be interested in cases in which the hedonic account and the informed-preference account are in apparent agreement. To repeat an extreme example, suppose that A is dying of thirst, while B's throat is a little parched. It seems reasonable to say both that a glass of water would increase A's happiness more than it would increase B's happiness, and that A's preference for a glass of water is more intense.

Interpersonal Comparisons in Intuitionist Theory

There are two ways of making IPCs based on hypothetical examples: the right way and the wrong way. The right way is similar to the way in which we make IPCs in life. The author presents the facts of the example and concludes, based on these facts, that one person most likely has more welfare than another, or most likely would benefit more from resources. The reader can then evaluate the suggested IPC and can reject it if she finds it unconvincing. The wrong way, by contrast, involves something that one never encounters in life: a *stipulated* IPC that is supposed to be taken on faith and that may or may not be supported by the facts of the example.

If an IPC is convincingly based on the facts of an example, it may further our intuitive evaluation of rival theories; if it is merely stipulated, it may hinder intuitive evaluation. Suppose I want to test the intuitive appeal of resource egalitarianism against the intuitive appeal of welfare egalitarianism. I might imagine a situation in which there are two claimants, A and B, for a scarce resource. A has fewer resources and B has less welfare. Therefore, resource egalitarianism would tell us to

distribute the scarce resource to A, while welfare egalitarianism would tell us to distribute the scarce resource to B.

This hypothetical example involves a level IPC: B has less
welfare than A. If this IPC is convincing, the example may help
us to determine whether resource equality is a more appealing
goal than welfare equality.

But suppose the IPC is not convincing. Suppose I describe
a situation in which the *facts* seem to indicate that A, who has
fewer resources, *also* has less welfare. I then stipulate, at seem-
ing variance with the facts, that B, who has *more* resources, really has less welfare. For example, A, who is poor, is also physically disabled, appears to be emotionally depressed, is jobless,
homeless, and cut off from any family relations. B, who is rich,
is also physically healthy, shows no outward signs of depression, has a high-status job and also an outwardly happy family
life. But wait, I add—B actually has less welfare than A! Since
B has less welfare than A, welfare egalitarianism calls for distributing additional resources to B (rich, physically healthy,
high-status job, etc.) and away from A (poor, physically sick,
homeless, etc.). Isn't it obvious that welfare egalitarianism is
less appealing than resource egalitarianism?

The problem with an example containing such an unconvincing stipulated IPC is that we cannot be sure that our
moral intuitions are responding only to the *stipulated* IPC,
which is at apparent variance with the facts, and that our intuitions are not at all responding to the contrary IPC suggested
by the facts themselves. If welfare egalitarianism has intuitive
appeal, then facts suggesting that A has less resources and *also*
less welfare than B will enlist both resource-egalitarian intuitions *and* welfare-egalitarian intuitions toward distributing a
scarce good to A instead of B. If we then stipulate, at apparent
variance with the facts, that A really has more welfare than B,

we may be commandeering the intuitive appeal of welfare egal-itarianism and turning that intuitive appeal against welfare egalitarianism itself.

Unconvincing stipulated IPCs are often used in arguments against utilitarianism. As the above example shows, however, unconvincing IPCs can also be deployed against other theories. In Chapter 9, I discuss another example of an unconvincing stipulated IPC that could distort moral intuition, this time one that might be offered in *favor* of utilitarianism (illegitimately) and against prioritarianism.

The most famous and spectacular example of an un-convincing stipulated IPC is Robert Nozick's utility monster. Nozick writes that "utilitarian theory is embarrassed by the possibility of utility monsters who get enormously greater gains in utility from any sacrifice of others than these others lose. For, unacceptably, the theory seems to require that we all be sacrificed in the monster's maw, in order to increase total utility."[7]

Nozick's example is meant to test utilitarianism against rights-based theories. We think of a situation where some per-son would benefit more from resources, while other people have an asserted moral right to those resources. The example involves an increment IPC: the utility monster would benefit more from the unlimited sacrifice of others than those others would suffer. If this IPC is convincing, the example may help us to determine whether a rights theory such as libertarianism is more convincing than utilitarianism.

Of course, the IPC is not convincing. An unlimited sacri-fice of people for the benefit of some other person would mean a drastic reduction in aggregate welfare. Therefore, when we recoil in horror at the specter of the utility monster, we cannot be sure that our moral intuitions are responding only to the *stipulated* IPC, which is at apparent variance with the facts, and that our intuitions are not at all responding to the contrary IPC (massive reduction of welfare) suggested by the facts themselves. If utilitarianism has intuitive appeal, then facts suggesting that people have rights to resources and *also* that they will suffer horribly by making an unlimited sacrifice of those resources will enlist both deontological intuitions *and* utilitarian intuitions. If we then stipulate, at apparent variance with the facts, that the utility monster will actually benefit more than the sacrificed people will suffer, we may be commandeering the intuitive appeal of utilitarianism and turning that intuitive appeal against utilitarianism itself.

There may be some people, of course, whose reaction to Nozick's example is not based on this kind of phenomenological ju-jitsu; possibly some people find the specter of the utility monster horrifying only because it suggests a violation of rights and not at all because it suggests a massive reduction in welfare. But since it is also possible that the example provokes a utilitarian intuitive response and then turns that response against utilitarianism, it is not a fair example by which to test utilitarianism against a theory of rights.

I am not optimistic about my ability to convince normative theorists—especially those opposed to utilitarianism—that unconvincing stipulated IPCs are illegitimate. Some doubtless will continue to see nothing wrong in stipulated IPCs. Others, perhaps, will think that it would be illegitimate to use unconvincing stipulated IPCs against welfare egalitarianism and on behalf of resource egalitarianism (as illustrated above), and it would be illegitimate to use unconvincing stipulated IPCs against prioritarianism and on behalf of utilitarianism (as illustrated in Chapter 9), but it is perfectly legitimate to use unconvincing stipulated IPCs against utilitarianism.

So be it. I have explained why I believe unconvincing stipulated IPCs do not fairly test moral intuition. The better moral theorists, in my estimation, do not use stipulated IPCs.[8] In my examples I will also abjure stipulated IPCs, except to demonstrate why they are illegitimate. Just as I will submit my examples to the reader's moral intuition, I will also submit them to the reader's hedonic intuition (if I may so call it).

Here, then, is my response to Wiseacre, the character I introduced earlier in this chapter: You, Wiseacre, are not convinced that someone who is dying of thirst has less welfare and would benefit more from a drink of water than someone whose throat is a little dry? Fine; then you can reject my example. I do not expect hedonic unanimity, just as I do not expect moral unanimity. And I certainly grant that readers less frivolous than Wiseacre can take moral exception to my examples, or can take hedonic exception, or both.

Fanciful Settings

While I am committed to use IPCs that are convincing (to me, at any rate), I will sometimes situate my examples in an unrealistic setting. I will imagine, for example, that there are only two classes in society, that there is only one kind of disability, and so on. One reason I will use such fanciful hypothetical examples is in *order* to achieve convincing IPCs.

There is always some reason for caution when confronting examples that veer away from reality. Nevertheless, convincing IPCs in a fanciful setting, I would claim, are more reliable in focusing our intuitions than unconvincing IPCs in a realistic setting. Suppose that A is dying of thirst, while B's throat is a little parched. Both A and B have just arrived at a refugee camp, A having walked 100 miles across the desert and

B having walked from the other side of a small village. But wait! Person B (throat a little parched) is actually a "utility monster," so he would benefit more from a glass of water than would person A (dying of thirst). Here, the setting is more or less realistic, but the unconvincing IPC can confound moral intuition; it can illegitimately and misleadingly commandeer the intuitive appeal of one theory (namely utilitarianism) and assign it to an opposing theory.

On the other hand, suppose again that A is dying of thirst, while B's throat is a little parched. This time, A is located on the planet Zruk a thousand light-years away, while B is situated in the magical elven kingdom of Rivendell in the land of middle-earth. We can send a glass of water to A (dying of thirst) through a wormhole in space or, alternatively, we can send a glass of water to B (throat a little parched) by waving a magic wand. Here, the extraneous details do not add anything to the example, and may by their fanciful nature blunt the moral force of the situation somewhat, but they do not similarly risk confounding our intuitions.[9]

Examples Real and Hypothetical

Some of the examples in this book are real examples, in the sense that they concern policies that exist or might be adopted in the United States or other countries. Other examples are purely hypothetical. Hypothetical examples are a staple of distributive theory because they are often necessary to draw clear distinctions between opposing theories.

Many current policy disputes do not draw clear distinctions between utilitarian and egalitarian theories. In many cases, there are utilitarian arguments on both sides and also egalitarian arguments on both sides. One such dispute, for example, involves the employer's duty of accommodation under the Americans with Disabilities Act (ADA). Some conservative critics of the ADA have argued that the accommodation duty has actually reduced the employment rates of disabled people relative to the employment rates of nondisabled people.[10] I am skeptical of this argument.[11] But if it were true, it could support reexamination of the employer's accommodation duty on utilitarian grounds (because the losses of welfare may outweigh the gains) and also on egalitarian grounds (because some of those who are worse off are being harmed). If I were to take utilitarianism for granted and write only about the application of utilitarian theory, I would discuss such policy disputes. Since my goal is rather to test utilitarianism against egalitarian theories, I choose instead examples, real and hypothetical, in which the theories more clearly diverge.

III
Disability and Welfare

Both moral intuition and hedonic intuition can be influenced by our knowledge of the world. In this chapter I consider what we can know about the effect of disability on welfare.

First, what is disability? This is a surprisingly difficult question; there is no agreed-upon definition.[1] The Americans with Disabilities Act defines "disability" as "a physical or mental impairment that substantially limits one or more of the major life activities."[2] Under this definition, pain might not be a disability if it did not impair function. Indeed, one prominent distributive theorist—G. A. Cohen—has suggested that pain alone would not be a compensable disability under the theory of another prominent theorist—Ronald Dworkin, though Dworkin has recently rejected that interpretation of his theory.[3]

I consider pain to be a disability because of its negative effect on welfare. In a sense, then, my subject is not disability as such, but health-related conditions that might be expected to reduce welfare. In addition to disability narrowly construed, my subject includes pain, illness, and injury.

There are certainly differences between disability, pain, illness, and injury. My concern, however, is with questions that cut across these categories. Does the condition in fact reduce welfare, and if so by how much? Can we increase the welfare of people in the condition by allocating additional resources to them, and if so by how much? And so on. I will continue to use the term "disability" as a broad marker for my subject, but those who consider my usage inapt are free to read instead "health-related conditions that might be expected to reduce welfare" or "disability, pain, illness, and injury."

In discussions of disability and distributive justice, it is almost universally assumed that disabled people have on average less welfare than nondisabled people. Resource egalitarians assume that the disabled have less welfare when they claim that welfare egalitarianism would require virtually unlimited redistribution to the disabled. Welfare egalitarians assume that the disabled have less welfare in their criticism of resource egalitarianism for allocating too few resources to the disabled, and also in their criticisms of utilitarian policy toward the disabled (as discussed below in Chapter 4).

Does disability reduce welfare? I have not assumed the answer to this question by describing disability as a health-related condition that might be *expected* to reduce welfare. With this vague description I am expressing a common-sense view of disability, but common sense can be wrong.

Different disabilities have different effects on the welfare of people, and different people may also react differently to the same disability. Anecdotally, some disabled people have stated that they would "give anything" to be nondisabled,[4] while others have claimed that they would not choose to become nondisabled even if they could do so by taking a "magic pill"[5] or a simple medication.[6] The attitude of preferring to be disabled is perhaps most credible in the case of deafness, which for many is not just a disability, but also a culture. Indeed, some deaf people do not identify as being disabled at all.[7]

Some insight into the effect of disability on welfare can perhaps be gained from psychological studies that attempt to compare the welfare levels of disabled and nondisabled people. The psychological instruments employed in these studies do not actually use the term "welfare"; they seek to measure happiness, or subjective well-being, or subjective quality of life, or life satisfaction, or satisfaction with various life domains, or psychological conditions such as depression. I adopt these various terms where appropriate, but I continue also to use the term "welfare" as an overarching description of what is sought to be measured.

Physical Disability

The disability that has been most often studied in terms of its effect on welfare is probably spinal cord injury (SCI). If a single conclusion can be drawn from these studies, it may be that SCI victims do report lower levels of welfare, on average, than nondisabled people, but the difference is not as great as one might expect. Marcel Dijkers has summarized the literature on subjective well-being among SCI victims as finding that "subjective well-being among persons with SCI was lower than in the population at large, but . . . the difference was not dramatic."[8] Such findings have been interpreted by some psychologists as evidence of "hedonic adaptation," the ability of people to maintain relatively high levels of welfare in the face of adverse events that might be expected to reduce welfare drastically.[9]

Two caveats about hedonic adaptation among SCI victims should be considered. First, suicide rates among SCI victims in the United States are about five times greater than rates among the U.S. general population.[10] Second, while the self-reported welfare levels of SCI victims appear to be not that much lower, on average, than the self-reported welfare levels of nondisabled people, this *inter*personal comparison is belied somewhat by *intra*personal comparisons that SCI victims tend to make, given the opportunity, between their current level of welfare and their pre-injury level of welfare. I will review two famous studies in which this phenomenon occurs.

One often-cited study that appears to evidence hedonic adaptation is the article "Lottery Winners and Accident Victims: Is Happiness Relative?," by Philip Brickman et al.[11] In this study 29 SCI victims (11 paraplegics and 18 quadriplegics), 22 lottery winners, and 22 controls were asked to rate their present and past happiness on a scale of 0 to 5, with 5 representing the happiest state. As Brickman et al. explain, "respondents were asked to rate how happy they were (not at this moment, but at this stage of their life). They were also asked to rate how happy they were before winning (for the lottery group); before the accident (for the victim group); or 6 months ago (for the control group)."[12]

The mean present happiness of the victims was 2.96, and the mean present happiness of the controls was 3.82. The difference between the present happiness of the victims and the controls (0.86 on a 6-point scale) was viewed as surprisingly small by many, including Brickman et al. The authors note that "the [victim] rating of present happiness is still above the midpoint of the scale and . . . the accident victims did not appear nearly as unhappy as might have been expected."[13] On the other hand, Shane Frederick and George Loewenstein opine that a difference of 0.86 on a 6-point scale "seems to be a substantial difference, especially considering the tendency for subjects to avoid extreme response categories."[14]

In any event, the difference between the victims' *past* and *present* happiness was considerably greater than the difference between the victims' present happiness and the present happiness of the *controls*. The mean pre-accident retrospective happiness rating of the victims was 4.41, so the difference between their past and present happiness was 1.45 on a 6-point scale, which seems quite substantial. Brickman et al. describe the victims' high rating of their past happiness as a "nostalgia effect."[15] Brickman et al. appear to assume that the victims mistakenly inflated their past, pre-accident happiness. That could be, but it could also be that the *intra*personal comparison is more relevant than the *inter*personal comparison in showing how SCI affects the happiness of people.

Another famous study is the 1985 article by Richard Schulz and Susan Decker entitled "Long-Term Adjustment to Physical Disability: The Role of Social Support, Perceived Control, and Self-Blame."[16] Schulz and Decker studied 100 SCI persons living in the Portland, Oregon, metropolitan area. They administered to the SCI persons three well-established psychological tests that had previously been given to general-population samples. They concluded that the SCI subjects "reported a mean degree of well-being that was only slightly lower than that of other nondisabled adult populations."[17]

However, Schulz and Decker also asked the SCI subjects to compare their current life to their life before disability, and the answers to these questions suggested that perhaps SCI had lowered the welfare of the SCI subjects more than was indicated by their answers on the established psychological tests. Schulz and Decker constructed an index of five items, including two items that involved *intra*personal comparisons: "Respondents rated how good their current life situation was in comparison with those of 'most people,' 'others the same age,' and 'others with a similar disability,' and in comparison with 'their life before the disability' and with what it 'would be like without their disability.'"[18]

Schulz and Decker report that "for the three items requiring comparisons with other persons, the mean response was on the favorable side of the midpoint."[19] However, "for responses based on intrapersonal comparisons, the mean response was on the unfavorable side of the midpoint."[20] The mean response for the index as a whole was 14.9, very slightly below the midpoint of 15.[21] Therefore, the two unfavorable intrapersonal comparisons actually outweighed the three favorable interpersonal comparisons in their effect on the mean. Unfortunately, however, Schulz and Decker do not report mean responses on all five index items, so it is impossible to tell exactly how unfavorable the intrapersonal comparisons were.

Another question the SCI subjects were asked was, "Considering the best and worst things that could happen to you in your lifetime, where does your disability fit?"[22] Schulz and Decker report that "on a scale ranging from 1 (*worst that could happen*) to 5 (*best that could happen*), the mean response was 2.2."[23]

Nondisabled people may have an exaggerated idea of how drastically their welfare would be reduced if they became SCI victims. Studies that compare the welfare levels of SCI victims and nondisabled people are a useful corrective in this respect. However, the SCI studies may go too far in the other direction to the extent they suggest that SCI has on average only a slight effect on welfare.

Frederick and Loewenstein have pointed to the problem of "scale norming," using SCI as a hypothetical example:

> An obvious problem arises if factors that affect respondents' 'true' happiness also affect their use of scales. Suppose, for example, that a sample of quadriplegics and control subjects both rate their happiness as 80 on a 100-point scale. This number may accurately represent the happiness levels of the two groups. However, it may also overstate the happiness of the quadriplegics if they implicitly rate their own happiness relative to that of other quadriplegics . . . or elevate their current rating to reflect the contrast to their extreme despair immediately following the onset of their disability, or if they have adopted lower standards for the intensity of positive affect that warrants the rating 80. All of these forms of norming could lead researchers to overestimate the degree of adaptation to paralysis.[24]

The disjunction between the interpersonal comparisons made by SCI subjects and the *intra*personal intertemporal comparisons they also make, when given the opportunity, suggests that scale norming may in fact be occurring.

SCI is of course only one of many physical disabilities. I have discussed SCI at length for illustrative purposes; I will not attempt to canvass the results of studies involving all the other physical disabilities. It is worth noting, however, that while SCI is a relatively stable condition, many other physical disabilities and diseases involve progressive deterioration. Many psychologists believe that hedonic adaptation is more difficult in diseases that involve progressive deterioration, such as multiple sclerosis.[25]

Emotional Disability

Emotional disabilities, particularly depression, can greatly reduce welfare. Some psychologists go so far as to equate depression with unhappiness, though others reject such an equation.[26]

A large Finnish study of life satisfaction among 1,204 psychiatric patients (inpatient and outpatient) found relatively low levels of life satisfaction. As the authors report, "We found that psychiatric patients in general were rather dissatisfied. Depression was the major correlate of dissatisfaction, followed by lack of social support and low economic status. On the other hand, patients with schizophrenia were on average more satisfied than other psychiatric patients."[27]

The Finnish psychiatric study used a 4–20 scale, with higher scores indicating less satisfaction.[28] Subjects who record a score of 12 or higher are considered "dissatisfied." The same instrument had been used in a Finnish twin study, and the psychiatric researchers noted that the psychiatric patients were more dissatisfied than the twins: "We found that 52% of our patients were dissatisfied. In the Finnish twin study, the corresponding value was only 18% . . . Regardless of diagnosis, therefore, psychiatric patients are markedly more dissatisfied than members of the general population."[29]

Intellectual Disability

Intellectual disability (ID) is often lumped together with emotional disability, as in the reference to "mental impairment" in the Americans with Disabilities Act.[30] But while emotional disabilities such as depression clearly reduce welfare under any conception of welfare, it is not at all clear that ID reduces welfare. It is not easy to compare welfare levels of people with ID and nondisabled people, as people with ID may not understand scaled psychological tests, referred to by psychologists as Likert-scaled instruments (not that people without ID necessarily understand such tests either). In a recent study, Verri, Cummins, et al. dealt with this problem by pre-testing respondents with mild-to-moderate ID to "evaluat[e] the extent of Likert-scale complexity each respondent can reliably handle."[31] Verri, Cummins, et al. truncated their scales to match each respondent's capability, down to a two-point scale when necessary. Using this approach, they found that Italians and Australians with ID reported somewhat higher levels of life satisfaction than Italians and Australians without ID. However, they caution that the "magnitude of the [ID] satisfaction data . . . may be exaggerated as a result of the [truncated] scale characteristics."[32]

The finding that people with mild-to-moderate ID do not report lower levels of welfare than nondisabled people is consistent with common sense and common observation. Children with Down syndrome, for example, are stereotypically viewed as happy. Under a conception of welfare as happiness or life satisfaction, there is little reason to say that ID lowers the welfare of people with ID, though ID may tend to reduce the welfare of family members.

On the other hand, there are doubtless some people who would prefer to be depressed, paralyzed, and in pain rather than to be intellectually disabled. Under some kind of preference-based conception of welfare, then, we might say that the welfare of such people (from the perspective of their current preferences) would be vastly reduced if they became intellectually disabled.

Robert Cummins has hypothesized "the presence of a homeostatic mechanism that operates to control the human sense of well-being such that it generally remains positive."[33] He writes that "perhaps life satisfaction is controlled in an analogous manner to other homeostatic systems. Blood pressure, for example, is normally maintained within the very narrow range of 80–120 mmHg."[34]

The Cummins homeostasis hypothesis seems generally consistent with the theory of hedonic adaptation adverted to above.[35] Reviewing the effect of disability on welfare in light of Cummins's imagery, we might say that traumatic events such as SCI can shock the hedonic regulatory system, but that most people can recover a sense of well-being that is not drastically reduced. Progressive deterioration, in diseases like multiple sclerosis, is a series of continuing shocks to the hedonic regulatory system, which may make homeostasis more difficult to maintain. Depression is not just a shock to the hedonic system; it is a defect of the system itself, and so can drastically reduce welfare. Finally, intellectual disability does not directly affect the hedonic regulatory system at all.

IV
Utilitarianism and Distribution to the Disabled

I n this chapter I discuss some basic aspects of the utilitarian approach to the distribution of resources between disabled people and nondisabled people, and among people with different disabilities.[1] I do not try to resolve all the problems of utilitarianism.[2] I do, however, try to show that some of the supposed problems of utilitarianism are actually among its strengths. Though my focus is on utilitarianism, I also draw some contrasts between utilitarianism and egalitarian approaches.

The Greater-Benefit Criterion

Utilitarianism seeks to maximize welfare. The first-order distributive principle of utilitarianism is to distribute resources to the people who would most benefit from those resources, "benefit" being understood here as an increase in welfare.[3] Absent secondary considerations, the distribution of resources to the people who would most benefit from those resources will maximize welfare. I will refer to the principle that resources should be distributed to the people who would most benefit from them as the greater-benefit criterion.

The determination of who would benefit more from a resource involves an increment IPC. Because of the centrality of the greater-benefit criterion to utilitarianism, utilitarians are far more interested in increment IPCs than in level IPCs.[4] Suppose there are two candidates, A and B, for scarce good X. Further suppose that we know A would benefit more from X than would B, and that distributing the good to one of the candidates will have no welfare effects other than conferring a greater benefit on A or a smaller benefit on B. Then we can be sure that it would maximize welfare to distribute the good to A. We can be sure that distribution to A would maximize welfare regardless of whether A or B is at a higher level of welfare and regardless of whether the welfare levels of A and B can even be compared: a larger increase in welfare will always produce a greater sum of welfare than a smaller increase in welfare.

Harsanyi has often emphasized that the key distributive principle of utilitarianism is that resources should be distributed to the people who would most benefit from those resources.[5] The greater-benefit criterion also figures prominently in the work of Singer[6] and other utilitarian writers. Nevertheless, the centrality of the greater-benefit criterion to utilitarianism is insufficiently appreciated. Utilitarianism is the only theory that will always and only use the greater-benefit criterion to make distributive judgments, assuming again that the only effects of distribution on welfare are the benefits that people would derive from the distributed goods.

Many philosophers, including economists writing as philosophers, use the term "benefit" in the same way I do, to denote (or at least embrace) an increase in welfare. However, in the field of cost-benefit analysis, economists generally use the term "benefit" differently, to denote an increase not in welfare, but in wealth. While utilitarianism is a welfare-maximizing theory, cost-benefit analysis, as generally performed by economists, is a wealth-maximizing theory. Cost-benefit analysis can be useful to utilitarians, but cost-benefit analysis should not be confused with utilitarianism.

BOUNDARY PROBLEMS

Every distributive theory faces boundary problems. Who is to be included as a beneficiary of the theory, and are all to count equally? One boundary problem involves the scope of the theory across nations; another boundary problem involves the scope of the theory across species.

To its credit, utilitarianism is often associated with a concern to reduce all suffering, including the suffering of foreigners and non-human animals. Some utilitarians, most prominently Peter Singer, believe that utilitarianism should be applied universally, across nations and across species.[7] While other utilitarians are more willing to entertain a priority for humans over animals, and perhaps also for citizens over foreigners, it is safe to say that utilitarians tend to apply their theory more universally than do devotees of other theories of distributive justice. There has been some movement among egalitarian theorists toward an application of egalitarianism across nations,[8] but egalitarians on the whole are still less internationalist than utilitarians.

The utilitarian tendency toward universal application is not a matter of logical necessity. Rather, utilitarians tend to be more universalist because a universal application of utilitarianism is more plausible than a universal application of other theories. Resource egalitarians could advocate the equalization of resources across species, and welfare egalitarians could advocate the equalization of welfare across species. They do not do so because a cross-species application of their egalitarian theories would seem silly. It is not quite so silly to say that that the suffering of an animal is as great an evil as the equally intense suffering of a human being—though of course, not everyone would agree.

From a perspective that is impartial as between species, the suffering of an animal is indeed as great an evil as the suffering of a human being. From a perspective that is impartial as between nations, the suffering of a foreigner is as great an evil as the suffering of a citizen. The question posed by boundary problems is whether morality requires us to adopt these impartial perspectives. Boundary problems are thus different from most of the ethical issues discussed in this book; those issues assume an impartial perspective and ask what impartial morality requires. (We will, however, return to an issue of partiality—between self and other—in Chapter 5).

My own view on the application of utilitarianism across nations and across species is not completely developed. I am convinced that rich nations should do a lot more to alleviate suffering in poor nations (hence my advocacy of an international food stamp plan).[9] I am convinced that human societies should do a lot less to cause suffering among non-human animals. Beyond these relatively vague statements, I do not express a view on the application of utilitarian theory across nations and across species.

In my discussion of distributive justice and disability, I ignore inter-species issues. Further, I assume that utilitarianism and its egalitarian rivals would for the most part be applied within nations, not across nations. I make this assumption for simplicity of analysis, and also because it reflects current social reality.[10]

AMELIORATION OF DISABILITY

In the distribution of resources between the disabled and the nondisabled, the most important utilitarian consideration is the amelioration of disability. If resources can be used to cure or ameliorate disability, the disabled may gain a large amount of welfare from those resources. The potential for large welfare gains if resources can cure or ameliorate disability is implied by the assumption that disability makes a person's welfare lower than it would otherwise be. If paraplegia substantially reduces a person's welfare, then curing his paraplegia will substantially increase his welfare. Even ameliorative measures that fall far short of a cure can substantially increase the welfare of the disabled. If one reason paraplegia reduces welfare is that it makes it difficult for people to get around, the provision of wheelchairs to paraplegics can substantially increase their welfare, as can modification of their physical environment.

Some disabled people and advocates for the disabled believe that disability does not in itself reduce welfare; they maintain society's treatment of the disabled is what reduces their welfare. Utilitarianism can accommodate this view to some extent. The key point is that welfare has been reduced, whether by disability or by social treatment, and that welfare can accordingly be increased by various forms of assistance.

As resources used to ameliorate disability can greatly benefit the disabled, utilitarianism may support a redistribution of resources to the disabled, in order to provide those benefits. Of course, it must first be determined how many resources are necessary to provide a particular benefit, and how they could otherwise be used to benefit other people (including other disabled people). Motorized wheelchairs can provide great benefits to some paraplegics, especially if they cannot easily operate manual wheelchairs. But what if the resources necessary to provide motorized wheelchairs could instead be used to feed a large number of people who would otherwise live in a state of constant hunger? Utilitarians would then not necessarily advocate the provision of motorized wheelchairs.

In wealthy societies, it can hardly be doubted that redistribution is justified to provide relatively inexpensive aids such as wheelchairs, and even relatively expensive aids such as dialysis, at least to those disabled people who cannot otherwise afford these items. At some point, of course, the cost of aiding the disabled is so great and the benefit or expected benefit to the disabled is so small that redistribution is no longer justified. At that point, which may be the subject of controversy and difficult to ascertain, utilitarianism will call a halt to redistribution in favor of the disabled and will direct resources elsewhere.[11] As noted in Chapter 5, welfare egalitarianism will be unable to do the same.

One form of disability that is widely acknowledged to be inimical to welfare is illness.[12] As illness often greatly reduces welfare, medical care that can counteract the effect of illness often greatly increases welfare. Utilitarianism will seek to minimize situations in which people are denied beneficial medical care. Accordingly, there is a strong utilitarian argument for national health insurance, a health-care system in which the government pays the basic medical expenses of all citizens. Although I support national health insurance, I will not argue for it here; the utilitarian case for national health insurance depends on empirical matters beyond the scope of this book. It is obvious, however, that utilitarianism requires, at the very least, some medical subsidy for people who cannot afford medical care or who cannot afford private medical insurance.

DIMINISHING MARGINAL UTILITY
OF NON-MEDICAL CONSUMPTION

The potential of resources to ameliorate disability is, as I have said, the most important consideration bearing on the distribution of resources between the disabled and the nondisabled. A related consideration is that if disabled people spend some of their own money on medical and other disability-related expenses, they will have less money to spend on other things than nondisabled people who begin with the same income.

Most who would grant that interpersonal comparisons have any validity would also grant that as between a poorer individual and a richer individual, the poorer individual is likely to benefit more from an additional unit of income. This is the principle of diminishing marginal utility, a principle I have elsewhere defended.[13] Because the poor on average benefit more from additional money than the rich, utilitarians almost always support some degree of redistribution from rich to poor.

But what if an individual with a higher income has to spend most of her income for necessary medical treatment, so that she actually has less money, after medical expenses, than a lower-income individual? It seems reasonable that in comparing the incomes of two individuals to see who most likely benefits more from a marginal dollar, we should deduct income spent for beneficial medical care. This diminishing marginal utility of non-medical consumption has been pointed to as a justification for income tax deductions for medical expenses.[14] Amartya Sen makes a somewhat similar point from the perspective of his own "capabilities" approach: "Income is only one factor among many that influence the real opportunities people enjoy. For example, person A may be richer than person B in terms of income, and yet be more 'hard up' than B if a big part of her income has to go for medical attention she needs because of some chronic illness."[15]

We have reviewed two convincing and broadly applicable reasons why disabled people may benefit more from additional resources than nondisabled people. One reason is that disabled people may use additional resources to ameliorate their disability; another reason is that after using some of their resources to ameliorate disability, disabled people may have fewer resources left over.

BENEFITS TO THE NONDISABLED OF AID TO THE DISABLED

Often aid to the disabled benefits the nondisabled as well. Ramps designed to accommodate wheelchairs are more often used by people with baby carriages and wheeled suitcases. If special education and employment programs enable the disabled to work, society benefits in various ways. There is an insurance aspect of much aid to the disabled, as all nondisabled people are potentially disabled, and most nondisabled people become disabled to some extent with age. There is also a public-goods aspect of much aid to the disabled, in that many people want to live in an inclusive society. Such considerations are of course relevant to utilitarian distributive policy, even if the main issue is the extent to which the disabled themselves benefit from aid.

When Would Utilitarianism Distribute Less to the Disabled?

The major theme of this book is that utilitarianism is a golden mean between resource egalitarianism, which would distribute too few resources to the disabled, and welfare egalitarianism, which would distribute too many resources to the disabled. But it might be objected that there are circumstances under which utilitarianism would distribute *fewer* resources to the severely disabled than to nondisabled people, on the ground that the disabled would derive *less* benefit from those resources. The result, seemingly unfair, would be that some disabled people receive fewer resources and *also* have far less welfare than some nondisabled people.

The objection that utilitarianism would unfairly distribute a less-than-equal share of resources to the disabled is most associated with Sen;[16] it has also surfaced in the work of T. M. Scanlon,[17] Jon Elster,[18] John Roemer,[19] Marc Fleurbaey,[20] and Jerome Bickenbach.[21] I will argue that this objection is based on a misunderstanding of the circumstances under which the disabled would benefit less than the nondisabled from additional resources. In those limited circumstances in which the disabled really would benefit less from resources, I will argue, it does not seem unfair to allocate fewer resources to them.

LOW WELFARE DOES NOT IMPLY LOW MARGINAL WELFARE FROM RESOURCES

Egalitarian opponents of utilitarianism sometimes suggest that the physically disabled would as a rule derive less benefit from resources than nondisabled people. However, it appears that in making this suggestion, egalitarians fallaciously assume that low welfare implies low *marginal* welfare from resources. In his book *On Economic Inequality,* Sen considers an example in which "one person A derives exactly twice as much utility as person B from any given level of income, say, because B has some [physical] handicap." Fleshing out this example, Sen presents a diagram in which both B (the disabled person) and A have downward-sloping marginal utility curves for income, but in which "B's marginal utility schedule is exactly half that of A."[22] Accordingly, if B and A had the same income, A would always derive twice as much utility from an additional dollar as B. B would only derive as much utility as A from a marginal dollar if B had a much lower income than A.

As the utilitarian objective of maximizing utility is reached when marginal utilities are equalized, utilitarianism would in Sen's example require that B receive a much lower income than A. This result, Sen indicates, is doubly unjust: "Even if income were equally divided, under the assumptions made A would have received more utility than B; and instead of reducing this inequality, the utilitarian rule of distribution compounds it by giving more income to A, who is already better off."[23]

In Sen's example, B's *disability* is intended to support two assumptions about the relative welfare of A and B. First, B will always have less welfare than A, if B and A have the same income. Second, B will always derive less welfare from a marginal dollar if B and A have the same income. Only the second assumption—low marginal welfare from resources—is directly relevant to a utilitarian distributive analysis. The fallacy of Sen's example is that it glides too easily from the assumption of low welfare, which may be plausible, to the assumption of low marginal welfare from resources, which is not so plausible.

Suppose, with Sen, that A and B have the same income. They earn enough for basic necessities, with some additional income left over. Now suppose that the remaining income is enough for B, a paraplegic, to purchase a motorized wheelchair on credit (B cannot operate a manual wheelchair). It is easy to believe that B would derive greater benefit from the ability to move himself about than A would derive from any use he might find for his own discretionary income. Therefore, while B would (we may assume) have less welfare than A *at* the same income, he would not get less marginal welfare than A *from* his discretionary income; B's welfare from his discretionary income would in fact be *higher* than A's. Moreover, after spending his discretionary income on a wheelchair, B's income for non-medical consumption would be far lower than A's, so B would likely get more marginal welfare from any further *addition* to his income.

Or suppose that B's wheelchair is provided by the government, so that B can spend his discretionary income on other things. B and A both spend all their discretionary income on music; they are avid music enthusiasts. Assuming, once again, that B clearly has less welfare than A, who would benefit more from a marginal musical experience, A or B? It is certainly possible that an ambulatory music enthusiast would benefit more from music than a paraplegic music enthusiast, but it is also possible that a paraplegic music enthusiast would benefit more. The answer is not at all obvious.

In sum, Sen's stipulation that B is physically disabled gives us reason to believe that B has less welfare than A, but B's disability gives us no reason at all to believe that B derives less marginal welfare from resources. Quite the reverse: if all we know about A and B is that B is physically disabled and A is not, the reasonable assumption is that B would derive *more* marginal welfare than A from resources (at the same income), because B could use those resources to ameliorate his disability, and because having done so, B would have less discretionary income left over.

Sen's book *On Economic Inequality* was originally published in 1973; it was republished in 1997 with an "Annexe" by Sen and James Foster. In the 1997 Annexe, Sen once again uses disability-based terminology to criticize utilitarianism: "The utilitarian maximand discriminates against a person who is uniformly handicapped in converting income into utility (since she would be seen as an 'inefficient' utility maker, with a low utility-generating ability). The utilitarian logic is insensitive to the fact that giving her less income would *compound* the lowness of her utility-generating capacity: she would get a lower total income in addition to having lower utility *per unit* of income."[24]

If what Sen means by "a person who is uniformly handicapped in converting income into utility" is "a person who derives less benefit from income," his description of the utilitarian approach is technically accurate. However, Sen's terminology perpetuates the misleading impression, created in the original edition of *On Economic Inequality,* that a *physically* handicapped person is by reason of his physical handicap also "handicapped" in converting income into utility.

Consider again Sen's original example, as I have embellished it. Two people earn the same income. One, A, is not disabled; the other, B, is a paraplegic. I have suggested that if B uses his discretionary income to purchase a motorized wheelchair, he will quite plausibly derive more marginal welfare from that income than A derives from his own discretionary income. In that case, which of the two people should be considered "handicapped" in converting income into utility? It would be the nondisabled person, A, who is "handicapped" in this way. No matter what A does with his small discretionary income, he cannot possibly convert that income into utility as efficiently as B, who spends his discretionary income on a motorized wheelchair. Moreover, it is precisely B's *handicap* that makes him more efficient, or less "handicapped," in converting income to utility! The incongruity of these conclusions brings out the misleading character of Sen's terminology.

Depression

It will be granted, I hope, that physical disability does not as a rule imply less marginal welfare from resources, contrary to the careless assumptions of some egalitarian theorists. It might be thought, however, that the emotional disability of depression does imply less marginal welfare from resources. Here the issue is complicated, but there is reason to believe that this view of depression falls into the same fallacy just discussed, in a subtler guise.

Depression certainly implies a low *level* of welfare— more so, probably, than most physical disabilities. Does depression also imply less marginal welfare from resources? It might be thought that the welfare of those who are depressed is not only low, but also relatively fixed, that their welfare is raised less by good fortune and lowered less by bad fortune than the welfare of those who are not depressed.

There may be some truth to this view, but it is not shared by many psychologists and psychiatrists who treat and study depressed patients. Some medical professionals believe that good fortune can be a "fresh start" event for the depressed, and can help to raise them out of their depression.[25] Some also believe that bad fortune can make depressed patients even more unhappy, possibly leading them to suicide.[26] The psychological literature does not yield clear answers on these issues. Pending such answers, it would be rash to assume that depressed people as a rule get less marginal welfare from resources than people who are not depressed.

In any event, the same two factors that generally suggest that the disabled get *more* marginal welfare from resources also apply to depression. As depression manifestly reduces welfare, the use of social resources to cure or alleviate depression has a high social value. Few developments have so increased aggregate welfare (in wealthy societies, at least) as the introduction of drugs that for many can cure or alleviate depression. These drugs are often expensive, as is other medical assistance for the depressed, so depressed people may once again end up with less purchasing power than other people with the same income, suggesting once again a higher marginal welfare from additional income.

LESS BENEFIT BY REASON OF DISABILITY

It is important to clear away the fallacy that less welfare necessarily implies less marginal welfare from resources. Having done so, we can begin anew and look at the limited range of cases in which it is plausible that disabled people *do* derive less marginal welfare from resources than nondisabled people, because of their disability. In general, such cases involve specialized resources that a disability renders a person unable or less able to use or enjoy. Thus, for example, while there is nothing about paraplegia that renders someone inherently less able to benefit from money, there is something about paraplegia that renders someone less able to benefit from an ordinary bicycle: paraplegics cannot operate an ordinary bicycle. In cases where a person's disability really does disable him from enjoying a particular resource, it does not seem unfair, I believe, to discriminate against him in the allocation of the resource.

Suppose that two new patients enter a nursing home. One patient, B, is old and almost completely blind; the other, A, is old but not particularly disabled. The nursing home has two different single-occupancy rooms available. One room has a beautiful view, while the other faces a brick wall. Both patients want the room with the beautiful view. B can only barely tell the difference between the two rooms, but he is still slightly aware that one room has more light, and he prefers that room. To which patient should the nursing home distribute the room with the beautiful view?

Here, I would not think it wrong to distribute the preferred room to A, who would benefit more from it, even though A is already (I assume) better off. Similar examples could be concocted involving the distribution of gourmet food between the nondisabled and those barely able to taste; the distribution of fine music between the nondisabled and those barely able to hear; and so on.

More significantly, there are cases in which a person's disability, or the extent of his disability, renders him less able to benefit from specialized medical resources. Suppose that a poor country must ration rehabilitation therapy. One candidate for treatment is severely injured and could at most recover some slight movement with therapy; another candidate for treatment is less severely injured and could probably, with therapy, regain the ability to walk. It does not seem at all wrong to distribute the scarce treatment to the candidate who could most benefit from it, even though he is already better off.[27]

Strictly speaking, triage cases of the type just illustrated do not involve the distribution of resources between the disabled and the nondisabled. In such cases, the better-off person who would benefit more from the specialized medical resource is also disabled or sick, or would be so if we denied treatment to him. Nevertheless, triage cases of this type demonstrate that when someone who is worse off really would benefit less from scarce resources, it may seem fair to deny him those resources in favor of someone who would benefit more from them.

SAME BENEFIT, GREATER EXPENSE

What if a person's disability does not make it impossible for her to obtain the same benefit from resources as nondisabled people, but instead makes it more expensive? Surely, it might be thought, here is a scenario that supports the position of Sen and other egalitarian critics of utilitarianism. If disabled people need more resources to obtain the same benefit, then they are less efficient at converting resources to utility. Utilitarianism would therefore allocate fewer resources to them, and this result seems unfair.

In fact, utilitarianism does not always require, in a greater-expense case, that the disabled receive fewer resources. And when it does so require, I contend, the result does not seem unfair. In order to dispel misunderstandings about greater-expense cases, it may be useful to draw some sharp distinctions through the use of a paired set of imaginary examples. I will refer to these examples as Poor Two-Disability Society and Rich Two-Disability Society.

Poor Two-Disability Society

Let us first consider a greater-expense case in which utilitarianism would in fact distribute fewer resources those who are worse off. Everyone in society is afflicted with an incurable disease that if untreated causes severe pain for one day (24 hours) per month, 12 days per year. In this society, there is no scarcity of food or shelter, but there is a shortage of medical resources. Medical resources are centrally produced and centrally allocated each year. If medical resources were allocated equally per person, the amount of resources allocated to each person each year would be E.

Most people in society (the "less-disabled") can obtain one day of complete pain relief from an expensive drug, RX1, that costs 0.1E per dose. If the less-disabled were each allocated E medical resources, they would each get 10 doses of RX1 per year, which would provide them 10 days of pain relief per year. Because of the scarcity of medical resources, the less-disabled would still suffer 2 days of severe pain per year.

Unfortunately, 1 out of 11 people in society (the "more-disabled") can obtain no relief at all from RX1, because of an additional genetic disability. The only pain relief the more-disabled can get comes from an even more expensive drug, RX2, which costs E per dose. What is worse, one dose of RX2 will provide only one hour of pain relief to a more-disabled person. Accordingly, if the more-disabled were each allocated E per year, they would each get one dose of RX2 per year, which would provide them with one hour of pain relief. In that case each of the more-disabled would still suffer from 11 days and 23 hours of severe pain per year.

Here, the more-disabled are far less efficient at converting medicine to pain relief than are the less-disabled. It is 240 times more expensive for a more-disabled person to obtain one day of pain relief than it is for a less-disabled person to obtain one day of pain relief (24 doses of RX2 at E per dose versus 1 dose of RX1 at 0.1E per dose). Because there is a scarcity of medical resources, if we give one day of pain relief to a more-disabled person, we will be denying 240 days of pain relief to

less-disabled people. If we give one hour of pain relief to a
more-disabled person, we will be denying 10 days of pain relief
to less-disabled people. In this situation, it does not seem at all
wrong (to me, at any rate) to distribute all the medical resources to the less-disabled and to distribute no medical resources to the more-disabled. The less-disabled (10 out of 11
people in society) would then each receive 1.1E medical resources per year, which would gain them 11 days of pain relief
per year. The more-disabled would receive zero pain relief.

Intuitions about cases differ. Perhaps some readers will
believe that it would be right to devote some medical resources
to the more-disabled in this case, even though by giving one
hour of pain relief to a more-disabled person we will be denying 10 days of pain relief to less-disabled people.[28] I hope, however, that even readers who reject the utilitarian course will
concede that it does not seem obviously unjust.

Rich Two-Disability Society

Let us now consider a situation in which the disabled (or more-
disabled) are less efficient at converting resources to utility,
but utilitarianism would *not* allocate fewer resources to them.
Modify the above example so that society is far richer. It is still
240 times as expensive to afford a day of pain relief to a more-
disabled person as to a less-disabled person, but now there are
easily enough resources to provide every less-disabled person
with 12 days of pain relief per year; the major question of distributive policy is whether society should *also* provide each
more-disabled person with 12 days of pain relief per year, at a
cost that is 240 times as great, or should instead devote those
resources to some other purpose.

Now it is plausible and, I think, quite likely, that the
welfare-maximizing course would be to provide every more-

disabled person with 12 days of pain relief per year, because no other use of resources would provide as much benefit to people overall. Of course, we cannot be sure unless we know how else the resources might be used, but it is hard to think of any use that would increase welfare more than relieving every more-disabled person from 12 days of severe pain per year. In this modified example, therefore, utilitarianism would not allocate fewer resources to the more-disabled; it would allocate *240 times as much* pain-relieving resources to the more-disabled, per capita, as to the less-disabled!

How can this be? Are not the more-disabled in Rich Two-Disability Society just as inefficient at converting resources to utility as the more-disabled in Poor Two-Disability Society? The answer, of course, is that while the more-disabled in the second example are still less efficient utility converters than the less-disabled *on average,* they are no longer less efficient *at the margin.* After the less-disabled have already gotten full and cheap relief from pain, it is efficient to spend 240 times as much, per person, to relieve all pain among the more-disabled, as no alternative use of the resources would yield as great an increase in welfare.

Special Education in Rich and Poor Nations

I can offer another example to the same effect as Poor Two-Disability Society and Rich Two-Disability Society, one that does not have all the same thematic elements, but is a tad more realistic. In the United States, disabled children have rights to educational assistance under the Individuals With Disabilities Education Act.[29] Sometimes there is need for a sign language interpreter who interprets for only one child in a class. Sometimes an educational assistant is assigned to an intellectually disabled child—once again, on a one-to-one basis.

To the extent that they need one-to-one assistance, disabled children are less efficient converters of educational resources than are nondisabled children. However, disabled children are not necessarily less efficient *at the margin*. In rich countries, the provision of an educational assistant to one disabled child does not mean that many nondisabled children will receive no education at all. There are enough resources to provide a basic public education to all nondisabled children; the question is whether to devote additional resources to special education or instead to use those additional resources in some other way.[30]

I do not believe that the United States devotes too many resources to special education. This impressionistic judgment could be challenged on utilitarian grounds; some other utilitarian observer might think that if fewer resources were devoted to special education, those resources could and would do more good elsewhere. However, the opposing view certainly could not claim to be an obvious conclusion.

In many poor countries, by contrast, it is obvious that special education services of the type described—one-to-one assistance—can rarely be justified on utilitarian grounds. Of course, some resources of poor countries should be allocated to the benefit of the disabled in those countries (and some resources of rich countries should be allocated to the benefit of the disabled in poor countries). Nevertheless, many poor countries do not provide a primary education to all children. If the choice is between providing an educational assistant to one disabled child and providing a teacher to twenty nondisabled children, the teacher should be provided. In these circumstances, the disabled child who needs one-to-one educational assistance is inefficient at the margin, and it therefore does not seem unfair to deny extra resources to that child, in accordance with utilitarianism.

I suspect that when critics say utilitarianism is unfair in distributing fewer resources to inefficient utility converters, they are thinking, confusedly, of examples like Rich Two-Disability Society or special education in rich countries, not of examples like Poor Two-Disability Society or special education in poor countries. The critics do not really have in mind a case in which utilitarianism would demonstrably distribute fewer resources to the disabled, for example a case in which granting a benefit to the disabled would deprive many other people of the same benefit. Rather, they have in mind a case in which it would be more expensive to provide disabled people with a benefit that nondisabled people *already* enjoy. The critics cavalierly assume that utilitarianism would shortchange the disabled in this second kind of case. But it is simply false to think that the greater expense of providing a benefit to the disabled would in itself lead utilitarians to deny that benefit. The disabled are often more efficient utility converters at the margin even when they are less efficient utility converters on average. The question, as always, is whether the disabled will benefit more than the nondisabled from additional resources, and the answer is often "yes."

After all, the common case in which society allocates additional resources to the disabled in order to ameliorate disability can be seen as a variant of the second kind of greater-expense case. In order to move around, disabled people may need special assistance, such as wheelchairs or trained guide dogs. Undoubtedly, utilitarianism endorses the social provision of such assistance (at least to those who cannot themselves afford it). Such assistance brings great benefits to people and is relatively cheap. And yet, it is even cheaper for the *nondisabled* to move around; they can do so without help, at virtually no cost. Thus, almost all assistance to the disabled can be seen as the more expensive provision of benefits that the nondisabled already enjoy.

V

Egalitarianism and Distribution to the Disabled

There are many kinds of utilitarianism, but there are even more kinds of egalitarianism. The distinction I most stress in this book is that between resource egalitarianism, which would distribute too few resources to some who are disabled, and welfare egalitarianism, which would distribute too many resources to some who are disabled. The common fault of both these egalitarian theories is that they do not consider the extent to which people can benefit from resources. Because resource egalitarianism is insensitive to relative benefit, it distributes too few resources to disabled people who could benefit greatly from additional resources. Because welfare egalitarianism is insensitive to relative benefit, it distributes too many resources to those severely disabled people who are considered to have least welfare, even when they would benefit only infinitesimally from additional resources.

In this chapter I also draw a number of other distinctions between various egalitarian theories. This chapter is not intended to be a catalog of egalitarian theories;[1] I focus on distinctions that are most relevant to my argument. Many distinctions considered important by egalitarians are not particularly relevant to my argument. I note some of these distinctions, but only to show that my argument against egalitarianism is unaffected by them.

It may be useful, at the outset, to make a general tripartite distinction among egalitarian theories that is highly relevant to my argument, but that egalitarians themselves are unlikely to make. There are three kinds of egalitarianism. First, there are egalitarian theories that are so extreme that they lack even initial plausibility. Second, there are egalitarian theories that have initial plausibility, but lose that plausibility when one considers how they would deal with the disabled. Third, there are egalitarian theories that maintain plausibility in dealing with the disabled, but only because they coincide to some extent with utilitarianism, because they find some way of becoming sensitive to relative benefit.

As I discuss the problems faced by egalitarian theories, the reader may sometimes wonder: isn't this also a problem for utilitarianism? I keep this question in mind and draw some parallels to utilitarian theory.

My discussion in this chapter is thematic. Although I refer by name to a number of egalitarian theorists, I defer any detailed discussion of specific theorists until the next few chapters. As I demonstrate in those chapters, egalitarian theorists tend to compromise their theories when dealing with disability. Resource egalitarians find some way to distribute extra resources to the disabled, and welfare egalitarians find some way to halt redistribution to the disabled. Indeed, it is so rare to find a theorist who advocates unalloyed egalitarianism in dealing with the disabled that my thematic discussion here may seem a little surreal, especially with respect to welfare egalitarianism. Nevertheless, there may be some value in exploring what would happen if we actually tried to apply egalitarian ideas to the problem of disability.

Extreme Egalitarianism

One way in which an egalitarian theory can be extreme is if it advocates what has been called "levelling down."[2] A welfare-egalitarian theory might counsel us to reduce everyone's welfare in order to make welfare more equal; a resource-egalitarian theory might counsel us to reduce everyone's resources in order to make resources more equal.[3]

Another way in which an egalitarian theory can be extreme is if it does not limit itself to the distribution of material resources (what I am calling simply resources), but advocates also the redistribution of body parts. Some have suggested that a consistent egalitarianism would require the redistribution of one eye or one kidney from people who have two to people who have none.[4] Larry Temkin, who is an egalitarian, has suggested that a pure egalitarian theory would require that we blind sighted people. This proposal combines both kinds of egalitarian extremism: it would take away people's body parts, and it would make everyone, including the blind, worse off. Temkin does not of course advocate blinding the sighted; while he suggests it would be required by egalitarianism, he considers it wrong because it traduces other important values that he recognizes, such as liberty and utility.[5]

I am not too interested in the more extreme forms of egalitarianism. They do not have much intuitive plausibility, and I do not consider them to be serious competitors to utilitarianism. Thus, when I use the term "egalitarianism" in this book, I generally do not have in mind egalitarian theories that would require leveling down or the redistribution of body parts. Egalitarians generally do not advocate such things, and it is not my job to tell them that they must do so if they want to be "pure" egalitarians. It is only my job to tell egalitarians when they have departed from their own theories, as they themselves have specified those theories, in order to deal with the problem of disability.

The "leveling down" of welfare is not of course a problem for utilitarianism; the idea of reducing everyone's welfare is anathema to utilitarianism. Arguably, there may be unusual situations where utility would be increased if everyone's *resources* were reduced. I do not dwell on this possibility, however, as it seems farfetched and has not in any event been raised by opponents of utilitarianism.

The opponents of utilitarianism have on occasion argued that it could require the redistribution of body parts. This is a problem for utilitarianism, but not as much as it is a problem for egalitarianism. As regards body parts that are not necessary to life, such as one kidney or one eye, there are utilitarian arguments against redistribution that may not be available to egalitarians. The prospect of having their bodies invaded and body parts forcibly removed would cause considerable insecurity among many nondisabled people. People would go to great extremes to avoid or escape the obligation to donate body parts, giving rise to heavy avoidance and enforcement costs. Utilitarianism can take such consequences of body-part redistribution into account; egalitarianism cannot take them into account as long as people with no kidneys or no eyes would still be worse off than people with two kidneys or two eyes.

Opponents of utilitarianism also sometimes conjure up examples in which utilitarianism would supposedly favor the redistribution of body parts that *are* necessary to life; in the famous Transplant case, a surgeon can secretly kill one patient and use his organs to save the lives of five other patients.[6] I refer to this as the Karlovian Transplant Case, because one may imagine Boris Karloff in the role of the surgeon ("What I do is for the greatest benefit of humanity. Come, Igor!").

Once again, the Karlovian Transplant Case may be a problem for utilitarianism. But as noted below in Chapter 11, it is a worse problem for egalitarianism: egalitarianism might require a doctor to kill *five* patients in order to save *one* patient.

In any event, I am concerned in this book with egalitarian theories that do not support leveling down or the redistribution of body parts. Therefore, the most extreme form of egalitarianism I consider is a maximin egalitarianism that limits itself to the distribution of material resources. A maximin welfare egalitarianism would distribute material resources so as to maximize the welfare level of those who have the least welfare, regardless of whether those who have more welfare would benefit more from additional resources. A maximin resource egalitarianism would distribute material resources so as to maximize the resource level of those who have the fewest resources, regardless of whether those who have more resources would benefit more from additional resources.

The term "egalitarianism" has been given different meanings by different distributive theorists. In recent years some theorists have taken to using the term to refer *only* to a theory that would "level down," that would reduce the welfare of the better-off without doing anything for the worse-off, or that would reduce everyone's welfare to achieve greater equality. I do not adopt this usage, as it would exclude most distributive theorists who have considered themselves egalitarians over the years.

Moderate Egalitarianism

What about egalitarian theories that are *less* extreme than maximin egalitarianism? Mixed egalitarian-utilitarian theories are sensitive to relative benefit to some extent. They give some preference to those who are worse off, but they still distribute resources to those who are better off if the better-off can derive sufficiently more benefit from the contested resources. I take up the contest between utilitarianism and mixed egalitarian-utilitarian theories in Chapter 9. At this point, however, and throughout most of this book, I attempt to isolate the three theories at issue—resource egalitarianism, welfare egalitarianism, and utilitarianism—so that they reflect three completely separate distributive criteria: help those who have fewer resources, help those who have less welfare, and help those who can most benefit. When I use the term "egalitarianism" in this book, I generally do not have in mind a theory that mixes egalitarian and utilitarian elements.

Another way in which an egalitarian theory can be more moderate than maximin egalitarianism is if there are intermediate claimants for resources, between the best-off class and the worst-off class. Suppose we must choose, under welfare egalitarianism, whether to raise considerably the welfare of the class with the *next*-to-least welfare, or whether instead to raise only slightly the welfare of the class with the least welfare. Or, to make the situation even more difficult, suppose that the only way we can slightly raise the welfare of the lowest class is to *reduce* considerably the welfare of the next-to-lowest class. It could be argued that welfare equality itself, aside from utilitarian considerations, can justify avoiding a large welfare loss by the next-to-lowest class at the cost of giving up a slight welfare gain by the lowest class. If so, a greater-benefit criterion has been given sway in welfare egalitarianism, purportedly on egalitarian grounds rather than utilitarian grounds.

Unfortunately for egalitarians, there is no obvious stopping point. Under one conception of welfare egalitarianism, everyone but the person or class with the most welfare has an egalitarian complaint.[7] If we combine this view with the greater-benefit criterion, we get a distributive theory that is identical to utilitarianism in distributive matters involving everyone in society except the person or class with the most welfare. Resources would be distributed to the class with the next-to-*most* welfare, instead of the class with the *least* welfare, as long as the class with the next-to-most welfare could gain a slightly greater increase in welfare from those resources. While it is unlikely that anyone who calls himself an egalitarian would advocate such a system, there is no obvious way to limit the scope of the greater-benefit criterion once it is introduced on "egalitarian" grounds. We would probably end up with a theory that is identical in most respects to the mixed egalitarian-utilitarian theories considered in Chapter 9.

An egalitarian theory that incorporates some form of the greater-benefit criterion as a way of dealing with intermediate claimants for resources can achieve some plausibility and can sometimes be hard to distinguish from utilitarianism. However, if there are no intermediate claimants, such an apparently moderate theory collapses into maximin egalitarianism. Its sensitivity to relative benefit is lost, and it yields implausible results in cases involving disability. We can then see clearly that such an apparently moderate theory is plausible only to the extent it can coincide with utilitarianism. Later in this chapter I consider an example of this type, and I return to the issue of intermediate claimants in my discussion of Ackerman's work in Chapter 8. Throughout most of this book, however, I ignore the possibility of egalitarian theories that use a greater-benefit criterion to deal with intermediate claimants. Because theories more moderate than maximin egalitarianism lose their distinctly egalitarian character, I focus on maximin resource egalitarianism and maximin welfare egalitarianism. So not only is maximin egalitarianism the most extreme form of egalitarianism I consider; it is also, for the most part, the least extreme form of egalitarianism I consider.

At the beginning of this chapter I suggested that egalitarian theories can be divided into three types: those that are so extreme as to lack initial plausibility; those that appear plausible until one considers how they deal with the disabled; and those that maintain plausibility in dealing with the disabled by borrowing elements of utilitarianism. I have now narrowed my focus, at least temporarily, to theories of the second type: maximin-egalitarian theories.

Included in the set of maximin-egalitarian theories are leximin-egalitarian theories. Suppose that it is not possible to give any further help to members of the worst-off class. Does a maximin-egalitarian theory then proceed to maximize the welfare or resources of the next-to-worst-off class? Many theorists have thought that it should do so; they have given the name "leximin" egalitarianism to maximin-egalitarian theories that concern themselves with successively better-off classes after doing all that they can for those who are worse off.

A leximin-egalitarian theory still gives absolute priority to the worst-off class, as long as anything can be done for that class. If the treatment of better-off classes has any effect whatsoever on the worst-off class (which is usually the case), a leximin-egalitarian theory becomes identical to a maximin-egalitarian theory that has no concern at all for those who are not worst off.

Also included within the set of maximin-egalitarian theories are theories that consider it an egalitarian improvement to reduce the membership of the worst-off class. Suppose it is no longer possible to help *every* member of the worst-off class, but it is possible to help *some* members of that class, or to prevent some people from falling into that class. Should maximin egalitarianism seek to minimize the membership of the worst-off class? The leximin issue just addressed does not precisely answer this question. Even a maximin-egalitarian theory that was indifferent to the fate of everyone but those in the worst-off class could favor helping *some* of those in the worst-off class if it were impossible to help everyone in the class. And while a leximin theory certainly might consider it an egalitarian improvement to reduce the membership of the worst-off class, it need not do so.

To me it seems only logical that a maximin-egalitarian theory should seek to reduce the membership of the worst-off class if it cannot further help everyone in that class. I will not impose this view on my maximin-egalitarian friends, but I will take note, in subsequent chapters, of some situations in which this issue is relevant.

Resource Egalitarianism and the Disabled

Now let us return to our two main suspects: resource egalitarianism and welfare egalitarianism. Resource egalitarianism provides too little help to some who are disabled, and welfare egalitarianism provides too much help to some who are disabled. But the analysis of both theories is quite complicated. Both can be specified in different ways.

One element that divides resource-egalitarian theories is how ambitious they are in maintaining resource equality on an ongoing basis. The least ambitious resource-egalitarian theory is what Dworkin has called the "starting-gate theory of fairness."[8] There is an initial equal distribution and no subsequent redistribution; one could say there is egalitarianism at T1 and libertarianism thereafter. At the other end of the spectrum is a theory like Rawls's, that continually redistributes income so as to maximize the resources of the least-advantaged class. In the middle are theories that call for an initial equal distribution and redistribution upon the death of old citizens and the birth of new ones.[9] Or perhaps there is a redistributive social minimum, as with Rawls, but it is not available to people who had the opportunity to earn more than the social minimum and squandered that opportunity.

There is also a time dimension to the very definition of resource equality. Probably the predominant temporal approach of resource egalitarians is to equalize total resources over a complete life. Other possible approaches are to equalize average resources over a complete life, or to equalize resources in every year.

All such resource-egalitarian theories are vulnerable to the criticism that they distribute too few resources to disabled people who could benefit greatly from additional resources. To be sure, resource egalitarianism would actually *help* many disabled people in comparison with current distributive regimes. There are doubtless disabled people in many countries, perhaps all countries, who have fewer resources devoted to them than what a resource-egalitarian system would provide. But many disabled people would also doubtless do worse under any resource-egalitarian system than they do now.

In general, resource egalitarianism can compensate the disabled for an inability to work, but it cannot compensate them for medical expenses. The precise amount of help available to the disabled, in a resource-egalitarian system, depends

in part on the nature of the disability and on the version of resource egalitarianism that the system embodies. I begin by
considering the help that a resource-egalitarian system can give
to people with disabilities that are not life-threatening.

Resource egalitarianism will provide a minimum income.
The disabled poor, as well as the nondisabled poor, will receive
income subsidies to raise them to the level of the minimum income. In one respect, the disabled poor will actually receive a
kind of preference. If the system is sensitive to issues of opportunity, some of the nondisabled poor will not receive the
full minimum income; people of working age who fail to work
will generally receive no income subsidy, or will receive a reduced income subsidy. The disabled poor will generally be immune from this penalty; if someone is unable to work because
of disability, he will receive the full minimum income even
without working.

The problem for resource egalitarianism is that if the disabled poor are compensated for medical and other disability-
related expenses, they would receive more resources than
nondisabled poor people who receive the full minimum income. Any special government expenditures on behalf of the
disabled would tend to reduce the funds available to pay general income subsidies to the poor. By paying special subsidies
to the disabled, a resource-egalitarian system would move away
from resource equality.

Some resource inequalities are permitted in a resource-
egalitarian system: those inequalities that raise the income of
those who have least income. I assume, with most egalitarians,
that a resource-egalitarian system will not achieve, or even aim
for, full resource equality. Some market-driven inequality will
be permitted in order to maintain incentives for production;
there will be some limit to redistribution corresponding to

Rawls's difference principle. Could subsidies for the disabled be similarly justified under a productivity rationale?

An initial problem with the productivity rationale for subsidies to the disabled is that even a resource-egalitarian system that permits market inequalities might not permit differential subsidies. In many resource-egalitarian theories, there is a strong view that the government should not encourage or discourage, by subsidy or penalty, particular uses of resources. People should be free to do whatever they like with their equal resource allotments. But I will assume that the system evaluates subsidies to the disabled under the same criterion as market-driven inequalities: if a subsidy raises the minimum income affordable to the poorest citizens, the subsidy should be given.

Even so, the scope for redistribution to the disabled would be very narrow. Any dollar paid out to support the disabled would be a dollar less available for general income subsidies. So aid to the disabled would have to more than pay for itself in the amount of money generated for general income subsidies. This is a demanding standard; it would exclude even most aid to the working disabled and would especially preclude aid to the non-working disabled. In sum, people who have non-life-threatening disabilities would likely receive little help, in a resource-egalitarian system, beyond the general income subsidy.

For life-threatening disabilities, the scope of redistribution to the disabled may be greater. A resource-egalitarian system that seeks to equalize total resources over a complete life will seek to keep people from dying before they receive a minimum lifetime income. A complete-life total resource egalitarianism will be especially solicitous of young people who have life-threatening or terminal conditions. A person who dies young has usually received, by the time of death, far less than the lifetime minimum income. A complete-life total resource

egalitarianism will seek to avoid this great inequality by chan-
neling extra resources to young people facing death. If the
young people facing death have a medical condition that can
be cured with expensive care, they may fortuitously receive
enough resources to obtain a cure. If the young people facing
death have a medical condition that cannot be cured, they may
receive a large cash grant.

Here we can see, incidentally, something of a convergence
between welfare egalitarianism and the version of resource
egalitarianism that seeks to equalize total resources over a complete life. While the general problem of resource egalitarianism is that it distributes too few resources to the disabled, a
complete-life total resource egalitarianism would distribute too
many resources to some young people with terminal conditions. Suppose that a twenty-year-old poor person is terminally ill. Nothing can be done to prolong his life. He is receiving medical care, but it is not very expensive, and further care
will not be very beneficial. In such a case, complete-life total
resource egalitarianism would be moved to make a large cash
grant to the terminally ill young person to bring him up to the
minimum lifetime income before he dies. In a rich country,
such as the United States, such a cash grant could total in the
hundreds of thousands of dollars. This redistribution to the
terminally ill young seems excessive. Of course, it is not *as* excessive as the redistribution that the terminally ill young might
receive under welfare egalitarianism. The limit to resource-
egalitarian redistribution would be the lifetime minimum income; the limit to welfare-egalitarian redistribution would be
much higher, as discussed below.

In any event, the more serious problem, even under complete-life total resource egalitarianism, is not excessive redistribution to those with fatal and incurable medical conditions,

but inadequate redistribution to those with life-threatening but curable conditions. Suppose that a person has a life-threatening illness that *can* be successfully treated. If she has already received, throughout her life, more than the minimum lifetime income, she likely would receive no help under a resource-egalitarian system. The system would pay to keep her alive only if it could use her as a means to increase the guaranteed lifetime income for everyone, if it could more than make up for the cost of treatment by collecting future taxes from her.

Under other temporal versions of resource egalitarianism, there often would be even less scope for helping those with life-threatening conditions. Take, for example, a system that tries to equalize average yearly resources over a complete life rather than total resources over a complete life. Such a resource-egalitarian system would generally not provide help even to a young person with a life-threatening illness if she had already received, on average, more than the minimum income for the years she had been alive. As before, resource egalitarianism would help such a disabled person only if it could use her as a means to increase the average lifetime income for everyone.

Under every version of resource egalitarianism, poor disabled people who are uninsured or underinsured would be forced to spend their own money on highly beneficial medical care and other aids. After paying for these items, the disabled poor would be left with less money than the nondisabled poor. Some expensive life-saving and life-improving care, such as dialysis and heart surgery, might be completely beyond the reach of the disabled poor (and "poor" here includes people who were not poor to begin with, but who exhausted their resources to pay for medical care). Under resource egalitarianism, there would be unnecessary suffering and unnecessary death.

Many, I'm sure, would find resource egalitarianism appealing if only it could provide greater help to the disabled, and in particular if it could subsidize the medical expenses of (at least) the disabled poor. Let us therefore look more closely to see if there is any way for a resource-egalitarian system to accomplish this objective. First, however, let us examine the impulse to provide additional resources to the disabled in a resource-egalitarian system. If you are a resource egalitarian, you believe that resources should be distributed equally regardless of differences in the benefit people get from resources, and regardless of differences in their level of welfare. Either you do not care about these differences, or you believe they cannot be measured, or you believe they are irrelevant to distributive justice. Why, then, would you want to distribute extra resources to the disabled? Is it not obvious that it is because the disabled would benefit more from additional resources, or because they have less welfare, or both?. On the face of it, the impulse to distribute additional resources to the disabled is an impulse to move away from resource egalitarianism toward utilitarianism, or welfare egalitarianism, or some mix of the two.

Could a resource-egalitarian system attend to the medical needs of the disabled by giving everyone an "equal" entitlement to medical care rather than an equal amount of cash? This question is relevant to Dworkin's system of hypothetical insurance, discussed in Chapter 7, and also to the modified difference principle that Rawls advances in *Justice as Fairness: A Restatement,* discussed in Chapter 6. The short answer to the question is no: universal medical coverage is not a genuine resource-egalitarian scheme. Under any system of universal medical coverage, benefits will be distributed unequally. Those who obtain covered medical treatment will receive more resources than the nondisabled poor; often, they will receive more than the lifetime average income. As a system of universal medical coverage distributes medical resources unequally, "equal entitlement to medical care" means unequal entitlement to resources.

It might be argued that while the distribution of resources in a system of universal medical coverage is unequal when benefits are received, it is equal "ex ante," when people receive the entitlement to medical care, at birth or before. At that time, it is not known how much medical care people will need. But this argument proves too much. With such an "ex ante" perspective, we could say that any unequal distribution of resources, based on any eventuality of life, is really an equal distribution of resources.

We could say, for example, that the government maintains equality of resources when it pays a one million dollar bonus to every person who grows to be taller than seven feet. Suppose the government entered into an arrangement with insurance companies in which it made an equal premium payment, on behalf of all newly conceived persons, that guaranteed a payment of one million dollars to every person who exceeded the height of seven feet. All of this rigmarole would not change the reality that the government had instituted a resource inequality benefiting people taller than seven feet (and also, perhaps, benefiting insurance companies).

It might be objected that no one ever really has an equal chance of exceeding seven feet in height. Some people have genes that predispose them to be tall, and of course men are usually taller than women. But a similar objection could be leveled against the pretense that people have an equal chance of receiving medical resources under a system of universal medical coverage. Some people have genes that predispose them to suffer from expensive illness.

Universal medical coverage is a sensible idea, whereas

million-dollar bonuses for people who are taller than seven feet is a silly idea. But that does not mean that universal medical coverage is a kind of equality of resources; it is a sensible, rather than silly, inequality of resources.

Let us try another tack in our attempt to make resource egalitarianism more favorable to the disabled. Maybe medical care is a special use of resources, one that should not be counted when we determine a person's resource share. In Chapter 4, I discussed two important reasons why utilitarianism is inclined to help the disabled. First, medical care and other disability aids can often greatly benefit the disabled. Second, after spending some of their own money on these highly beneficial items, poor disabled people have less money than poor nondisabled people who started out with the same income; therefore, poor disabled people would benefit more from additional money.

Resource egalitarianism cannot rely on the first of these two grounds: It is committed to distributing resources equally regardless of whether some people benefit more from additional resources than other people. But what about the second? If a poor disabled person has to pay medical expenses, isn't she really poorer than a nondisabled person with the same income?

The problem is that the second ground alone does not distinguish between medical expenses and other expenses. A poor person who spends half his income gambling at a casino is left with the same resources as a poor person who spends half his income on medical care. A utilitarian system will subsidize medical care and not gambling because medical care is more beneficial to people. Resource egalitarianism cannot make this distinction.

The negative verdict on resource egalitarianism stands. Resource egalitarianism means unnecessary suffering and unnecessary death. Suffering and death will of course occur under any system, including utilitarianism. However, utilitarianism is committed to preventing these harms if prevention can be achieved without causing greater harm. Resource egalitarianism would permit suffering and death even if the cost of avoiding them was relatively low.

I have so far neglected an argument against resource egalitarianism that is commonly put forward by utilitarians and others. Resource egalitarianism, its opponents argue, can result in redistribution to the poor that is vastly resource-inefficient and also welfare-inefficient.[10] Suppose a resource-egalitarian system with market-driven inequalities that have been thought necessary to maximize the resource holdings of the poorest class. Suddenly it is discovered that with massive redistribution from the great majority of citizens, it is possible to achieve a further, very tiny increase in the resources of the poorest class. Even though the new scheme is vastly inefficient, it must be put into place: under a resource-egalitarian system, even the tiniest gain to the poorest class must be seized, whatever the cost to others.

I actually do consider this a telling argument against resource egalitarianism and in favor of utilitarianism. Utilitarianism itself would permit *some* resource-inefficient redistribution. Because the poor benefit more from additional money than do the rich, utilitarianism would endorse redistributive schemes in which there is some leakage of resources in the course of redistribution from rich to poor. But utilitarianism would not permit welfare-inefficient redistribution; it would only endorse redistributive schemes in which, despite the leakage of resources, the poor still gain more welfare than the rich lose (and there are no other negative effects of redistribution to offset the net gain in welfare). A redistributive scheme that is vastly resource-inefficient would probably be welfare-inefficient as well, especially if the poor have attained a moderate standard of living.

Nevertheless, there are drawbacks to the argument conjuring up a sudden and vastly inefficient resource-egalitarian redistribution. Such arguments have a bad pedigree. They recall false predictions of disastrous effects made by opponents of greater redistribution. The most prominent recent example in the United States involved President Clinton's 1993 budget, which raised income taxes on richer Americans. Republican opponents of Clinton confidently predicted disaster, but instead the 1993 tax hike on the rich ushered in a period of great prosperity. There are issues here that go far beyond the scope of this book, but the upshot is that the scenario of a sudden and vastly inefficient redistribution is one that might possibly occur under resource egalitarianism, not one that would certainly or even probably occur.

The intuitive selling point of utilitarianism is that often it seems right to distribute resources to those who will most benefit; when opposing theories require distribution away from those who will most benefit, they often seem wrong. But to fully evoke utilitarian moral intuition against an opposing theory, we must also have the appropriate hedonic intuition: we must believe that the opposing theory really does distribute resources away from those who will most benefit. As argued in Chapter 2, this hedonic conclusion must be based on the facts of the case, not on bald stipulation.

The hypothesis of a sudden and vastly inefficient redistributive scheme purports to be a case where resource egalitarianism takes resources from those who would benefit more (the rich), destroys most of those resources, and distributes a tiny remnant to those who would benefit less (the poor). We may not be convinced, however. Because the assumption of vast inefficiency is speculative and freighted with associations to discredited claims, it may be difficult to summon up the hedonic intuition that the rich really do lose more, in welfare, than the poor gain.

In the area of disability, by contrast, the interpersonal comparisons can be immediately convincing. Resource egalitarianism would deny additional resources to some disabled people who would die or be in horrible pain without those additional resources; resource egalitarianism would distribute the resources instead to the nondisabled poor, who would benefit less. We do not have to hypothesize a vast leakage of resources in the course of redistribution; we do not have to hypothesize any leakage at all.

Resource egalitarianism would make more sense if people were basically alike and their life situations were basically similar. In that event, people would get more or less the same benefit from resources. Even if there were some minor differences, it would not be worthwhile to investigate them for purposes of varying resource holdings.

Interestingly, resource egalitarians do not argue for their theory on the ground that people are alike; they argue for it on the ground that people are very different. People are so, so, different, the resource egalitarian tells us, that it is impossible to make interpersonal comparisons of welfare among them. How can we tell whether a pacific nature lover would get more benefit from additional resources than a competitive sportsman?[11] All we can measure about people, with respect to distributive justice, is how much material resources they have. Therefore, we might as well divide resources equally.

The problem for resource egalitarianism is that it breaks down when it encounters people who really are convincingly different. When we add to the pacific nature lover and the competitive sportsman a third candidate for additional resources, one who would die or be in horrible pain without them, interpersonal comparison is suddenly quite easy. So while resource egalitarians argue for their theory on the ground that people are different, the intuitive appeal of resource egalitarianism seems to rest on our assumption that most people are really the same. When that assumption is convincingly refuted, as with disabled people who could clearly benefit more than others from additional resources, the intuitive appeal of resource egalitarianism disappears.

Welfare Egalitarianism and the Disabled

If resource egalitarianism would distribute too few resources to disabled people who could benefit greatly from additional resources, welfare egalitarianism would distribute too many resources to disabled people who could benefit only infinitesimally from additional resources. This criticism applies to all varieties of welfare egalitarianism.

The theorists that I class as welfare egalitarians do not all describe themselves as welfare egalitarians. Sen advocates equality of "capabilities" to achieve "functionings,"[12] and G. A. Cohen advocates equality of "access to advantage."[13] Richard Arneson at one time advocated equality of "opportunity for welfare."[14]

These distinctions do not matter much in the context of distribution to the disabled. All such theories are vulnerable to the criticism that they set no acceptable limit on redistribution to the disabled. Equality of capabilities to achieve functionings would result in excessive redistribution of resources from the nondisabled to the disabled, as would equality of access to advantage, as would equality of opportunity for welfare.

A number of welfare-egalitarian theorists, including Sen, Cohen, Arneson, and Roemer, stress issues of opportunity and responsibility. The idea, once again, is that we will raise the welfare of people who did not have the opportunity to raise their own welfare. But of course, denying redistribution to people who are responsible for their own low welfare does not limit redistribution to the disabled, except perhaps in circumstances where we might blame the disabled for causing their own disability. Opportunity and responsibility may be very relevant to some issues treated by welfare egalitarians, but these concepts do not help welfare egalitarians to avoid unlimited redistribution to those disabled people who have very low welfare through no fault of their own. Just as a sensitivity to opportunity does not enable resource egalitarians to avoid inadequate redistribution to the disabled, a sensitivity to opportunity does not enable welfare egalitarians to avoid excessive redistribution to the disabled.

EXTENT OF WELFARE-EGALITARIAN REDISTRIBUTION

Many theorists, including some welfare egalitarians, agree that a pure welfare egalitarianism would entail excessive redistribution to the disabled. Assessing the manner and extent of such redistribution, however, is a complicated matter. Before addressing this matter I will describe three different kinds of redistribution that now benefit the disabled in many countries, and that could have a place under any welfare-egalitarian system.

First, there is unconditional income or wealth redistribution; the disabled are given additional resources to use however they see fit. In a hypothetical initial distribution, this might be the only kind of redistribution or (more accurately) more-than-equal distribution to the disabled. The disabled would get extra manna, or clamshells, or dollars, or whatever.

Second, there is medical redistribution, which would involve medical research and the provision or reimbursement of medical and rehabilitative goods and services. Third, there is environmental redistribution; society might spend resources to alter the public and private environment of people with disabilities, so as to improve their lives in various ways. These are doubtless rough categories.

I will now list four limits to redistribution under welfare egalitarianism. If any one of these limits is reached, redistribution will stop:

1. Satiation
2. Counterproductivity
3. Equalization of welfare
4. Sympathy

To simplify an exploration of these limits, imagine that there is only one disability in society; its victims suffer constant severe pain. There is no currently known cure or alleviative treatment for the disability or the pain. But while additional resources cannot currently relieve the pain of the disabled, additional resources can improve their welfare in much the same way additional resources would improve anyone's welfare: by enabling them to get things they want. Also, a cure or treatment may be possible, though none has yet been found.

Now a maximin-welfare-egalitarian system (which, it will be remembered, I am treating as synonymous with welfare egalitarianism) would not redistribute resources from the nondisabled to the disabled if the disabled would not benefit at all from those resources. If there is a point at which additional resources would not improve the welfare of the worst-off class *at all,* even though they continue to have the least welfare, re-distribution would stop. This would be the point of satiation.

Would there be any point of satiation in the scenario described? In part, the answer depends on what conception of welfare the welfare-egalitarian system follows. It may be a preference-based system, under which a person's preference (or informed preference) for additional money means that additional money would increase his welfare. Under such a system, there probably would be no satiation; there are few people, of any income level, who would say they have no desire for additional money.

On the other hand, the governing conception of welfare may be a hedonic one. Under a hedonic conception of welfare, it is somewhat plausible that the worst-off disabled class could reach a point of satiation, at least with respect to unconditional income redistribution. Some social scientists, including Robert Lane, question whether present-day wealthy people in ad-vanced societies get *any* increase in happiness, however slight, from a marginal dollar.[15] Presumably, the same view about hedonic satiation could be advanced about disabled wealthy people as about nondisabled wealthy people.

But under a hedonic view, it is unlikely there would be any plausible point of satiation with respect to medical redis-tribution. Even if there is no current cure for some painful dis-ability or disease, a cure can always be sought. All medical re-search projects that offered some possibility of finding a cure or ameliorative treatment would increase the *expected* welfare of the worst-off disabled class. Such an increase in expected welfare, however slight, would justify continued redistribution under the hedonic account.

Satiation is not a very promising limit to redistribution under welfare egalitarianism. Let us move on to the counterproductivity limit. Possibly the redistribution of resources to the disabled will reach such a point that any attempt at further redistribution will actually decrease their welfare. This maximin-welfare-egalitarian limit to redistribution is analogous to the maximin-resource-egalitarian limit to redistribution contained in Rawls's difference principle. But the counterproductivity limit does not operate the same way under welfare egalitarianism as under resource egalitarianism. For example, it is commonly assumed that too-high taxes on the rich, in a resource-egalitarian system, would be counterproductive from a redistributive standpoint, reducing work and investment incentives. In a welfare-egalitarian system, by contrast, redistributive taxation could be so extreme as to leave most or all nondisabled people poor, as long as they had higher welfare than the worst-off disabled. A redistributive scheme so extreme that it reduced rich people to poverty might *generate* work and investment incentives, on balance, rather than depressing them, at least as long as nondisabled people could benefit to some extent from their work and investment. Obviously, we are now in the realm of ideal theory (a realm we have long since entered), so we need not consider how to enforce a draconian system of redistribution that could reduce the vast majority of citizens to poverty.

The third limit to redistribution under welfare egalitarianism is equalization of welfare. Possibly the worst-off disabled class will receive sufficient additional resources so that they are no longer worst off. At that point redistribution will stop, at least as between the disabled and those nondisabled people with whom they have reached welfare equality.

It is often assumed, in discussions of disability and distributive justice, that some disabling and painful conditions are uncompensable.[16] Suppose that the test of compensation is preference-based, and the issue is whether the worst-off disabled would say (if they answered honestly) that a certain amount of redistribution could make them indifferent between disability plus redistribution and a hypothetical state of no disability and no redistribution (or whatever lesser redistribution they would receive in a nondisabled state). Different disabled people might view this issue differently. The disability we are now imagining is one that causes constant severe pain. This disability of course has analogues in the real world; there are people in the real world, not just in philosophers' examples, who suffer from constant severe pain. It seems unlikely that many such people, in the real world or in our imagined setting, would consider any amount of resources to be adequate compensation for constant severe pain. Possibly no one would think such a condition compensable, at least as compared to a nondisabled state with some modicum of resources.

As noted, however, in a welfare-egalitarian system, nondisabled people need not have a modicum of resources. There is a way of achieving welfare equalization that relies not so much on compensation of the disabled as on immiseration of the nondisabled. It is possible that as more and more resources are redistributed to disabled people, they do get *some* slight benefit from those resources, but nondisabled people simultaneously experience enormous decreases in welfare—sometimes going hungry, for example. This would not be a process of "leveling down," which we have ruled out as inconsistent with maximin welfare egalitarianism. Everyone would not be made worse off, and the better-off nondisabled class would not be made worse off unless doing so could increase the welfare of the disabled class. Still, the equalization of welfare would occur not because of the slight benefits the disabled would continue to gain from redistribution, but because the nondisabled would be made miserable.

This may be an auspicious point at which to reintroduce the problem of intermediate classes. Suppose there is a class of poor nondisabled people who are made so miserable by welfare-egalitarian redistribution that their welfare declines to the same level as the now-rich disabled. But suppose that other nondisabled people in society are not poor; there is a class of rich nondisabled people.

At this point it might be argued that the immiseration of the nondisabled poor is not wrong because it produces misery, which is the utilitarian position. Rather, it might be said, the immiseration of the nondisabled poor is wrong because it creates greater *inequality* between the nondisabled poor and the nondisabled rich. To evaluate this argument, imagine now that there are not two or several nondisabled classes, but one nondisabled class; all nondisabled people are equally miserable. Would it be acceptable if all nondisabled people, instead of some nondisabled people, were immiserated en route to welfare equality? I think not. This exercise demonstrates again that egalitarian theories more moderate than maximin egalitarianism depend, for their apparent moderation, on the presence of intermediate classes. If there are intermediate classes, such theories can arguably coincide with utilitarianism to some extent. However, if there are only two classes, the apparently moderate theories become indistinguishable from maximin egalitarianism and subject to the same utilitarian objections.

A final possible limit to redistribution under welfare egalitarianism is sympathy. This is counterproductivity with a twist. Suppose that the disabled continue to benefit, however slightly, from more and more resources, as far as their own personal well-being is concerned. The nondisabled poor are suffering substantial welfare losses as a result of redistribution, but they have not yet become so miserable that their welfare is no higher than that of the disabled rich. Before the nondisabled poor are actually immiserated to the level of welfare equality, the disabled rich might reach a point where further immiseration of the nondisabled poor would reduce their *own* welfare, because of sympathy, more than additional redistribution would increase their welfare. Even though the disabled rich still have less hedonic welfare than the nondisabled poor, the disabled rich would prefer that they *not* receive additional resources from the nondisabled poor, because the nondisabled poor could derive so much more benefit from those resources. Welfare-egalitarian redistribution to the disabled would then end because the disabled had partially internalized the utilitarian greater-benefit criterion.

ADDITIONAL COMPLICATIONS

While welfare egalitarianism clearly has counterintuitive implications for the distribution of resources between disabled and nondisabled people, the precise distributive results of a welfare-egalitarian theory are hard to specify, even in a relatively simple model. Adding some real-life complexity introduces more problems. The biggest question for welfare egalitarianism is: who has least welfare? There are in reality a number of candidates. Perhaps the people with least welfare are the ones who appear to be in the most physical pain or who are terminally ill. Perhaps the least-welfare distinction goes instead to depressed people who have seriously attempted suicide, thus revealing a

low amount of life satisfaction. Or perhaps those who are severely intellectually disabled have the least welfare.

As with resource egalitarianism, there is a temporal dimension to the definition of welfare equality and inequality. Is
welfare is to be equalized across simultaneous points in time,
across complete lives, or in some other way? A simultaneous-
point approach could invest enormous resources on behalf of
people who are now in the most pain, or are now on the point
of death, even if the benefit or expected benefit to them is tiny.
On the other hand, a whole-life approach could ignore the
people who are now most in pain, even if they might benefit
substantially from additional resources, unless and until their
pain reduces their whole-life welfare sufficiently.[17]

There is also the issue of how narrowly the least-welfare
class should be defined. In the Introduction, I suggested that
young people with terminal cancer might be considered to have
the least welfare in a welfare-egalitarian system. I made this suggestion because young people with terminal cancer are worse
off than others in several ways: they are currently suffering,
they will suffer for the rest of their lives, and their lives will be
short. So the class of young people with terminal cancer is itself at the intersection of at least two classes that might claim
to be worst off: people suffering from pain and young people
with a terminal medical condition. We might narrow the least-
welfare class further, for example by making it young people
with terminal cancer who suffer from severe "breakthrough"
pain (pain that breaks through medication) and also suffer
from severe depression. We could in fact attempt to establish
individual welfare rankings, identifying the one person with
least welfare, the one person with next-to-least welfare, and so
on. But I will assume a class-based approach.

Once the least-welfare class is defined, welfare egalitarianism will lavish resources on that class unless and until one of the limits to redistribution, discussed above, is reached. As there will be several classes of severely disabled people, the equalization limit may be easier to reach in real life than in the single-disability model I presented. Possibly, after the expenditure of vast sums on the least-welfare disabled, another class will become the least-welfare disabled and will in turn receive massive redistribution. But it is also possible that the equalization limit will never be reached, and many classes of severely disabled people will never be considered worst off. It might be determined that no amount of redistribution to young people with terminal cancer can raise their welfare to the level of people with severe intellectual disability (or vice versa).

Suppose young people with terminal cancer are identified as the worst-off class. The considerations bearing on redistribution to this class would be similar to those I outlined above, with some additional complications because of the life-shortening nature of the disability. There would be massive medical redistribution. Vast sums would be devoted to medical research to find cures and treatments for terminal cancer. Vast sums would also be devoted to medical treatment to prolong life and relieve pain.

Assume that a complete cure is not found. There continue to be young people with terminal cancer, and they continue to be identified as the worst-off class. Further medical redistribution would not benefit the cancer victims significantly; the expenditure of further vast sums would only obtain for some of them tiny life extensions, or a tiny increase in the probability of finding additional cures and treatments. At this point society might still continue with further medical redistribution, since any benefit to the worst-off class, however, tiny, justifies further redistribution. Or there might be a shift to unconditional wealth redistribution. The worst-off might receive large cash grants, over and above the cost of medical treatment. The case for cash grants is especially strong if the worst-off class is comprised of people who will die soon. In that event, it can be known that many members of the worst-off class will get no benefit at all from medical research projects, even if they are to any extent successful.

In a rich society, such as the United States, members of a relatively small worst-off class, such as young people with terminal cancer, could expect to receive cash grants in the millions of dollars. What would happen to the unspent money when they die? Possibly their relatives would be allowed to inherit; it might increase the welfare of terminally ill young people to know that their relatives will become rich.

In our one-disability model, we saw that the nondisabled poor are valuable, in a welfare-egalitarian system, only as a means to increase the welfare of the severely disabled (unless the nondisabled poor should become so miserable that they no longer have more welfare than the severely disabled). Where there are multiple classes of disabled people, this purely instrumental status extends to many disabled people as well. Those disabled people who are not considered to have least welfare would actually do worse under welfare egalitarianism than under resource egalitarianism. While resource egalitarianism can be faulted for failing to grant the disabled poor more resources than the nondisabled poor, resource egalitarianism would at least guarantee to the disabled poor the same minimum income to which everyone in society is entitled. Under welfare egalitarianism, there would be no income guarantee to anyone who is not worst off. Those disabled people who could not work might not be able to survive. If the worst-off class is defined as young people with terminal cancer, old people with terminal cancer might receive no help at all.

Thus far I have casually assumed that every member of the worst-off class under welfare egalitarianism would be a disabled person. This assumption, though widely shared by distributive theorists, may not be strictly accurate.[18] Nevertheless, any inaccuracy would not weaken the case against welfare egalitarianism.

If the worst-off class is defined as those who are in the most physical pain, then every member of the worst-off class would indeed be a disabled person; under my broad definition of disability, physical pain is always a disability. Similarly, if the worst-off class is defined as the terminally ill young, every member of that class would be disabled; under my broad definition of disability, illness is always a disability. However, if the worst-off class is defined as people with the least life satisfaction, or people who are on the point of committing suicide, not every member of that class would be a disabled person. Those who are on the point of suicide because of a broken hedonic regulatory system (that is, chemical depression) would be disabled, but those who are on the point of suicide because of a broken heart would not necessarily be disabled.[19]

In any event, under any sincere definition of the worst-off class, welfare egalitarianism would end up distributing resources to people who derive hardly any benefit from those resources, instead of to people who could benefit greatly from additional resources. Either people in the worst-off class can be raised out of that class, or they cannot. If they cannot be raised, welfare egalitarianism will concentrate all its redistributive energy on them, as long as they can benefit at all from additional resources. If they can be raised, welfare egalitarianism will raise them and then move on to the next candidates for re-distribution, ultimately settling on a class of people who cannot be raised to equality of welfare with the class above them, but can continue to benefit from additional resources. Thus, for example, when welfare egalitarianism is first instituted, the worst-off class might include both people who are dying of starvation and young people with terminal cancer. Assuming that society is at least moderately wealthy, welfare egalitarianism will raise starving people out of the worst-off class by providing them with the means to obtain food. Welfare egalitarianism will then concentrate all its redistributive energy on young people with terminal cancer, who cannot be so easily helped.

In Chapter 2, I claimed that those who summon up the specter of the utility monster as an argument against utilitarianism are making a deceptive and illegitimate argument; they are in reality evoking utilitarian intuitions and turning those intuitions against utilitarianism. We do not really believe that a person could be a utility monster, that he could gain more from all sacrifices of others than those others lose. So when we decide that the supposed utility monster should not receive all the world's resources, this intuitive moral judgment is a utilitarian one; it is based on the assumption that sacrificing everyone to the utility monster would lead to a massive reduction in welfare, rather than (as unconvincingly stipulated) an increase in welfare.

The true and legitimate home of the utility monster is not utilitarianism, but welfare egalitarianism. Under welfare egalitarianism, those who are worst off have a massive claim on the resources of others. This claim does not depend, as it would under utilitarianism, on the unconvincing stipulation that the worst-off would actually benefit *more* from all the sacrifices of others than those others lose. The claim of the worst-off under welfare egalitarianism is good as long as the worst-off derive *any* benefit from the sacrifice of others, while still remaining worst-off. It is quite easy to believe that the worst-off would derive *some* benefit from massive sacrifices of those who are better off. Hence, welfare egalitarianism turns the worst-off into credible utility monsters.

The implausibility of welfare egalitarianism is so great that one is moved to modify its strictures—not in order to render it plausible (that is impossible), but in order to lessen its absurdity. Possibly a welfare-egalitarian system will not choose between contending conceptions of welfare, but will compromise between them. If some say that young people with terminal cancer have least welfare and others say that those with severe intellectual disability have least welfare, perhaps the system will split its massive redistribution between these groups.

Perhaps also the absolute priority of maximin egalitarianism will be relaxed, at least as to people who are severely disabled. The system could extend some help to classes of disabled people other than those with least welfare, and could adopt something like a utilitarian greater-benefit criterion to make tradeoffs. The system could decide, for example, that it is more important to give a significant benefit to older people with terminal cancer than to give only an insignificant benefit to younger people with terminal cancer. The farther a welfare-egalitarian system travels in the direction of utilitarianism, the more plausible it will be. But welfare egalitarianism can travel very far in the direction of utilitarianism and still remain implausible. A welfare-egalitarian system could extend help to many classes of disabled people and still maintain the nondisabled poor in a state of destitution.

WELFARE EGALITARIANISM
AND THE HAPPY DISABLED

A common resource-egalitarian critique of welfare egalitarianism is that welfare egalitarianism would not deal satisfactorily with the happy disabled. This is actually a resource-egalitarian comeback to the welfare-egalitarian critique of resource egalitarianism. Welfare egalitarians join utilitarians in complaining that resource egalitarianism would not allocate any more resources to the disabled than to the nondisabled. Resource egalitarians respond: "Aha! What about disabled people who are happier than nondisabled people? Welfare egalitarianism would not allocate additional resources to those happy disabled people; it would allocate *fewer* resources to them." A common example involves Tiny Tim and Scrooge.[20] Tiny Tim is happier than Scrooge, even though Tiny Tim is poor and disabled and Scrooge is rich and nondisabled. Doesn't welfare egalitarianism therefore have to redistribute resources from Tiny Tim to Scrooge instead of the other way around?

I would not dismiss the interpersonal comparison in this example as something that could only be dreamed up by Wiseacre (a character I introduced in Chapter 2). Although the disabled have on average less welfare than the nondisabled, there are undoubtedly many disabled people who have more welfare than many nondisabled people. On the other hand, it seems unlikely that in any practical welfare-egalitarian system (if such a thing could exist) the purposes of welfare egalitarianism would be served by seeking to determine which disabled people were temperamentally happy and should therefore receive fewer resources.

In any event, however much the happy disabled are a problem for welfare egalitarianism, they are less of a problem for utilitarianism. Utilitarians are concerned with how much welfare can be raised, not how low it is. The violinist Itzhak Perlman is a victim of childhood polio. He can walk only painfully and with difficulty, using elbow crutches.[21] Yet I would not claim that I have more welfare than Itzhak Perlman; if I had to guess, I would say it is probably the other way around. I would claim, however, that anything which enabled polio victims to move around more easily would benefit them greatly, even if they already enjoyed a high level of welfare. Utilitarians can assume with some confidence that if distributive policy leads to a cure or substantial amelioration of disability, virtually every affected disabled person will experience an increase in welfare.

In the Tiny Tim example, utilitarianism would distribute additional resources to Tiny Tim, even though he has more welfare than Scrooge, because he can also benefit more from resources than can Scrooge. To be sure, it is possible to *suppose* that a rich nondisabled person (such as Scrooge) can benefit more from resources than a poor disabled person (such as Tiny Tim), just as it is possible to suppose that a rich nondisabled person is less happy than a poor disabled person. But the first supposition is far less plausible than the second. We could easily be convinced, after meeting a rich nondisabled person and a poor disabled person, that the poor disabled person is happier; it is unlikely that we could be convinced that the poor disabled person would benefit less from additional resources.[22]

The analysis of resource egalitarianism and welfare egalitarianism has proved to be complicated, but the negative verdicts on both these theories stand. All versions of resource egalitarianism give too little to some disabled people, and all

versions of welfare egalitarianism give too much to some disabled people. Nevertheless, we have uncovered some surprises.
A thoroughgoing welfare egalitarianism is very unfavorable for
disabled people who are not considered to have the least welfare, as well as for the nondisabled poor. A resource egalitarianism that seeks to equalize total resources over a complete life
actually gives too much to some disabled people.[23] All this is an
example of how egalitarianism, lacking a sensitivity to relative
benefit, oscillates between inadequate redistribution and excessive redistribution to various classes.

It is also interesting that of the three contending theories—utilitarianism, resource egalitarianism, and welfare egalitarianism—only utilitarianism can even potentially support
national health insurance. In the previous chapter, I noted
that there is a strong utilitarian argument for national health
insurance, and that utilitarianism would at the very least subsidize the medical expenses of the poor. Neither resource egalitarianism nor welfare egalitarianism can even get as far as
subsidizing the medical expenses of the poor. Resource egalitarianism, as we have seen, cannot in general allow the disabled poor more resources than the nondisabled poor. Welfare
egalitarianism lavishes medical care on those disabled people
who have least welfare, but cannot in general provide for the
medical needs of others. Both egalitarian theories can help
people outside their favored groups only as a means to help
people inside the favored groups. This instrumental approach
can justify some subsidized medical care, on productivity
grounds, but it cannot come close to a general subsidy for
medical care, or even a medical subsidy for the poor.[24] Utilitarianism, by contrast, treats every person (or at least, every
person's welfare) as an end in itself, not solely as a means.

Marginal Egalitarianism

Before leaving behind the taxonomy of egalitarian theories, we should consider marginal egalitarianism, a theory that would not be acknowledged as egalitarian by everyone. Marginal egalitarianism tells us to distribute equally whatever resources are available for redistribution at a given point in time. I take the term "marginal egalitarianism" from Douglas Rae, who is one of the few scholars to analyze it.[25]

Suppose that we have two dollars to distribute among two claimants: Donald Trump and a homeless person (this is assuming that Donald Trump has not himself been reduced to homelessness through the vicissitudes of the real estate market). The three theories with which I am most concerned—utilitarianism, resource egalitarianism, and welfare egalitarianism—would all counsel us to give two dollars to the homeless person and nothing to Donald Trump. Marginal egalitarianism, however, would counsel us to give one dollar to each.

Marginal egalitarianism is closer to resource egalitarianism than to welfare egalitarianism. What I am calling marginal egalitarianism is actually marginal resource egalitarianism. There could theoretically be a marginal welfare egalitarianism; such a theory would tell us to increase, by equal amounts, the welfare of all those whose welfare we can increase. If we are distributing money between a rich person and a poor person, marginal welfare egalitarianism would tell us to give more money to the *rich* person, because the poor person can get a larger welfare increase from any given amount of money.

Marginal welfare egalitarianism has no intuitive appeal. However, marginal resource egalitarianism (what I am calling simply marginal egalitarianism) does have some intuitive appeal, even perhaps in extreme examples such as the Trump/ homeless person example, and more so in examples that are less extreme. When it is aligned with another theory of distributive justice, marginal egalitarianism can make the result favored by that theory more appealing. The most frequent beneficiaries of alignment with marginal egalitarianism are resource egalitarianism and welfare egalitarianism. But as demonstrated by the following example, marginal egalitarianism can be aligned with utilitarianism against one of the other egalitarian theories.

Suppose there are two patients suffering from persistent pain. Patient A is in pain 15 hours a day, and patient B is in pain 20 hours a day. We have two pills that will, somewhat magically, provide permanent but partial relief from pain to both patients, to a different extent. If patient A receives 1 pill, he is relieved of 10 hours of pain per day; if he receives 2 pills, he is relieved of an additional 30 minutes of pain per day. If patient B receives 1 pill, he is relieved of 1 hour of pain per day; if he receives 2 pills, he is relieved of an additional 1 hour of pain per day.

Here, the welfare-egalitarian course is to give both pills to patient B, for 2 hours of pain relief from 20 hours of pain per day. The utilitarian course is to give 1 pill to each patient, so that patient A gets 10 hours of pain relief from 15 hours, and patient B gets 1 hour of pain relief from 20 hours (This is the utilitarian course if we assume that patient A benefits more by being relieved of 10 hours from 15 than patient B benefits by being relieved of 1 hour from 19).

The marginal egalitarian course is in this case the same as the utilitarian: 1 pill to each patient. Therefore, if we think it right to distribute 1 pill to each patient, we cannot be sure whether we are endorsing utilitarianism, or marginal egalitarianism, or some combination of the two.

It is important to notice when marginal egalitarianism is in the picture. For example, resource egalitarians often begin their argument by hypothesizing the initial distribution of unowned material resources to people who have no other material resources. In this setting, resource egalitarianism is aligned with marginal egalitarianism: both tell us to distribute the unowned resources equally. If we think this approach is right, we may be responding to the intuitive appeal of marginal egalitarianism rather than, or in addition to, the intuitive appeal of resource egalitarianism.

Whence the surprising intuitive appeal of marginal egalitarianism? In part, it may be due to laziness of moral thought. An equal division of whatever is being distributed is a very prominent and easy-to-administer solution. If we seize upon that solution, we do not have to concern ourselves with difficult and controversial assessments of contending claims. Another possible reason for the appeal of marginal egalitarianism is that it draws on libertarian intuitions, or on intuitions related to the security of existing holdings. If everyone is assumed to be entitled to whatever she currently has, it is easier to ignore the current pattern of holdings in making distributive decisions.

Marginal egalitarianism is not very prominent in core debates over distributive justice, except as a hidden ally of one of the other egalitarian theories. Marginal egalitarianism is more prominent in the field of bioethics. In that field, it may seem more reasonable to consider resources on hand and available for distribution (such as a heart for transplant) as subject to special rules. Even in the bioethics field, however, theorists sometimes ignore the distinction between marginal egalitarianism and other egalitarian theories.[26]

The Strains of Egalitarian Commitment

One of my favorite examples in moral philosophy comes from Peter Singer's book *Practical Ethics*. I will refer to this example as the Singer Earthquake Case, and I will present a number of variations on Singer's original example in this chapter and in Chapter 9.

After an earthquake, Singer imagines, we come upon two victims, one more severely injured than the other:

> The more severely injured victim, A, has lost a leg and is in danger of losing a toe from her remaining leg; while the less severely injured victim, B, has an injury to her leg, but the limb can be saved. We have medical supplies for only one person. If we use them on the more severely injured victim the most we can do is save her toe, whereas if we use them on the less severely injured victim we can save her leg.[27]

Most people, I hope, will agree with Singer that here we should distribute the scarce medical supplies to the person who can most benefit from them, even though the other candidate is worse off. In other words, we should follow the utilitarian course rather than the welfare-egalitarian course.

We can modify the example so that utilitarianism is opposed not only to welfare egalitarianism, but also to a version of resource egalitarianism. Suppose that person A (who has already lost a leg and risks losing a toe on her remaining leg) is obviously poor, while person B (who risks losing a leg, but has no other injury) is obviously rich. I will refer to this as the Modified Singer Earthquake Case. Most people, I hope, will persist in thinking that in the Modified Singer Earthquake Case, we should still distribute the scarce medical resources to person B, who will most benefit from them, even though she already has more welfare *and* more resources.

The Modified Singer Earthquake Case does not necessarily bring utilitarianism into conflict with all versions of resource egalitarianism. Resource egalitarians are often unwilling to apply their theory in small-scale triage situations. Rawls, for example, tells us that "the maximin criterion is not meant to apply to . . . how a doctor should treat his patients or a university its students."[28]

Resource egalitarians might have no theory for triage cases, or they might incorporate elements of other theories for application to such cases. Resource egalitarians might, for example, apply utilitarianism to small-scale distributive problems. While any application of utilitarianism would certainly be a step in the right direction, there are other possibilities as well. Resource egalitarians might think that the only resources which should be equalized, in a case like the Modified Singer Earthquake Case, are the specialized medical resources that both candidates need. In other words, resource egalitarians might apply marginal egalitarianism to triage cases.

In both the Modified Singer Earthquake Case and the original Singer Earthquake Case, it is impossible to divide the scarce medical resources: they must be used on one candidate or the other. We can modify the example further by stipulating that the medical resources can be divided in half, in which case they will be half as effective: Person A will lose half a toe and person B will lose half a leg. So, in what I will call Modified Singer Earthquake Case #2, we now have the following choices:

1. We can use all the medical supplies on person A, a poor person who has already lost a leg and will also lose a toe if we do not help her. Then person A's toe will be saved.
2. We can use all the medical supplies on person B, a rich person who will lose a leg if we do not help her, but has no other injury. Then person B's leg will be saved.
3. We can divide the medical supplies in half. Then person A will lose half a toe, and person B will lose half a leg.

Most people, I hope, will agree that we should not divide the medical supplies, but should instead use them all on person B, who will benefit most. In this example, then, utilitarianism seems right even though it is opposed by not one, but *three* different egalitarian theories. The golden mean of utilitarianism is not yet tarnished, and egalitarian theories seem implausible even when they are aligned together against utilitarianism.

Egalitarian critics of utilitarianism sometimes claim that utilitarianism imposes too great a demand on people at the bottom of society. If helping people at the bottom means that those who are better off must forgo greater benefits, no help will be forthcoming under a utilitarian system. Rawls, T. M. Scanlon, and Thomas Nagel, among others, have expressed such sentiments. Nagel appeals to a "fundamental psychological fact" that "it is easier to accept sacrifices or forgo advantages for the sake of those worse off than you than for the sake of those better off than you."[29]

Nagel's view has some initial plausibility. It does seem that it must be easier to accept sacrifices or forgo advantages for the sake of those who are worse off than you than for the sake of those who are better off than you. Of course, utilitarianism only requires worse-off people to accept sacrifices and forgo advantages for the sake of better-off people if the better-off people would thereby obtain *greater* advantages or avoid *greater* sacrifices. There is also some ambiguity in the terms "worse off" and "better off." Do we mean worse off in terms of resources or worse off in terms of welfare? While Rawls is a resource egalitarian, Nagel is more of a welfare egalitarian.

The Modified Singer Earthquake Case can help to test the view that utilitarianism imposes more unreasonable demands on people than do various forms of egalitarianism. Do we think, in this example, that it would be easier for person A (poor person who has already lost a leg and is about to lose a toe) to forgo treatment in favor of person B? Or do we think it would be easier for person B (rich person who is about to lose a leg, but has no other injury) to forgo treatment in favor of person A? Doubtless it would not be easy for either person to forgo treatment. But as to the *relative* ease or difficulty of sacrifice, the answer, to me, is obvious: it would be easier for the person who is worse off, in both welfare and resources, to forgo an advantage (saving a toe) so that the person who is better off can obtain a greater advantage (saving a leg).

I contend that egalitarian critics of utilitarianism hold false views about the strains of commitment and the relative burden of sacrifices under egalitarianism and utilitarianism. It is not true, as a general matter, that it is "easier to accept sacrifices or forgo advantages for the sake of those worse off than you than for the sake of those better off than you."[30] The initial plausibility of this claim depends on its partial coincidence with utilitarianism: often those who are worse off than you would benefit more from your sacrifice. But when utilitarianism diverges from egalitarianism, as in the examples here discussed, the egalitarian claim loses its plausibility. Contrary to Nagel's view, the most accurate simple statement we can make about the relative burden of sacrifice is that it is easier to accept *lesser* sacrifices so that others can avoid *greater* sacrifices, and it is easier to forgo *lesser* advantages so that others can obtain *greater* advantages.

Of course, egalitarian critics of utilitarianism probably do not have in mind examples like the ones here discussed. They probably have in mind a tableau of fat and satisfied rich people[31] claiming that nothing should be done to alleviate the misery of the poor; if taxes are raised, it will merely reduce the work and investment incentives of those satisfied rich people. In other words, egalitarian critics of utilitarianism have in mind a situation in which better-off people claim that they would have to forgo greater advantages to help the poor, but in which that claim is not particularly convincing. As argued in Chapter 2, that is not the way to do moral philosophy.

MAXIMALLY DEMANDING THEORIES

A number of moral theorists have asked whether morality allows individuals a zone of partiality, and how wide such a zone might be.[32] Both utilitarianism and egalitarianism could accommodate a zone of partiality; both could allow individuals, in some or most circumstances, to advance their own interests rather than the distributive goals of the theory. On the other hand, both utilitarianism and egalitarianism could be maximally demanding; both could deny individuals any zone of partiality. A maximally demanding utilitarianism would tell people to give up their resources to others who could benefit more from those resources (assuming no offsetting reduction in welfare). A maximally demanding egalitarianism would tell people to give up their resources to others who are in some way worse off than them.

Mostly, the demand of both utilitarianism and egalitarianism is for the those who are better off to give resources to those who are in various ways worse off. But in unusual circumstances, a maximally demanding utilitarianism can require those who are worse off to give their resources over to people who are better off, as long as those who are better off can also benefit more. Leaving aside the question of whether *any* theory should be maximally demanding, is such a maximally demanding utilitarianism less plausible than a maximally demanding egalitarianism?

The Modified Singer Earthquake case can once again shed some light on this question. Let us modify that example further by dispensing with the disinterested, benevolent, uninjured person who happens to have medical supplies. Let us suppose, alternately, that each of the two earthquake victims herself possesses the scarce medical supplies, and faces the question of whether to give those supplies to her fellow victim instead of using them herself. I will refer to this version of the example as Modified Singer Earthquake Case #3.

A maximally demanding utilitarianism would say that person A (poor person who has already lost a leg and is about to lose a toe) has a moral obligation to give, or perhaps sell, her medical supplies to person B (rich person who is about to lose a leg, but has no other injury). A maximally demanding egalitarianism would say that person B (rich person who is about to lose a leg, but has no other injury) has a moral obligation to give her medical supplies to person A (poor person who has already lost a leg and is about to lose a toe). Put another way, maximally demanding utilitarianism would say that person A has a moral obligation to give up a toe so that someone better off can avoid losing a leg, while maximally demanding egalitarianism would say that person B has a moral obligation to give up a leg so that someone worse off can avoid losing a toe.

Possibly we think that both maximally demanding theories are implausible. Possibly neither earthquake victim would have a moral obligation to give up scarce medical supplies that she needs. Surely, however, maximally demanding egalitarianism is far less plausible than maximally demanding utilitarianism. Even if it is sometimes wrong to say that people should give up their resources to others who would benefit *more*, it is certainly wrong to say that people should give up their resources to others who would benefit *less.*

I am inclined to think that utilitarianism should not be maximally demanding, that there should be a zone of partiality in utilitarianism. However, I do not try to justify this view here, and I do not venture to suggest how wide the zone of partiality should be. Throughout most of this book I assume away issues of partiality; I assume that a decision has already been made to view distributive issues from an impartial perspective.

VI
Rawls

In this and the following two chapters, I discuss the major resource-egalitarian theorists John Rawls, Ronald Dworkin, and Bruce Ackerman. In dealing with disability, resource egalitarians actually oscillate between resource egalitarianism, welfare egalitarianism, and utilitarianism. They begin by trying to maintain the ideal of resource equality. They realize, however, that it would be unfair not to distribute additional resources to disabled people who would suffer horribly without those additional resources. They modify their theories in order to justify extra resources for the disabled, but these modifications threaten to push them all the way to welfare egalitarianism. They then search for some way of limiting redistribution to the disabled, sometimes settling on a form of utilitarianism. I group together Rawls, Dworkin, and Ackerman as resource egalitarians because they begin as such, even though all of them depart from resource egalitarianism to some degree.

In this chapter I discuss Rawls's treatment of disability.[1] This aspect of Rawls's work has not escaped the notice of commentators—no aspect of his work has—and I take some note of what others have said. It might be wondered: what is the point of another discussion of Rawls? While nothing I say is revolutionary, I believe I give a fuller account than others of the oscillation in Rawls's theory between inadequate provision for the disabled and excessive redistribution to the disabled. Also, I consider at length some new positions and new arguments advanced by Rawls in his book *Justice as Fairness: A Restatement*.[2] *Justice as Fairness* was published in 2001, the year before Rawls's passing.

My discussion of Rawls is perhaps less central to my argument than my discussion of Dworkin in the next chapter. I give Rawls pride of place because of his status as the preeminent egalitarian political philosopher of the twentieth century.

Basics of Rawls's Theory

Rawls believes that the fundamental task of political philosophy is to specify principles of justice that are "fair terms of social cooperation."[3] These principles should be chosen from behind a "veil of ignorance," from an "original position of equality," in which "no one knows his place in society . . . [or] his fortune in the distribution of natural assets and abilities, his intelligence, strength, and the like."[4] The parties in the original position should see themselves as representing citizens whose characteristics they do not know, but who "have to the minimum sufficient degree the two moral powers and other capacities enabling them to be normal cooperating members of society over a complete life."[5] The two moral powers are a capacity for a sense of justice and a capacity for a conception of the good.[6]

Many have thought that parties choosing principles of justice from behind a veil of ignorance would choose to be governed by some form of utilitarianism. This was the posi-

tion of Harsanyi, who made use of a device like the veil of ignorance before Rawls did. I will not rehash that dispute here; I
will wait to rehash it until I discuss Dworkin's theory in the
next chapter.

Rawls, of course, believes that parties in the original position would agree upon his famous two principles of justice.
Rawls's two principles, as set forth in *Justice as Fairness,* read as
follows:

> (a) Each person has the same indefeasible claim to
>   a fully adequate scheme of equal basic liber-
>   ties, which scheme is compatible with the same
>   scheme of liberties for all; and
> (b) Social and economic inequalities are to satisfy
>   two conditions: first, they are to be attached to
>   offices and positions open to all under condi-
>   tions of fair equality of opportunity; and sec-
>   ond, they are to be to the greatest benefit of the
>   least-advantaged members of society.[7]

Under Rawls's system, the first principle—the principle
of liberty—is lexically prior to the second: the second principle cannot require even the slightest violation of the first, at
least under reasonably favorable conditions.[8] Moreover, the
first condition of the second principle (fair equality of opportunity) is lexically prior to the second condition of the second
principle. The second condition of Rawls's second principle—
inequalities must be to the "greatest benefit of the least advantaged"—he terms the difference principle.[9]

Who are the least advantaged? Rawls's answer, in the
most general sense, is that the least advantaged are those who
have the fewest social "primary goods," goods which "are gen-

erally necessary to enable citizens adequately to develop and fully exercise their two moral powers, and to pursue their determinate conceptions of the good."[10] In *Justice as Fairness,* Rawls lists the primary goods as follows:

(i)   The basic rights and liberties . . .
(ii) Freedom of movement and free choice of occupation against a background of diverse opportunities . . .
(iii) Powers and prerogatives of offices and positions of authority and responsibility . . .
(iv) Income and wealth, understood as all-purpose means . . . generally needed to achieve a wide range of ends whatever they may be.
(v)   the social bases of self-respect.[11]

Though Rawls in general defines the least advantaged as those with the fewest primary goods, in interpreting the difference principle he focuses on the primary goods of income and wealth. He essentially defines the least advantaged as the poorest class, as "specified by the level of income and wealth."[12] Under this definition, the difference principle requires society to maximize the income and wealth of the poorest citizens, subject to the priority of liberty and to fair equality of opportunity.[13]

Changes in Rawls's Theory

Rawls's principles of justice have not changed very much from *A Theory of Justice* (1971) to *Political Liberalism* (1993) to *Justice as Fairness* (2001). There has been some change in the first principle (the liberty principle), and as discussed below the difference principle is reinterpreted, in *Justice as Fairness,* so as to allow the provision of extra resources to those who are temporarily disabled.

There is a much-remarked change in the way Rawls conceives of his system, one that is fully present in *Political Liberalism* and continued in *Justice as Fairness.* Rawls stresses, in both of the later works, that he does not see his system as a comprehensive doctrine; he sees it as a less ambitious "political" doctrine that he hopes can gain the adherence of an overlapping consensus of reasonable comprehensive doctrines.

There are also changes in the way that Rawls purports to derive his principles of justice. These changes are present to some extent in *Political Liberalism,* but they are more pronounced in *Justice as Fairness.*

In *A Theory of Justice,* Rawls appeared to believe that all of his principles were the result of the maximin decision rule as applied by parties in the original position.[14] The maximin decision rule tells us to make the worst possible outcome as good as possible. In *Justice as Fairness,* Rawls continues to use the maximin rule to argue for his first principle, but he claims that the difference principle relies not at all on the maximin rule.[15] This is a surprising shift, as the difference principle—socio-economic inequalities must be to the greatest benefit of the least advantaged—is the only Rawlsian principle that has the same *form* as the maximin rule.

The other major change in the derivation of Rawls's principles is that the content of those principles is now determined in major part by the two moral powers (a capacity for a sense of justice and a capacity for a conception of the good). The two moral powers are the key features of what Rawls call his "normative and political" conception of the person.[16] In *Justice as Fairness,* the two moral powers are used to derive both the list of liberties protected under the first principle[17] and the list of primary goods.[18] In *A Theory of Justice,* by contrast, Rawls seemed to take a more general view of citizens as human beings; primary goods were there described as "things which it is supposed a rational man wants whatever else he wants."[19]

Rawls evidently believes that his political conception of the person follows from his political conception of justice. But a doctrine can draw moral conclusions about the nature of persons as human beings and still limit its strictures to the political realm. Such an approach would seem more likely to connect with the adherents of diverse comprehensive doctrines. They can readily engage with Rawls in a conversation about what people as people would want or do in the original position. When Rawls insists that the principles of justice be chosen in order to further the two moral powers, he risks alienating from the start those who deny that the two moral powers are the only morally relevant features of persons that bear on political justice. In *Justice as Fairness,* Rawls in fact acknowledges that his shift toward a political conception of the person may make it *more* difficult for his theory to achieve an overlapping consensus.[20]

An Alternate Rawlsian Vision: The Disabled as Least Advantaged

As originally formulated, Rawls's theory appeared to require that the disabled poor receive no more social resources than the nondisabled poor. This result was criticized as unfair by Sen and others.[21] Rawls could have partly avoided the problem of inadequate provision for the disabled if he had identified the severely disabled, rather than the poor, as the least-advantaged class. Then, however, he would have faced the problem of excessive redistribution to the disabled.

Many commentators have thought that Rawls erred in identifying the least advantaged, and that the disabled, rather than the poor, should indeed be considered least advantaged under a Rawlsian system.[22] Parties in the original position who accepted this alternate definition and remained concerned with promoting the life prospects of the least advantaged would adopt principles requiring quite extensive redistribution to the disabled. Rawls's system would transpose from resource egalitarianism into something like welfare egalitarianism.

Different principles might be consistent with this alternate Rawlsian vision, and might be considered by parties in the original position. To facilitate analysis, I assume that parties in the original position would retain the liberty principle and fair equality of opportunity, but would replace the poor-centered difference principle with a disabled-centered difference principle. In fact, it would not even be necessary to change the language of the difference principle, though its meaning would change drastically. The difference principle, it will be recalled, requires that social and economic inequalities must "be to the greatest benefit of the least-advantaged members of society."[23] In a poor-centered system, this means that inequalities may favor the *non*-poor only to the extent they benefit the poor. In a disabled-centered system, it means that inequalities may favor the disabled to the extent they benefit the disabled. Unlike poor-centered maximin egalitarianism, disabled-centered maximin egalitarianism permits the least-advantaged class to receive a greater-than-equal share of material resources and to remain the least-advantaged class.[24] Whereas Rawls's poor-centered difference principle stops redistribution short of absolute equality, the analogous limit in a disabled-centered system would stop redistribution short of the disabled getting everything.

In Chapter 5, I discussed the various possible limits on redistribution to the disabled under a thematic welfare-egalitarian system. These limits would also apply in a disabled-centered Rawlsian system. There might also be additional limits to redistribution, based on the particular features of a Rawlsian system. One possible limit derives from Rawls's idea that the problem of justice is to divide the gains from social cooperation.[25] Given this conception, each nondisabled person might be entitled to a social minimum representing slightly more than she would achieve under the no-agreement point of noncooperation or, as Rawls terms it, general egoism.[26] Yet another possible limit, based on Rawls's theory, is that a certain social minimum is necessary for people to discharge their functions as cooperating citizens.[27] The liberty principle and fair equality of opportunity might also impose limits. Nevertheless, a disabled-centered Rawlsian system would doubtless require what most would consider to be excessive redistribution to the disabled.

So why are the disabled not least advantaged? Rawls has devoted remarkably little attention to this question. Perhaps the clearest explanation he has offered for not identifying the disabled as least advantaged is that this would be inconsistent with his concept of justice as a system of fair cooperation. As noted, parties in the original position are instructed to assume that the people they represent are fully cooperating members of society over a complete life.[28]

But prohibiting parties in the original position from considering that they may represent persons who are not fully cooperating citizens does not eliminate the issue of whether the least-advantaged class should be defined as those with severe disabilities who *are* cooperating citizens. Blind people can work, as can people who are in wheelchairs, as can people who are depressed or in severe pain. And Rawls adamantly rejects any idea of basing distributive shares on the contributions citizens make to society: "There is no question of determining anyone's contribution to society, or how much better off each is than they would have been had they not belonged to it, and then adjusting the social benefits of citizens by reference to these estimates."[29]

Therefore, Rawls's strictures on representatives in the original position would not prevent them from defining the least-advantaged class as those with severe disabilities *who can work*. Such a definition would still result in massive redistribution to the disabled.

In fact, Rawls's exclusion of non-cooperating citizens from the original position could result in a system that is even less palatable than disabled-centered maximin egalitarianism. As discussed below, Rawls's theory is less favorable to the *non*-cooperating disabled than commonly supposed; it is plausible that the non-cooperating disabled would receive no assistance at all under a Rawlsian system. So if the cooperating disabled were identified as least advantaged, we could see the worst of both egalitarian worlds: millions for the cooperating disabled and starvation for the non-cooperating disabled.

There are hints and suggestions, at various points in Rawls's works, of a number of other justifications for choosing the poor and not the disabled as the least-advantaged class. To draw out and weigh these putative justifications would require a considerable effort in Rawls exegesis. I have elsewhere attempted this task.[30] I conclude that Rawls's critics are correct:

the severely disabled are at least as plausible as the poor as candidates for the least-advantaged class.

Modifying the Poor-Centered Rawlsian System

Rawls does not choose to provide for the needs of the disabled by identifying them as the least-advantaged class. However, in *Justice as Fairness* he does modify his poor-centered system somewhat. Rawls there addresses cases in which "citizens fall temporarily—for a period of time—below the minimum essential capacities for being normal and fully cooperating members of society."[31] In such cases, Rawls writes, society should provide medical care so as to enable people to "resume their normal lives as cooperating members of society";[32] such restorative care has "great urgency."[33]

REINTERPRETING THE DIFFERENCE PRINCIPLE

Welfare-egalitarian critics of Rawls have assumed that the difference principle, in regulating inequalities of income and wealth for the greatest benefit of the poorest class, rules out the provision of extra resources to the ill and disabled. In *Justice as Fairness*, Rawls repudiates this interpretation of the difference principle. He writes that "individuals' expectations of primary goods . . . can be the same ex ante, while the goods they actually receive are different ex post, depending on the various contingencies—in this case, on the illnesses and accidents that befall them."[34]

This is certainly a reinterpretation of the difference principle. Some members of the poverty-defined least-advantaged class can receive far more social resources than others, and the difference principle exerts no pressure to even out this difference, because all members of the least-advantaged class had the same ex ante expectation of social resources.

It is unclear whether Rawls means that there must actually be a point in time at which the expectations of the least advantaged are equal. If so, people with genetic disabilities may be left out. Some people are born with disabilities that call for expensive lifetime care. If they were entitled to the medical care needed to maintain them as fully cooperating members of society, they would have an expectation, at least from birth, of receiving *more* than the social minimum provided to nondisabled citizens.

An alternative interpretation is that we are products of a cosmic lottery in which we all have an equal chance of being disabled. But this interpretation would threaten to empty the difference principle of all meaning. People would also, under this interpretation, have an equal expectation of resources under a libertarian system: everyone would have the same ex ante chance of being talented, being born into a high social class, and so forth.

If equal expectation at some actual point in time is required, the difference principle would not become meaningless, but it would still fail to *require* the provision of restorative medical care. Such provision would be consistent with the difference principle, but so would the failure to provide extra resources to the temporarily disabled; then, too, every member of the least-advantaged class would have the same ex ante expectation of resources. It would also be consistent with the difference principle to provide extra resources to people based on any other contingency—to pick a frivolous example, those who won the lottery could have their winnings doubled from government funds, all without violating the difference principle.

MAXIMIN PRODUCTIVE LIFE

So the provision of restorative medical care must be motivated by some principle other than the difference principle. In *Justice as Fairness,* Rawls briefly suggests, as candidates, both the principle of fair equality of opportunity and the liberty principle. Once again, it would require a great deal of exegesis to determine how these principles can support the provision of restorative medical care.[35] I will bypass these exegetical issues because I believe Rawls's theory can indeed motivate a requirement for restorative medical care, and that the most natural way of doing so is through a principle prior to the difference principle and the principle of fair equality of opportunity, and prior even to the liberty principle.

How, it might be asked, can any Rawlsian principle be prior to the first principle, the liberty principle? Actually, Rawls himself suggests such a prior principle in *Justice as Fairness.* In a footnote, he writes that the first principle "may be preceded by a lexically prior principle requiring that basic needs be met, at least insofar as their being met is a necessary condition for citizens to understand and to be able fruitfully to exercise the basic rights and liberties."[36]

In the Rawlsian system of political liberalism, premature death must surely be considered worse than poverty or political oppression. Those who are poor or oppressed can still exercise the two moral powers to some extent; they can to some extent evaluate the justice of their institutions and pursue a plan of life. If you are dead, you cannot exercise the two moral powers at all. Just as bad as death, perhaps, is life at a very low level of capability, a level at which one cannot exercise the two moral powers or cannot be a cooperating member of society.

Life at such a low level of capacity might be equated to death under a "political" conception of death.

Rawls devotes remarkably little attention to death. In part, this may be because he operates in the realm of ideal theory; he assumes reasonably favorable conditions. Even under reasonably favorable conditions, however, some will have their lives cut short and will be unable to pursue their life plans at all.

Premature death can sometimes be avoided. Rawlsian contractors in the original position would presumably assign very high priority to the prevention of premature death and to the maintenance of citizens at a level where they could remain cooperating citizens and continue to exercise the two moral powers. If Rawlsian contractors followed the maximin decision rule, they might maximize the productive life of those who would have the shortest productive life. A Rawlsian injunction to maximin productive life could easily justify the social provision of restorative medical care.[37] Such care would of course go first to those below a certain age, who had not had much time to pursue their life plans.

MODIFIED RAWLSIANISM
AND UTILITARIANISM

Like the Rawlsian approach to medical care sketched out in *Justice as Fairness,* utilitarianism would give great priority to care that restored a person's capacity to be a cooperating citizen. Restorative care is care that benefits a person greatly: it raises her from a level at which she is unable to cooperate to a level at which she is once again a fully cooperating citizen. Utilitarianism might even give priority to restorative care above and beyond its direct effect on the welfare of recipients, because enabling people to work again benefits others also.

Rawls's current emphasis on restorative care introduces something like a greater-benefit criterion into his theory. If the choice is between helping someone who is worse off and someone who is better off, we are to help the person who is better off if she can benefit more, in the sense of rising from non-cooperative status to cooperative status.

In the following chapter I claim that Dworkin's theory surreptitiously incorporates large elements of utilitarianism. I do not make the same claim here regarding Rawls's emphasis on restorative care. This emphasis is partially coincident with utilitarianism, but it can be independently justified as following from Rawls's theory.[38]

Because restorative care benefits a person greatly, Rawls's new approach to medical care is partly immune from the usual utilitarian criticism of egalitarian theories, that they are insensitive to relative benefit. But Rawls is only partly immune. A system that gives priority to restorative care can still be insensitive to relative benefit, if a great expenditure will yield the benefit of restoration only for a short period of time, or if a great expenditure will yield only a small probability of restoration. It might be possible, at great expense, to increase only slightly the productive life of those destined to die or become incapacitated at a young age. It might be possible to invest vast sums in medical research projects that have only a tiny chance of permanently restoring young people to full cooperation. Such counterintuitive measures appear to be required under Rawls's new approach—unless they are blocked by the incorporation of utilitarian standards for the allocation of medical care. So we can say that where Rawls's priority for restorative care is plausible, it coincides with utilitarianism; where it does not coincide with utilitarianism, it is implausible.

THE NON-COOPERATING DISABLED

A further problem with Rawls's modification to his poor-centered theory is that it would benefit only the cooperating disabled, those who with assistance can be fully cooperating members of society. There is still no basis in Rawls's theory for aid to the non-cooperating disabled. As Rawls writes in *Justice as Fairness,* "I put aside the more extreme cases of persons with such grave disabilities that they can never be normal contributing members of social cooperation."[39]

The status of the non-cooperating disabled in Rawls's theory is actually even more precarious than Sen and other critics of Rawls have suggested. Because Rawls directs parties in the original position to assume that they represent cooperating citizens, it is not clear that the non-cooperating disabled would receive any social minimum at all. Under Rawls's theory, parties in the original position have no benevolent concern for citizens generally; they are concerned solely to represent the interests of their beneficiaries.[40] Only because parties in the original position do not know the identity of their beneficiaries do they consider the interests of all cooperating citizens; parties must realize that if they paid no attention to the interests of a certain group, it might turn out that the citizens they represent were members of precisely that group.

It follows, however, that when we instruct parties in the original position that their beneficiaries are *not* members of a certain group—here, non-cooperating citizens—they will choose principles of distributive justice which give no weight whatsoever to the interests of that group. The logical effect of Rawls's exclusion of the non-cooperating disabled, then, is that representatives in the original position, given the opportunity, will choose principles of justice that afford only such aid to the non-cooperating disabled as is likely to benefit groups *other* than the non-cooperating disabled. It is therefore plausible that representatives in the original position would choose to give no aid at all to the non-cooperating disabled. The non-cooperating disabled would not receive the amount generated by the difference principle for the nondisabled poor and the co-operating disabled poor. The non-cooperating disabled might not even be entitled to a social minimum representing what they would have received under the no-agreement point of general egoism, or representing what is necessary to be a full citizen; by assumption, the non-cooperating disabled are not fully cooperating citizens and would not be able to survive under a system of general egoism.

All this makes it important to determine who is a cooperating member of society and who is not. As Eva Feder Kittay has observed, Rawls does not clearly explain who is a cooperating citizen.[41] Rawls does make it clear, in *Justice as Fairness,* that a cooperating citizen can temporarily fall below the level of "minimum essential capacities,"[42] but he still does not explain what that level is. Probably the most natural interpretation is that a cooperating citizen is one who works during most of her adult life, either in or outside the home.

Rawls sees the non-cooperating disabled as beyond the pale of justice. For this reason alone, his theory is objectionable. Utilitarianism does not draw such boundaries between the subjects of justice, nor do some egalitarian theories.

We have seen that Rawls's theory oscillates between excessive redistribution to the disabled and insufficient redistribution to the disabled. Under a very plausible definition of the least-advantaged class as those with severe disabilities, Rawls's theory would lead to excessive redistribution to the disabled. Rawls avoids this extreme by defining the least-advantaged class as those who are poorest. But this definition seems to permit no extra help for the disabled. Rawls is aware of this deficiency in his theory, so he adds a requirement that society provide restorative care. But this modification of his resource-egalitarian system threatens to commit vast social resources to medical expenditures that will prolong only slightly the productive life of those who die or become incapacitated at a young age. And in all permutations of his theory, Rawls seems unable to provide for the non-cooperating disabled; they may receive no social minimum at all under his system.

This kind of oscillation is discernible in all resource-egalitarian theories. The enunciated principles differ, but resource egalitarians never reach a satisfactory position on disability unless they somehow manage to become sensitive to relative benefit, unless they find the golden mean of utilitarianism.

Rawls is too large a figure to be contained in only one chapter. In Chapter 10, I explore some illiberal implications of his theory and respond to his contention that utilitarianism has illiberal implications.

VII
Dworkin

Ronald Dworkin is well known as an opponent of utilitarianism.[1] Dworkin has purported to offer a nonutilitarian and intuitively appealing solution to the problem of redistribution to the disabled: hypothetical insurance.[2] The device of hypothetical insurance is a major element in Dworkin's book *Sovereign Virtue*, a collection of some of his important articles on distributive justice.[3]

In this chapter I argue that Dworkin's hypothetical insurance is actually a form of utilitarianism, though not the most attractive form.[4] I first show that hypothetical insurance makes use of a greater-benefit criterion, in a manner similar to utilitarianism. I next argue that hypothetical insurance can be considered a type of hypothetical-choice utilitarianism, similar to early efforts by utilitarian economists John Harsanyi and William Vickrey. Then, I argue that hypothetical insurance is only appealing to the extent that it seems an accurate device for the making of interpersonal welfare comparisons in aid of utilitarian judgments. I next argue that hypothetical insurance has no secure basis in what Dworkin presents as his wider egal-

itarian theory. Finally, I discuss Dworkin's attempts to distinguish his system from utilitarianism.

Hypothetical Insurance and
the Greater-Benefit Criterion
BASICS OF DWORKIN'S THEORY

According to Dworkin, his distributive principle is that resources, suitably defined, should be distributed equally. Dworkin
illustrates this principle by hypothesizing that a group of immigrants has landed on a previously unoccupied island. The
fairest scheme for dividing the resources on the island, he claims,
would be to distribute to each immigrant an equal number of
clamshells for use in bidding at an auction, and then to auction off all things of value on the island.[5] Such an auction,
if successfully concluded, would pass the "envy test," which
Dworkin posits as a provisional ideal for his conception of
equality of resources: "No division of resources is an equal division if, once the division is complete, any immigrant would
prefer someone else's bundle of resources to his own bundle."[6]

Dworkin would deal with disabilities through a system of
hypothetical insurance. We are to imagine that people do not
know whether they are or will be disabled, but they do know
the rate at which disabilities occur. We then ask how much insurance people would buy, from an initially equal stock of resources, against the risk of being disabled. The average level of
coverage and its corresponding premium amount would form
the basis of a system of redistribution to the disabled. The premium amount would be collected from each person as a tax,
and the revenue raised would be used to pay each disabled person, as compensation, the average level of coverage that hypothetically would have been purchased.[7]

Alternatively, Dworkin suggests, if we could figure out how much insurance each *individual* disabled person would have bought in a hypothetical market, we would award each of them the corresponding level of compensation. Dworkin notes that this individualized approach would actually be preferable if it were possible; the averaging assumption is a "second-best" solution.[8]

In addition to his system of hypothetical insurance against disability, Dworkin also puts forward a system of hypothetical insurance against the inability to earn various levels of income. This system of hypothetical income insurance generates a minimum income-earning ability or, in an alternative version suggested by Dworkin, a minimum income.[9] The premiums for Dworkin's system of hypothetical income insurance do not come from initial resources; they are paid out of future income, through a progressive income tax.[10]

Dworkin mentions the possibility that hypothetical insurance against disability might be undertaken on the same basis as hypothetical income insurance, with premiums taken out of future income instead of initial resources.[11] For ease of analysis, however, he assumes that his immigrants choose the simpler version of hypothetical insurance against disability, involving a "fixed premium," taken out of initial resources.[12]

Dworkin has more recently used the idea of hypothetical insurance to address two major distributive issues in health-care policy: what total amount of resources should be devoted to health care, and how should that care be distributed?[13] Dworkin proposes a "prudent insurance" test for fairness in health care.[14] We are to imagine, once again, that people do not know whether they will fall ill or be disabled, but they do know the rate at which illnesses and disabilities occur. We then ask what health insurance it would be prudent for most people to buy, from an initially equal stock of resources. If most people would prudently buy insurance covering certain kinds of medical care, a universal health-care system should provide such care.[15]

Dworkin's prudent insurance test does not generate any compensation for the disabled beyond the provision of health care. I will therefore concentrate, for the most part, on Dworkin's original and more general model of hypothetical insurance against disability.[16] However, I will return at times to the prudent insurance test; as I will demonstrate, "prudent insurance" is even more utilitarian than Dworkin's original model of hypothetical insurance.

HYPOTHETICAL INSURANCE
AND RISK ATTITUDES

Hypothetical insurance against disability is a means of distributing resources between people who are actually disabled and people who are actually nondisabled. The higher the average premium selected by the hypothetical insurance buyers, the greater will be the amount of initial resources distributed to the disabled; the lower the average premium, the smaller will be the amount of resources distributed to the disabled.

It is an intuitive selling point of hypothetical insurance that it seems to take a position intermediate between equality of welfare and strict equality of material resources. Equality of welfare, Dworkin observes, could theoretically require unlimited redistribution to the severely disabled: "It provides . . . no upper bound to compensation so long as any further payment would improve the welfare of the wretched."[17] On the other hand, a strict equality of initial resources would not provide any compensation to the disabled.

However, the intermediacy of Dworkin's hypothetical insurance is not inherent; rather, it is based on a not-entirely-explicit assumption that the decision criterion of hypothetical insurance buyers will be something close to risk-neutral welfare maximization. If hypothetical insurance buyers exhibit an extreme attitude to risk, hypothetical insurance will collapse into one of the straightforward egalitarian approaches.

Suppose that all people in Dworkin's hypothetical insurance market adopt the same maximin decision rule that Rawls, in *A Theory of Justice,* claims would be adopted in the original position.[18] Maximin represents an attitude of maximum risk aversion: it requires that we make the worst possible outcome as good as possible, no matter how unlikely that worst outcome is, no matter how slight an improvement in that outcome we can accomplish, and no matter how great a deterioration in other possible outcomes we must suffer in order to accomplish that slight improvement.

If everyone in Dworkin's hypothetical insurance market adopted the maximin criterion, they might devote all of their stock of initial resources to pay for insurance against being severely disabled, purchasing the highest possible level of coverage. They would allocate additional resources to their disabled state, by buying higher and higher coverage, as long as they believed that additional resources would improve their disabled state to any degree, without actually making their disabled state as good as their nondisabled state. The familiar and, by assumption, unacceptable result would be that all initial resources would be redistributed to the disabled, leaving no initial resources for the nondisabled.[19] Under maximin, then, hypothetical insurance collapses into equality of welfare.

To be sure, even under maximin hypothetical insurance might not lead to *unlimited* redistribution of initial resources to the disabled. Hypothetical insurance buyers might decide that past a certain point of insurance purchases, it would be worse to be nondisabled and poor than to be severely disabled and rich. Or they might decide that past a certain point of insurance purchases, additional insurance proceeds would not benefit them at all if they were disabled. But these are analogous to decisions that could similarly put a limit to redistribution under equality of welfare: perhaps poor nondisabled people, if poor enough, would have lower welfare than rich disabled people; perhaps additional resources would not increase the welfare of the disabled at all, past a certain point of redistribution. Despite these possible limiting conditions, it is generally assumed, by Dworkin and others, that equality of welfare would theoretically require an unacceptably high level of redistribution from nondisabled to disabled, and the same can be said of hypothetical insurance under maximin, for essentially the same reasons.

Things would also not turn out well if everyone in Dworkin's hypothetical insurance market followed a decision rule of maximal risk-seeking, or maximax.[20] Under a maximax decision rule, people would try to make the best outcome as good as possible. In the hypothetical insurance scenario, the best outcome is to be nondisabled rather than disabled. In order to make this outcome as good as possible, insurance buyers would buy no insurance at all against the possibility of being disabled,[21] to assure that they would have to pay no insurance premium and would have more resources if they turned out to be nondisabled rather than disabled. The result would be no redistribution at all to the disabled, even to pay for medical expenses. Everyone, disabled or nondisabled, would retain the same equal share of initial resources. Under maximax, hypothetical insurance collapses into strict equality of material resources. (It should be noted, however, that hypothetical insurance under maximax results in a strict equality of material resources only because the system precludes any distribution in which disabled people receive *fewer* initial resources than nondisabled people: you cannot insure against *not* being disabled. Without this constraint, maximax would result in the disabled getting no initial resources at all.)

THE GREATER-BENEFIT CRITERION IN HYPOTHETICAL INSURANCE AND UTILITARIANISM

If hypothetical insurance buyers follow the maximin decision rule, the system of hypothetical insurance leads to massive redistribution to the disabled, in a manner similar to equality of welfare. If insurance buyers follow the maximax decision rule, hypothetical insurance, like equality of material resources, permits no redistribution to the disabled. Thus, as I have said, our view of hypothetical insurance as intermediate between equality of material resources and equality of welfare is based on the assumption that hypothetical insurance buyers would not take an extreme attitude to risk, but would instead adopt a decision rule close to risk-neutral welfare maximization.

A decision rule of risk-neutral welfare maximization makes *intra*personal distributive decisions based on calculations of relative benefit. Return briefly to the maximin decision rule. Under maximin, considerations of *relative* benefit are irrelevant. The situation of the worst-state disabled must be improved as long as *any* benefit to that state is possible. Similarly, considerations of *relative* benefit are irrelevant under maximax. The best-case nondisabled state must be improved as long as any benefit to that state is possible. It is this insensi-

tivity to relative benefit that makes both maximin and maximax (and equality of welfare and equality of material resources) yield what seem to be unfair results.

A risk-neutral decision rule, by contrast, is completely
sensitive to calculations of relative benefit. Risk-neutral hypothetical insurance buyers will make insurance decisions solely
on the basis of whether the expected benefit of resources to
their disabled state (the benefit times the probability of receiving the benefit) is *greater* than the expected benefit of those resources to their nondisabled state. It is this greater-benefit criterion which allows hypothetical insurance to negotiate a path
between equality of welfare and equality of material resources.

Similarly, of course, a greater-benefit criterion allows utilitarianism to negotiate a path between equality of welfare and
equality of material resources. As previously noted, the first-
order distributive principle of utilitarianism is to distribute resources to those who will most benefit from those resources.
Ignoring for now any secondary considerations, utilitarianism
would redistribute resources from the nondisabled to the disabled to the extent that the disabled would benefit more from
those resources. Just as hypothetical insurance under risk neutrality compares the expected benefit of resources to the disabled state of the average insurance buyer with the expected
benefit of those resources to his nondisabled state, so utilitarianism compares the benefit that actual disabled people would
derive from resources to the benefit that actual nondisabled
people would derive from those resources.

There is obviously a close similarity between utilitarianism and hypothetical insurance under risk neutrality. Both
systems make distributive decisions based on a greater-benefit
criterion—a criterion that is completely foreign to both equality of welfare and equality of material resources.[22]

TERMINOLOGICAL DETOUR

I should specify here that I am speaking of risk neutrality (and risk aversion and risk seeking) with respect to utility or welfare, not with respect to wealth.[23] If someone is risk neutral with respect to wealth, she is indifferent between a certainty of receiving a given amount of money and a 50 percent chance of receiving twice that amount. If someone is risk neutral with respect to welfare, she is indifferent between a certainty of experiencing a given increase in welfare and a 50 percent chance of experiencing twice as great an increase. Risk neutrality with respect to welfare can take account of the diminishing marginal utility of money; someone who is risk neutral with respect to welfare can vastly prefer a certainty of receiving one million dollars to a 50 percent chance of receiving two million dollars, on the ground that receiving two million dollars does not bring twice as much benefit as receiving one million dollars.

My usage here is similar to that of Rawls, in his discussion of risk attitudes in the original position.[24] It is different from that of most writers on law and economics, who generally speak of risk preferences with respect to wealth, especially when discussing the incentive effects of alternative legal rules.[25]

Also, when I speak of risk attitudes with respect to welfare or utility, I mean subjective utility, not von Neumann–Morgenstern (VNM) utility. While it is possible to be risk averse or a risk seeker with respect to subjective utility, it is impossible to be anything but risk neutral with respect to VNM utility: the VNM utility scale is constructed by observing an individual's preferences over risky alternatives and then assigning utilities to outcomes so as to *make* the individual risk neutral with respect to those utilities.[26] Another way of saying that an individual is risk neutral with respect to subjective utility is to say that his subjective utility function is identical to his VNM utility function.

Dworkin assumes, I have said, that his hypothetical insurance buyers will not take an extreme attitude to risk. It does not follow, of course, that either Dworkin or his readers must assume that the average insurance buyer will be *strictly* risk neutral with respect to welfare. Dworkin does state that it makes sense to suppose that "most people would make roughly the same assessment of the value of insurance against general handicaps, such as blindness or the loss of a limb, that affect a wide spectrum of different sorts of lives."[27] This supposition suggests—to me, at any rate—that Dworkin has in mind an average attitude close to risk neutrality. In any event, Dworkin certainly assumes that hypothetical insurance will use a greater-benefit criterion, and that criterion appears most clearly in the decisionmaking of risk-neutral welfare maximizers.

HYPOTHETICAL INSURANCE AND POOR TWO-DISABILITY SOCIETY

As a demonstration of the similarity between hypothetical insurance (as we assume it will operate) and utilitarianism, consider what distributive results hypothetical insurance would reach in Poor Two-Disability Society, one of the examples I set forth in Chapter 4. In this example, 10 out of 11 people are "less-disabled" and 1 out of 11 people is "more-disabled." Everyone, if untreated, would suffer 12 days of severe pain per year. There is no scarcity of food or shelter, but there is a scarcity of medical resources; E resources per person (that is, an equal share) would provide 10 days of pain relief to each less-disabled person and only one hour of pain relief to each more-disabled person. It is therefore 240 times as expensive to provide an hour of pain relief to a more-disabled person as to a less-disabled person; for each one hour of pain relief provided to a more-disabled person, society must deny 240 hours of pain relief (10 days) to various less-disabled people.

Assume that both the less-disabled and the more-disabled would be considered "disabled" under Dworkin's system of hypothetical insurance.[28] If hypothetical insurance buyers bought no insurance against either disability, the result would be E medical resources for everyone. If hypothetical insurance buyers used all their initial resources to buy insurance against the lesser (less expensive) disability that afflicts 10 out of 11 people, the less-disabled would get all of the medical resources. If hypothetical insurance buyers used all their initial resources to buy insurance against the greater (more expensive) disability that afflicts 1 out of 11 people, the more-disabled would get all of the medical resources.

Here we are likely to assume that hypothetical insurance would reach, or at least approximate, the utilitarian solution to this problem: provide all medical resources to the less-disabled. Just as utilitarian allocators would not want to provide an hour of pain relief to the more-disabled at the cost of denying 240 hours of pain relief to the less-disabled, hypothetical insurance buyers would not want to provide an hour of pain relief to their hypothetical more-disabled state at the cost of denying 24 hours of pain relief to their hypothetical less-disabled state (which is 10 times as likely as their hypothetical more-disabled state).

As a formal matter, of course, hypothetical insurance need not track utilitarianism here. Hypothetical insurance buyers might be extremely risk averse: they might want to provide themselves with some pain relief in their more-disabled state at the cost of denying themselves 240 times as much pain relief in their less-disabled state. But such an attitude does not seem likely.

This exercise demonstrates how the greater-benefit criterion in Dworkin's system of hypothetical insurance causes his system to approximate utilitarianism—as long as hypothetical insurance reaches results based on the greater-benefit criterion and not based on risk seeking or risk aversion. Dworkin's system, like utilitarianism, distributes resources to people who would derive greater benefit from those resources, even if those people are already better off than others. This is precisely what sets a maximizing theory like utilitarianism apart from egalitarian theories. Dworkin's theory, as we and he understand it, is a maximizing theory, not an egalitarian theory.

Accordingly, Dworkin is inaccurate and misleading when he describes his theory as one that seeks equality of resources. Even granting that the originator of a theory must be allowed some deference in matters of appellation, the accurate term for Dworkin's theory of distributive justice is the one I have been using: hypothetical insurance.

Hypothetical-Choice Utilitarianism

Up to now I have only argued that Dworkin's hypothetical insurance is similar to utilitarianism. I will now argue that hypothetical insurance should be seen as a form of utilitarianism—specifically, a form of hypothetical-choice utilitarianism.

The most famous theorist of hypothetical-choice morality is of course Rawls. It is useful to contrast Dworkin's conception of hypothetical insurance to Rawls's original conception of the original position, advanced in *A Theory of Justice*. As a number of commentators have noted, hypothetical insurance is a modified original position, a device for making interpersonal distributive decisions based on personal, self-interested decisions that people would supposedly reach if they were in ignorance of their real situation.[29]

Now some features that appear to set Dworkin's scheme apart from that of Rawls may be largely superfluous. Dworkin posits an initially equal division of resources, while Rawls places everyone in ignorance of their economic standing. However, Dworkin's initial situation can result in any distribution of resources between the nondisabled and the disabled, depending on the average level of insurance hypothetically purchased; the only constraint is that the disabled cannot have fewer initial resources than the nondisabled. Therefore, Dworkin could drop his assumption of an initial equal distribution and instead ask his insurance buyers what level of compensation they would establish for the disabled if they did not know whether they would be disabled.

Nevertheless, there are some real differences between Rawls's version of the original position and Dworkin's. Most importantly, perhaps, Dworkin's hypothetical insurance buyers follow different decision rules than Rawls's parties in the original position. I have already noted that if Dworkin's hypothetical insurance buyers adopted the maximin criterion, hypothetical insurance would collapse into equality of welfare, with massive redistribution from the nondisabled to the disabled. By the same token, if the parties in Rawls's original position adopted the decision criteria of Dworkin's hypothetical insurance buyers, those parties would choose—or at least would be far more likely to choose—average utilitarianism, rather than Rawls's two principles, as a principle of justice.

In *A Theory of Justice*, Rawls considers the argument that parties in the original position would choose average utilitarianism. The argument for average utilitarianism, Rawls notes, depends on some key premises about the decisionmaking of the parties. One of these premises is that the parties would assume that each of them has an equal probability of being every actual member of society; this is the equiprobability assumption.[30] Another pro-utilitarian premise is that the parties would take a neutral attitude to risk.[31] If the equiprobability assumption is accepted, the expected welfare of a party in the original position is the same as the average welfare of society; parties in the original position would maximize their own expected welfare by maximizing the average welfare of society. If risk neutrality is accepted, the parties will choose to maximize their expected (subjective) welfare, and so will choose average utilitarianism as a principle of justice.[32]

Rawls rejects both the equiprobability assumption[33] and the idea that parties in the original position would be risk neutral with respect to welfare or utility.[34] Dworkin, however, comes very close to accepting both of these features. As noted, Dworkin assumes, somewhat implicitly, that the average attitude to risk will not be extreme, but will be something close to risk neutrality. Dworkin also instructs his hypothetical insurance buyers to assume that they have a probability of suffering from various disabilities which is the same as the frequency of those disabilities in society; this is similar, though not identical, to the equiprobability assumption rejected by Rawls.[35]

Is Dworkin's hypothetical insurance, then, a form of utilitarianism? It is not conventional utilitarianism, which I will define as any theory that seeks to maximize the welfare of *actual* people. If the parties in Rawls's original position chose average utilitarianism as their principle of justice, Rawls's theory would lead to conventional utilitarianism. The original position, having been used to derive a principle of justice, would be discarded; distributive decisions would be made by attempting to maximize the average utility of actual people.

Dworkin, by contrast, uses his modified original position not to derive principles of justice, but to make distributive decisions. I have previously noted the great similarity between the greater-benefit criterion that operates under Dworkin's hypothetical insurance, as he himself conceives that system, and the greater-benefit criterion that operates under utilitarianism. Nevertheless, the distribution that emerges from hypothetical insurance might not maximize welfare as between actual disabled people and actual nondisabled people, for reasons that I discuss below. Therefore, hypothetical insurance cannot be considered a form of conventional utilitarianism.

But other authors, including Harsanyi and Vickrey, have proposed distributive schemes involving hypothetical choice that are generally (if not universally) acknowledged as utilitarian, even though those schemes might not result in the maximization of welfare among actual people.[36] A full comparison between Dworkin's hypothetical insurance and the systems of Harsanyi and Vickrey is beyond the scope of this chapter.[37] Some parallels can be noted, however.

In their earliest treatments, in 1953 and 1945, respectively, Harsanyi and Vickrey do not require hypothetical choosers to assume that they have an equal probability of actually *being* every actual person, with all that person's feelings and preferences; rather, like Dworkin, they require hypothetical choosers to assume that they have an equal probability of being in the situation of every actual person. Thus, Harsanyi:

> [A] value judgment on the distribution of income
> would show the required impersonality to the high-

est degree if the person who made this judgment
had to choose a particular income distribution in
complete ignorance of what his own relative position (and the position of those near to his heart)
would be within the system chosen. This would be
the case if he had exactly the same chance of obtaining the first position (corresponding to the highest income) or the second or the third, etc., up to
the last position (corresponding to the lowest income) available within that scheme.[38]

Another important parallel to Dworkin is that it is theoretically possible, in the hypothetical-choice schemes of Harsanyi and Vickrey, for attitudes to risk to affect the distribution
of resources.[39] However, Harsanyi and Vickrey assume, sometimes more explicitly and sometimes less so, that people do
not or will not have extreme attitudes to risk. Harsanyi has on
occasion forcefully expressed his view that it would be irrational to follow a maximin decision rule, outside of special situations such as zero-sum games: "If you took the maximin
principle seriously then you could not ever cross a street (after
all, you might be hit by a car); you could never drive over a
bridge (after all, it might collapse); you could never get mar-
ried (after all, it might end in a disaster), etc. If anybody really
acted this way he would soon end up in a mental institution."[40]

Dworkin's hypothetical insurance, along with the systems proposed by Harsanyi and Vickrey, can be classed as
hypothetical-choice utilitarianism, as opposed to conventional
utilitarianism. Hypothetical-choice utilitarianism can plausibly be defined as a scheme for making distributive judgments,
based on hypothetical choice, that incorporates two features
similar to, but weaker than the conditions that Rawls believes

could lead to average utilitarianism in the original position. First, the hypothetical chooser must assume that he has an equal chance of being in the distribution-related situation of any actual person in society. So if resources are being distributed among classes, defined by health, income, or otherwise, the chooser must assume that he has a probability of being in any class that is the same as the percentage of the population represented by that class. Second, it is stipulated or assumed that the hypothetical chooser will take an attitude that is close to risk neutral; his choices between risky alternatives will be based for the most part on calculations of relative benefit rather than on attitudes to risk.

Hypothetical Insurance as a Device for Making Interpersonal Welfare Comparisons

A major ostensible difference between conventional utilitarianism and hypothetical insurance is that utilitarianism requires interpersonal welfare comparisons and hypothetical insurance does not. Indeed, Dworkin claims that there is "no place" in his theory for interpersonal welfare comparisons.[41] From a utilitarian perspective, this supposed difference between hypothetical insurance and utilitarianism is illusory. Utilitarians tend to think that people in the same broadly defined situation receive essentially the same benefit from resources. Therefore, the only interpersonal welfare comparisons that have to be made are those based on differences in situation, for example, wealth versus poverty, health versus disability. Dworkin's insurance buyers compare the benefit they would receive from resources in their nondisabled state to the benefit they would receive from resources in various disabled states. Dworkin's insurance buyers also compare the benefit they would receive from a larger amount of resources, in each of their nondisabled and disabled states, to the benefit they would receive from a smaller amount of resources. These are the only types of interpersonal comparisons that utilitarians are likely to think necessary in order to make distributive decisions among the nondisabled and the disabled.

But I will make a far bolder claim. To the extent that hypothetical insurance seems a fair means of distributing resources between nondisabled and disabled, it is only because it seems an accurate means of making interpersonal welfare comparisons in aid of conventional utilitarian judgments.[42] I will defend this claim by attempting to show that when hypothetical insurance does not seem to be an accurate means of making interpersonal comparisons, it no longer seems fair. Obviously, my argument here, even more than previously, depends on shared intuitions and shared interpretations of intuitions.[43]

A time-honored means of making interpersonal comparisons is to try to imagine oneself in another's situation. Suppose that two people are vying for a scarce resource. If the distributor of that resource is a utilitarian, he will want to determine who would most benefit from the resource. If there are no other considerations, the claimant who would most benefit from the resource will receive it.

The determination of relative benefit requires an interpersonal welfare comparison. How is the utilitarian distributor to make the comparison? As a heuristic device, in order to focus his intuitions and reason, the distributor may imagine that he has a 50 percent chance of being either claimant. In that situation, he would maximize his own expected welfare by distributing the resource to the claimant who would most benefit from it. And if he were risk neutral with respect to welfare, he would choose to maximize his expected welfare. An example substantially of this type is given by Hare in his book *Moral Thinking*.[44]

Let us consider how hypothetical insurance might diverge from utilitarianism, so that it would not be an accurate means of making interpersonal welfare comparisons. The major possible source of divergence between utilitarianism and hypothetical insurance has already been mentioned: extreme attitudes to risk. If the average insurance buyer is either extremely risk averse or an extreme risk seeker, hypothetical insurance will result in either massive redistribution to the disabled or no redistribution to the disabled, respectively. These results seem unfair, and Dworkin and his readers assume, as I have said, that the average attitude to risk would not be extreme and would not lead to these unfair results.

But *why* do the results of extreme attitudes to risk seem unfair, and why should we assume such attitudes away? A utilitarian is perfectly justified in stipulating that hypothetical choice, as a means of making interpersonal comparisons, must be strictly risk neutral: if hypothetical choice were not risk neutral, it would not determine maximum benefit and would thus fail of its purpose. For Dworkin, however, hypothetical choice is not a proxy for benefit, but supposedly an independent basis for making distributive decisions. Dworkin notes that actual insurance decisions are motivated in part by attitudes toward risk and that hypothetical insurance decisions would also be so motivated.[45] Thus, there is no reason, consistent with Dworkin's theory, to constrain the risk preferences of hypothetical insurance buyers.

It might be argued that the average attitude to risk just would not be extreme, and so the unfair results of an extreme average attitude to risk simply would not occur. This might be true, despite Rawls's view about how parties would reason in his version of the original position. Nevertheless, it should be remembered that pegging disability compensation to the average level of coverage in the hypothetical insurance market is only a second-best solution for Dworkin. The best solution, according to Dworkin, would be to determine what coverage each *individual* disabled person would have bought in the hypothetical insurance market, and compensate him or her accordingly.[46]

It is not farfetched to think that individual people would take widely varying attitudes to risk in the hypothetical insurance market, as they do take widely varying attitudes to risk in life. Suppose it could be determined what coverage two severely disabled people would have bought in the hypothetical insurance market. Larry, because of extreme risk aversion, would have devoted almost his entire stock of initial resources to buy insurance. Mary, a risk seeker, would have bought no insurance at all in the hypothetical insurance market. Larry and Mary do not evaluate differently the benefit they would derive from resources in their disabled state; they merely have extremely different attitudes to risk.

In this circumstance, Dworkin is committed to say that the ideally fair result is for Larry to receive an enormous amount of resources by reason of his disability, and for Mary to receive no compensation at all, simply because of the different decisions these two individuals *would* have made in a hypothetical insurance market.[47] This result does not seem fair to me, however, and I trust that it does not seem fair to most readers. Indeed, to paraphrase Kenneth Arrow, it seems almost the height of moral arbitrariness that the distribution of resources is to be governed by the tastes of individuals for gambling.[48]

Hypothetical insurance initially offers the promise of a position intermediate between equality of material resources and equality of welfare. But the above example shows that if we take seriously the idea of allowing hypothetical insurance decisions—whatever they are—to determine distributive shares, hypothetical insurance can fall prey simultaneously to the defects of *both* straightforward egalitarian approaches: it can result in massive redistribution for some and no help at all for others.

If hypothetical insurance initially seems fair, it is not, I would contend, because the choices people would make in a hypothetical insurance market determine the fair level of compensation for the disabled. Rather, the idea of choice in a state of ignorance seems congenial to us because we assume that the distribution people would establish between their disabled state and their nondisabled state, to maximize their expected welfare, is the same distribution that would maximize aggregate welfare as between *actual* disabled people and *actual* nondisabled people. Choice in a state of ignorance is merely a proxy for aggregate welfare maximization, and when idiosyncratic hypothetical choices do not appear to maximize aggregate welfare, we do not think the results fair—I do not, at any rate.

MISTAKEN PREDICTIONS OF BENEFIT

There are other possible differences between hypothetical insurance and utilitarianism. Dworkin has modified hypothetical insurance to minimize these differences, yet they still reflect unfavorably on hypothetical insurance and demonstrate that hypothetical insurance is only appealing to the extent it can mimic utilitarianism. One such difference is that hypothetical insurance could allow hypothetical insurance buyers to make mistakes about the benefit they would derive from resources in various conditions.

Utilitarianism is concerned with what will truly benefit people. Hypothetical insurance, on the other hand, even if we assume complete risk neutrality, considers only people's hypothetical *predictions* of what will benefit them. That, after all, is part of what constitutes an insurance-buying decision: a prediction of the extent to which resources will benefit the insurance buyer in various possible states of the world.

The problem is that predictions can be mistaken. Consider an example Dworkin gives of two sighted individuals with equal initial resources, one of whom buys insurance against blindness and one of whom does not. Among the reasons why these two individuals might make different decisions, Dworkin suggests, is that "one would count monetary compensation for the loss of his sight as worthless in the face of such a tragedy while the other, more practical, would fix his mind on the aids and special training that such money might buy."[49]

I actually think that *anyone* who declined to buy health or disability insurance because he thought he "would count monetary compensation for the loss of his sight as worthless in the face of such a tragedy" would be making a mistaken prediction. Here, however, I will only suggest that *some* such people could be mistaken in predicting the benefit they would derive from money should they become blind.

Suppose it could be determined that a blind person *would* have bought no insurance against blindness in Dworkin's hypothetical insurance auction, because he would have counted monetary compensation as worthless in the face of the tragedy of blindness. Suppose further that it could be determined that the insurance-buying decision the blind person *would* have made would have been mistaken. In fact, some monetary compensation can provide great benefits to him. My intuitive judgment, at least, is that it would not be fair to deny compensation to the blind individual because of a mistaken assessment of benefit he *would* have made.

Dworkin actually has taken steps to filter mistaken assessments of benefit out of his distributive system. Under his more recently devised prudent insurance test, he asks not what insurance people would in fact buy if they had equal material resources, but what insurance it would be "prudent for most Americans to buy."[50] He notes that "many people, particularly when young, do not make prudent decisions," explaining that "They do not, that is, make the decisions that best serve the plans, convictions, tastes, and preferences they would find, on reflection, that they already have."[51]

Possibly this attempt to filter out mistaken assessments of benefit can be justified as consistent with the idea of hypothetical insurance. Nevertheless, it is a step away from the model of *actual* insurance and toward a utilitarian mode of reasoning. Suppose that health-care allocators under a Dworkinian system were convinced that actual people behind the veil would buy insurance for a procedure that provides only minor benefits, instead of a procedure that provides major benefits. The Dworkinian allocators could (and presumably would) decide that this would not be a "prudent" decision, and that the health-care system should therefore provide the major benefits instead of the minor benefits.

COORDINATION PROBLEMS
AND INCENTIVE EFFECTS

Until now we have been considering a *distributive* model of compensation for disabilities: compensation is paid at the same time initial resources are distributed, and goes to determine the amount of initial resources received by the non-disabled and the disabled. In actuality, however, compensation would be *redistributive,* either under hypothetical insurance or under utilitarianism. People would earn income, and some of that income would be taxed away to support the disabled. Redistributive taxation would also be used to support the poor, both under Dworkin's hypothetical insurance of income-earning ability (which I have so far largely ignored) and under most utilitarian views.

Once the issue is framed as redistribution rather than distribution, further divergence between utilitarianism and hypothetical insurance is possible. Utilitarianism will consider the incentive effects of redistribution; hypothetical insurance may not.

From the perspective of hypothetical insurance buyers, incentive effects represent a coordination problem. The insurance buyers must (on one interpretation) arrive at a level of support for the disabled, and the poor, in ignorance of how their hypothetical decisions will interact with the hypothetical decisions of others. Therefore, hypothetical insurance buyers cannot consider the effect of their coverage decisions on work and investment incentives.

Dworkin shows some awareness of this coordination problem. "It might be," he notes, "that the costs in overall efficiency of [hypothetical insurance] would be so great that those who are prepared to compromise equality of resources either for general utility or in service of some strategy of making the worst-off as well-off as possible, would argue that even that much equality would be condemned by their more embracing conception of justice."[52] Dworkin does not appear to realize, however, that negative incentive effects can make hypothetical insurance an objectionable system from the point of view of hypothetical insurance buyers *themselves*. They might arrive at a level of coverage which, because of incentive effects, produces a result that they all would consider inferior to what would have been produced by a lower level of coverage.

The insensitivity of hypothetical insurance to incentive effects is the reason why Hal Varian finds, in his model of hypothetical income insurance, that hypothetical insurance buyers would insure to complete income equality.[53] This would be the result, moreover, even if it would make everyone worse off in absolute terms.

Another kind of coordination problem could result in too low a level of coverage for some medical conditions. Suppose there is a rare disease that can be successfully treated for one million dollars. Suppose further that the administrators of the Dworkinian health insurance system determine that one-half of the population would have bought full coverage behind the Dworkinian veil, and one-half would have bought no coverage. If the administrators give effect to this hypothetical choice, instead of labeling it imprudent, and if Dworkin's "prudent insurance" system remains true to the averaging approach of his original hypothetical insurance device, the result would be that those with the disease receive only one-half of the amount needed for treatment—a result that probably no hypothetical insurance buyer would have chosen.

It is presumably in order to avoid such results that Dworkin does abandon the averaging approach, in his "prudent insurance" system, in favor of providing full coverage for a condition where "most" people would have bought such coverage. But with this modification, "prudent insurance" no longer gives effect to the decisions every hypothetical insurance buyer would have made. It is hard to see how Dworkin's departure from his original model can be justified, except as a utilitarian choice to avoid the consequences of that model.

Yet another kind of coordination problem is well described by David Wasserman.[54] From the perspective of the hypothetical insurance buyer, many beneficial programs for the disabled have a public goods aspect; they do not involve individualized payments. There are medical research programs, accessibility requirements, and so on.

Neither Dworkin's original model of hypothetical insurance nor the later prudent insurance model can easily accommodate such programs. Suppose that people are asked, behind the Dworkinian veil, how much of their equal share of resources they would like to devote to medical research benefiting the entire society. Each hypothetical chooser would probably devote nothing to medical research, as each would get only an infinitesimal benefit from his own contribution.

We could ask people to decide, in ignorance of their own health condition, what portion of total social resources should go to medical research. But to effect this modification of Dworkin's system, we would have to drop his notion that hypothetical insurance buyers make decisions about their own hypothetically equal share of resources rather than about total social resources. Once again, we would be adjusting Dworkin's system because it had diverged from utilitarianism and reached a counterintuitive result.

Many years ago, before developing his own hypothetical-choice approach, Dworkin commented on Rawls's use of hypothetical choice. Dworkin then claimed that "hypothetical contracts do not supply an independent argument for the fairness of enforcing their terms. . . . you use the device of a hypothetical agreement to make a point that might have been made without that device, which is that the solution recommended is so obviously fair and sensible that only someone with an immediate contrary interest could disagree."[55] There is a great deal of merit to this claim. I would say, accordingly, that if Dworkin's own system of hypothetical insurance is intuitively appealing, it is not because we attach moral force to the counterfactual decisions people would have made in a state of ignorance, constrained by the requirement that they be prudent; it is because the distributive decisions resulting from that system approximate the utilitarian principle that resources should go to the people who would most benefit from them.

ROEMER AND FLEURBAEY ON HYPOTHETICAL INSURANCE AND UTILITARIANISM

In an early commentary on Dworkin's hypothetical insurance device, John Roemer noted the close connection between hypothetical insurance and utilitarianism.[56] In his more recent book *Theories of Distributive Justice*,[57] Roemer draws back from this insight. He lists various reasons why hypothetical choice might not maximize utility as between actual people in society, including some of the reasons I have discussed and also including other possible causes of divergence.[58] In a footnote, Roemer then "retract[s]" the implication that "Dworkin's insurance proposal . . . is closer to utilitarianism than [Dworkin] would like."[59]

While Roemer is undoubtedly correct in the formal-theoretic distinctions he draws between hypothetical insurance and utilitarianism, his earlier insight is still valid. It is true that hypothetical insurance can deviate wildly from utilitarianism; as I have noted, hypothetical insurance can result in zero redistribution to the disabled or virtually unlimited redistribution to the disabled. But the intuitive appeal of hypothetical insurance is not based on factors, such as a possible "enjoy[ment] of gambling,"[60] that can cause wild deviations from utilitarianism; it is based on the greater-benefit criterion, the way in which people compare the benefit they would derive from additional resources in their hypothetical disabled and nondisabled states. The greater-benefit criterion is what allows hypothetical insurance to converge with utilitarianism, and if we find hypothetical insurance plausible, it is because we assume that such convergence will occur.

Since Roemer's ill-advised reversal, I have taken up the banner of Dworkinian-utilitarian equivalence.[61] I am happy to note that I have now been joined by Marc Fleurbaey, who has independently come to the same conclusion.[62] But whereas I consider the imputation of utilitarianism to Dworkin a compliment, Fleurbaey considers it an insult. Fleurbaey argues that hypothetical insurance, like utilitarianism, will produce the "counterintuitive result" of favoring the nondisabled over the disabled when disabled people derive less marginal utility from income.[63] I responded to this argument in Chapter 4, where I observed that egalitarian theorists fallaciously exaggerate the conditions under which disabled people derive less marginal utility from income than nondisabled people. When it is truly convincing that the disabled would benefit less from additional income, it does not seem wrong to favor the nondisabled.

Equality of Resources versus
Hypothetical Insurance

I now will attempt to demonstrate that hypothetical insurance has no secure basis in Dworkin's wider egalitarian theory, and specifically that hypothetical insurance is inconsistent with the envy test of resource equality. This demonstration, if accepted, will support my position that hypothetical insurance represents a major element of utilitarianism in Dworkin's theory.

Dworkin's statement of the envy test, it will be remembered, is: "No division of resources is an equal division if, once the division is complete, any immigrant would prefer someone else's bundle."[64] How might the idea of equality of resources, as expressed in the envy test, be applied to disabilities? Consider first the idea that a person's resources include not only material resources, but also natural capabilities, and in particular health. If resources were defined in this way, the envy test would require that disabled people be allocated sufficient resources to make them indifferent between their bundles of natural and material resources and the bundles of nondisabled people. As Dworkin himself notes, however, no amount of material resources might be sufficient to make the severely disabled indifferent between their own bundles of natural and material resources and the bundles of the nondisabled.[65] It thus appears that if natural abilities are counted as resources, equality of resources collapses once again into something like equality of welfare.[66]

What if natural abilities are not counted as resources? Then the envy test would require only that each disabled person be indifferent between her material resources and the material resources possessed by each nondisabled person. The envy test would therefore be satisfied by an equal division of material resources by auction, with no compensation whatsoever for the disabled.

Thus, if health is treated as a resource, equality of resources demands too much redistribution; if health is not treated as a resource, equality of resources demands too little redistribution. And Dworkin's hypothetical insurance scheme does not correspond to either approach.

Dworkin actually does consider health to be a resource. He observes that "Someone who is born with a serious handicap faces his life with what we concede to be fewer resources, just on that account, than others do."[67] How, then, does Dworkin avoid applying the envy test so as to collapse equality of resources into equality of welfare?

One reason that Dworkin gives is simply that applying the envy test in this way "provides no upper bound to initial compensation," because, for example, "no amount of initial compensation could make someone born blind or mentally incompetent equal in physical or mental resources with someone taken to be 'normal' in these ways."[68] Now an opponent of egalitarianism might be excused for thinking that Dworkin takes too opportunistic an approach to determining what egalitarianism requires. If egalitarianism leads to a result that seems wrong, that arguably is a reason to reject egalitarianism as an ideal. Dworkin instead takes the questionable step of assuming that if a result seems wrong, it for that very reason cannot be required by egalitarianism; egalitarianism must instead require some different, more acceptable result.[69]

Another reason Dworkin gives for rejecting the view that the disabled should be made indifferent between their bundles of natural and material resources and the bundles of non-disabled people is that this view "requires . . . some standard of 'normal' powers to serve as the benchmark for compensation.

But whose powers should be taken as normal for this purpose?"[70] Dworkin here appears to misconceive what the envy
test requires or even, perhaps, to forget that it applies at all. If
we suppose, with Dworkin, that disabled people should be
considered to have fewer resources and thus "should be allowed to catch up, by way of transfer payments, before what
remains is auctioned off in any equal market,"[71] what is the
proper measure of whether a disabled person has been compensated sufficiently so as to "catch up"? Under Dworkin's own
theory, the proper measure would be the envy test. The envy
test, however, would not require that disabled people be made
indifferent between their bundles of natural and material resources and the bundles of some "normal" person; the envy test
would require that disabled people (and possibly all people) be
made indifferent between their resources and the resources of
any other person.

There certainly could be problems of measurement and
verification if one seriously tried to determine what (if any)
amount of material resources would make a severely disabled
person indifferent between her bundle of natural and material resources and the bundles of any other person. However,
there are also technical problems in determining what level of
coverage Dworkin's hypothetical insurance buyers would select, even under the second-best averaging assumption. As
Dworkin concedes, "any judgments that the officials of a
community might make about the structure of the hypothetical insurance market would be speculative and open to a variety of objections."[72]

Technical problems in achieving indifference are in any
case somewhat beside the point given Dworkin's acknowledgment that a straightforward application of the envy test would
require virtually unlimited redistribution to the disabled. The

view that excessive redistribution to the disabled is the *reductio ad absurdum* of egalitarianism is certainly not affected by any technical difficulty that might exist in effectuating the envy test.

In resisting a straightforward application of the envy test, Dworkin also draws a distinction between natural resources and material resources:

> Quite apart from these practical and theoretical inadequacies, the suggestion is troublesome for another reason. Though powers are resources, they should not be considered resources whose ownership is to be determined through politics in accordance with some interpretation of equality of resources. They are not, that is, resources for the theory of equality in exactly the sense in which ordinary material resources are. They cannot be manipulated or transferred, even so far as technology might permit. So in this way it misdescribes the problem of handicaps to say that equality of resources must strive to make people equal in physical and mental constitution so far as this is possible. The problem is, rather, one of determining how far the ownership of independent material resources should be affected by differences that exist in physical and mental powers, and the response of our theory should speak in that vocabulary.[73]

Some commentators have criticized Dworkin's easy assumption that his theory would not require the forced transplantation of body parts.[74] Nevertheless, it is not necessary for someone who sees the issue of redistribution to the disabled as the *reductio ad absurdum* of egalitarianism to claim that egalitarianism requires the redistribution of natural resources, such as eyes and kidneys, "so far as technology may permit." Accepting that the problem is "one of determining how far the ownership of independent material resources should be affected by differences that exist in physical and mental powers," the envy test appears to provide a clear—and unacceptable—solution to this problem if powers are defined as resources: independent material resources should be distributed so as to make people indifferent between their bundles of material and natural resources and the bundles of others.

So Dworkin doesn't do a good job of arguing that a straightforward application of the envy test, resulting in virtually unlimited redistribution to the disabled, would be contrary to his theory. Let us consider, then, how Dworkin arrives at hypothetical insurance. In elaborating the requirements of equality, Dworkin considers issues of luck and insurance. He distinguishes between two types of luck, "option" luck and "brute" luck: "Option luck is a matter of how deliberate and calculated gambles turn out—whether someone gains or loses through accepting an isolated risk he or she should have anticipated and might have declined. Brute luck is a matter of how risks fall out that are not in that sense deliberate gambles."[75] Dworkin notes that "insurance, so far as it is available, provides a link between brute and option luck, because the decision to buy or reject catastrophe insurance is a calculated gamble."[76]

Dworkin then argues that under his theory of equality of resources, there should be no redistribution from those favored by option luck to those disfavored by option luck. He supposes, for example, that "insurance against blindness is available, in the initial auction, at whatever level of coverage the policy holder chooses to buy."[77] He further supposes that "two sighted people have, at the time of the auction, equal chance of suffering an accident that will blind them, and know that they have."[78] Under these circumstances, Dworkin argues, equality of resources does not require redistribution to someone who buys no insurance and is blinded, either from someone who does buy insurance and is blinded or from someone who does buy insurance and is not blinded. Dworkin also intimates, though he does not actually say so, that there should be no redistribution to someone who buys no insurance and is blinded from someone who *also* buys no insurance, but is *not* blinded.

Dworkin recognizes, of course, that after the accident has struck, there is no equality of resources, as measured by the envy test. Someone who has been blinded will envy someone, with or without insurance, who has not been blinded, and someone without insurance who has been blinded will envy someone with insurance who has been blinded. However, Dworkin believes the appropriate point of reference, for purposes of distributive justice, is before the accident, when the envy test is indeed satisfied.

According to Dworkin, then, no compensation is due someone who has an equal chance of being disabled, buys no insurance, and is in fact disabled. I do not agree with this conclusion, but it is certainly a plausible elaboration of Dworkin's own theory. Even so, it is mysterious how Dworkin moves next to the conclusion that equality of resources endorses his hypothetical insurance scheme as the measure of appropriate redistribution to the disabled. He has by assumption established that if there is an *actual* situation in which the envy test is satisfied, and people make *actual* insurance decisions having different consequences, the resulting distribution will not be disturbed. How does Dworkin go on to conclude that even if there is *no* point in time when the envy test is satisfied, and there are *no* actual insurance decisions, the proper measure of redistribution under equality of resources is not to attempt to satisfy the envy test in actuality, but to establish a distribution that *would* have arisen from a nonexistent situation of equality? Dworkin does not offer any argument at all for this shift. He merely claims, blithely, that "the idea of a market in insurance provides a counterfactual guide through which equality of resources might face the problem of handicaps in the real world."[79]

It might be useful to state more succinctly two propositions at work here. The first proposition is that it is consistent with equality of resources to enforce gambles made at a point when the envy test is satisfied, even if the envy test will not be satisfied after the gambles are enforced. I will refer to this proposition as Enforce Gambles From Equality.

The second proposition is that when the envy test is not satisfied, the proper measure of redistribution, in an attempt to satisfy it, is to establish a distribution that would have arisen had everyone faced the same risk of suffering whatever loss is to be remedied, and had insurance against that loss been available. I will refer to this second proposition as Redistribute Per Hypothetical Gambles.

Enforce Gambles From Equality does not self-evidently lead to Redistribute Per Hypothetical Gambles. As Dworkin offers no argument from which we could conclude that the first proposition does lead to the second, it is hard to evaluate his reasoning.

It is possible, however, to offer a couple of arguments, based in Dworkin's own theory, that Enforce Gambles From Equality should not lead to Redistribute Per Hypothetical Gambles. One argument is that whether or not the envy test must be satisfied at every point in time, we surely cannot claim fidelity to that test if we do not even try to satisfy it at some actual point in time. This argument is well expressed by Jan Narveson: "The opportunity to participate in the insurance auction which underpins all this is purely hypothetical. The *fact* is that Smith is, in every measure that matters to him or to Jones, way behind Jones in the actual world. Can we hold with a straight face that the bundle of counterfactuals added to his bundle of de facto resources sufficiently 'compensates' him in the terms of a substantial theory of equality? I find this puzzling."[80]

Another argument focuses on the specific reasoning by which Dworkin arrives at Enforce Gambles From Equality. In rejecting the idea that there should be redistribution from those who gamble and win to those who gamble and lose, Dworkin says that "the possibility of loss was part of the life they chose . . . it was the fair price of the possibility of gain."[81] Similarly, in arguing that there should be no redistribution from those who gamble and win to those who "play it safe," Dworkin says that "the life chosen by someone who gambles contains, as an element, the factor of risk; someone who chooses not to gamble has decided that he prefers a safer life."[82]

The principle that people are responsible for their choices is a major theme in Dworkin's theory. Only by appealing to this principle can he reject the claim, which he considers quite powerful, that the envy test must be satisfied at every point in time. But the intuitive force of the principle that people are responsible for their choices seems to rely very heavily on the choices being *actual* choices. This feature is present in Enforce Gambles From Equality but not, of course, in Redistribute Per Hypothetical Gambles.

Ultimately, the jump from Enforce Gambles From Equality to Redistribute Per Hypothetical Gambles seems a form of wishful thinking.[83] It would be nice if everyone started out with an equal probability of being disabled and an equal opportunity to insure; that way, the envy test would be satisfied at the starting point, and it arguably would not require an unlimited transfer of resources from the nondisabled to the disabled, or indeed any transfer of resources beyond the enforcement of insurance contracts. But people do not start out in such equal circumstances, so a straightforward application of the envy test, once health is treated as a resource, does require massive redistribution.

I should emphasize here that I am not arguing that hypothetical insurance is unfair because it is inconsistent with the envy test. The envy test is a measure of equality, not, in my view, a measure of fairness. Hypothetical insurance is more fair than the envy test, because hypothetical insurance, like utilitarianism, incorporates a greater-benefit criterion. My point has been that to the extent that Dworkin represents himself as an egalitarian, his use of a greater-benefit criterion to avoid massive redistribution to the disabled is opportunistic; it is a major unacknowledged element of utilitarianism in his theory, not an elaboration of equality of resources or the envy test.

Dworkin's Attempts to Avoid the "U" Word

Dworkin has never come to grips with the similarity between his system and utilitarianism, the way in which both rely on a greater-benefit criterion rather than an egalitarian criterion of helping those who are worse off. One distinction Dworkin suggests is that hypothetical insurance is not the sole distributive element in his system.[84] He recalls the desert island story, in which clamshells are actually divided equally prior to an auction. But this is just a story. There is no situation in which Dworkin actually advocates, for current societies, an equal division of material resources and an application of the envy test. In actuality, all redistribution from market outcomes, in a Dworkinian system, would occur through the device of hypothetical insurance.

Dworkin also argues that hypothetical insurance buyers, making their separate decisions, cannot be seen as maximizing welfare under any single conception of what welfare is.[85] This distinction would have more force if Dworkin's theory drew normative distributive conclusions from the behavior of actual participants in an actual insurance market. But Dworkin does not seek to make distributive decisions based on the operation of actual insurance markets, nor would he even base distributive decisions on his best prediction of how people *would* behave in a counterfactual hypothetical insurance market. Dworkin would make distributive decisions based on his view of how most "prudent" people would behave in a hypothetical market. There is a conception of welfare here, albeit perhaps a vague one.

In any event, the distinction between maximizing welfare and equalizing welfare is far more important, for distributive purposes, than the distinction between conceptions of welfare. Utilitarians differ among themselves as to how welfare should be conceived: Is it a positive mental state? The satisfaction of informed preferences? Life satisfaction? These differences, however, would not prevent utilitarians from converging on a single position when the choice is between more welfare (on any conception of welfare) and less welfare. The same goes for hypothetical insurance, at least as it is interpreted by Dworkin.

Hypothetical insurance asks a question that has a superficially egalitarian sound: what would have happened from a situation of equal resources if people had an equal risk of suffering misfortune and an equal opportunity to insure? However, if what would have happened is that people would have applied a greater-benefit criterion in distributing resources between their possible different selves (as Dworkin essentially assumes), this initial situation of hypothetical equality results in a kind of utilitarian distributive scheme, as demonstrated above. Possibly Dworkin's theory can be seen as elucidating the idea that some form of utilitarianism is the best interpretation of the fundamental principle of equal respect for persons.

I stress again: I do not claim that Dworkin's system is identical to conventional utilitarianism. As a formal matter, Dworkin's system could result in no redistribution to the disabled or virtually unlimited redistribution. It could result in insurance coverage that pays only half the cost of a very expensive medical procedure. It could result in a level of income redistribution that would make everyone worse off. But if hypothetical insurance seems attractive to us, it is because we (including Dworkin himself) assume that it would approximate utilitarianism. Just as utilitarianism would distribute extra resources to the disabled if the disabled would benefit more from those resources than nondisabled people, so hypothetical insurance would in general distribute extra resources to the disabled if hypothetical insurance buyers believe they would benefit more from resources in their hypothetical disabled state than in their hypothetical nondisabled state. Just as utilitarianism would halt redistribution to the disabled when the disabled would no longer benefit more than the nondisabled from additional resources, so hypothetical insurance would in general halt redistribution when hypothetical insurance buyers believe that they would no longer benefit more from resources in their disabled state than in their nondisabled state. By approximating utilitarianism, Dworkin is able to achieve a relatively satisfactory intermediate position on redistribution to the disabled.

VIII
Ackerman

I In this chapter I discuss Bruce Ackerman's approach to compensating the disabled. At the end of the chapter I consider Philippe Van Parijs's adaptation of Ackerman's approach.

For Ackerman, equality of resources is a provisional default rule. In *Social Justice in the Liberal State*,[1] Ackerman argues that resource holdings and other forms of power are illegitimate unless they can be justified through "Neutral" dialogue. He posits a two-part principle of Neutrality:

> No reason is a good reason if it requires the power holder to assert:
>
> (a) that his conception of the good is better than that asserted by any of his fellow citizens, *or*
>
> (b) that, regardless of his conception of the good, he is intrinsically superior to one or more of his fellow citizens.[2]

To illustrate the operation of this principle, Ackerman imagines that a group of space explorers lands on an unoccupied planet. The planet contains a single resource called "manna." This resource, though scarce, is convertible to any material object people might want. In other words, manna is like money that is not owned by anyone.[3]

The explorers have to decide how to divide up the manna. They are constrained by Neutral dialogue: no claim for manna will be upheld if it violates Ackerman's two-part principle of Neutrality. The constraint of Neutrality is enforced by the Commander (a sort of self-restrained liberal dictator), who has a perfect technology of justice.[4]

A claim for equal resources, Ackerman argues, does pass the test of Neutrality. A person claiming equal resources can say, "Since I'm at least as good as you are, I should get at least as much of the stuff we both desire—at least until you give me some Neutral reason for getting more."[5]

According to Ackerman, a utilitarian justification for giving some people more than an equal share would *not* pass the test of Neutrality. Ackerman imagines a conflict between Manic and Depressive over resources. Manic would use the resources to climb and explore mountains while Depressive would use them to "pursue a life of leisured conversation and philosophical reflection."[6] Manic claims that he should get the resources because he would gain more happiness from mountaineering than Depressive would gain from philosophy.

After first raising the possibility that no such interpersonal comparison could be made, Ackerman assumes that Manic would in fact get more happiness from his use of the resources. Nevertheless, Ackerman concludes, Manic has not made a Neutral claim for resources because utility is not a Neutral yardstick. While life pursuits and conceptions of the good can be compared using the metric of utility, they can also be compared using other metrics. Depressive, for example, could say that resources should be distributed to the people who would use those resources to gain the most "philosophic wisdom."[7]

Ackerman's discussion of disability is mostly confined to genetic disability and is an outgrowth of his discussion of genetic engineering. He imagines a "Master Geneticist" who can make "test-tube babies on command" containing any combination of genes from the existing generation.[8] The Master Geneticist will be commanded not to produce a certain genotype if it is "genetically dominated" by another genotype. Genetic domination occurs only when every citizen affirms that a genotype would be at a relative disadvantage in pursuing that citizen's own conception of the good.[9]

When procreation is done without the aid of the Master Geneticist, there will be people who are genetically dominated by others, who are at a relative disadvantage at pursuing *any* conception of the good. Ackerman imagines that a person, Disadvantaged, is born with a "terrible birth defect" that makes him or her a victim of genetic domination.[10] He presents with approval Disadvantaged's claim for compensation:

> DISADVANTAGED: Since I'm at least as good as you are, I'm entitled to start out in life with a set of endowments that is at least as good as yours is.
>
> COMMANDER: Speak on, for I can detect no breach of Neutrality in your talk.
>
> DISADVANTAGED: Yet you yourself must recognize that my genetic endowment is inferior to the one with which many of my fellows have been endowed.

> COMMANDER: Yes. While you doubtless can do much that is good, there is no question that your genetic endowment makes it more difficult for you.
>
> DISADVANTAGED: But if this is a liberal state, an unjustified power disadvantage cannot be permitted to stand.[11]

Ackerman emphasizes that it is only someone who is genetically dominated by others who can demand compensation; there is no compensation in the "more frequent case" in which one citizen covets another's talents because they would best advance the first citizen's *own* conception of the good, as long as the citizen's talents would give him an advantage in pursuing *some* extant conception of the good.[12] As Ackerman puts it, "So long as there is *some* conception of the good at which you are comparatively advantaged, you cannot verbalize your sense of grievance in a way that survives the conversational constraint imposed by Neutrality."[13]

Ackerman favorably contrasts his own treatment of disability to that of Rawls. Ackerman aptly describes the oscillation between extremes to which Rawls's theory is subject, depending on which class is designated as least advantaged. Under Rawls's poor-centered definition of the least advantaged class, a victim of crippling genetic disability would be "only a submerged fragment of the 'worst-off class' as Rawls understands it."[14] But it is "simply grotesque," Ackerman claims, to respond to the plight of the genetically disabled person "by telling him all the good things that have been done for healthy white male proletarians."[15] On the other hand, if the least-advantaged class is defined as those people with severe genetic disabilities, "it would seem to follow that the *entire social universe* should be organized for the convenience of a small number of the world's worst basket cases."[16]

Unfortunately for Ackerman, his own theory is subject to the same criticism. Sometimes he would redistribute nothing to the disabled, even when they could benefit greatly. Sometimes he would redistribute vast amounts of resources to the disabled, even when they could hardly benefit at all. His theory suffers from the same kind of oscillation as does Rawls's, and for the same reason: he resists the golden mean of utilitarianism.

Achieving Redistribution

As an initial matter, it is not clear that genetic domination should suffice to justify redistribution (or as Ackerman says, compensation) under Ackerman's system. A nondisabled person who objects to redistribution could argue: "You say you are genetically inferior, but that does not make you morally superior. I am at least as good as you, so I should get at least as much resources." This appears to be a Neutral argument, just as it is a Neutral argument when Disadvantaged argues: "Since I'm at least as good as you are, I'm entitled to start out in life with a set of endowments that is at least as good as yours is."[17] The disabled claimant is making a Neutral argument of a welfare-egalitarian kind, while the nondisabled objector is making a Neutral argument of a resource-egalitarian kind.

Let us assume, however, that genetic domination does justify redistribution under Ackerman's system. The next problem for Ackerman is that genetic domination is so hard to establish: it can be vitiated by one sincere objection. If even one citizen denies that a genetic type is at a relative disadvantage at pursuing that citizen's conception of the good, there is no domination.

Ackerman himself gives a somewhat farfetched example of how a finding of genetic domination can be thwarted by people with unusual views. He imagines that citizens are deciding whether to create a genotype, B, representing a person who will be born "blind, deaf and crippled."[18] He then imagines that some citizens "happen to believe that people like B have the divine mark of approval emblazoned upon them. Blind, deaf, crippled though he be, B is understood as possessing a uniquely valuable insight into the meaning of the universe."[19] Under these circumstances, Ackerman concludes, a condition of "undominated diversity" exists between B and a "typical human specimen possessed of the powers of sight, hearing, locomotion, and so forth."[20]

Because there is no genetic domination in the example of the "B worshippers," the Master Geneticist cannot be ordered to exclude Bs from the genetic lottery. But it follows also that any Bs that might already exist or be created in the future are not entitled to any compensation by way of extra material resources; Ackerman makes it clear that a finding of genetic domination is necessary to justify such compensation.[21] Maybe the "B worshippers" would provide extra resources to any Bs that might exist—or maybe they would want to maintain Bs in as pristine a B-state as possible.

This is not an example I would have chosen to critique Ackerman's system. A far more plausible threat to compensation for the disabled under his system would be the "conceptions of the good" held by the disabled themselves. As indicated in Chapter 3, disabled activists have claimed that they would refuse to have their disability removed, even if they could do so by taking a "magic pill" or simple medication.[22] Joseph Shapiro also quotes one disabled activist as saying, "We want more disabled people, not fewer."[23] Doubtless these views are not held by all disabled people, but they are held by some, and that is enough to negate any finding of genetic domination under Ackerman's view of Neutrality.

Some disabled activists, then, take three positions that under Ackerman's system they could not combine successfully: they want compensation, they do not want to eliminate disabled genes from the gene pool, and they emphatically deny they are victims of genetic domination. Ackerman would say that if all genetically disabled people claimed they were victims of genetic domination, the genetically disabled could be eligible for compensation but would have to accede to the elimination of disabled genes. Since some disabled deny they are victims of genetic domination, they can prevent the elimination of disabled genes, but they can obtain no compensation.

We might ask genetically disabled people whether their disabilities *would* disadvantage them at pursuing their own conceptions of the good *if* they received no compensation or redistribution. If none of them denied such disadvantage, they could claim compensation, at least as long as no "B worshipper" piped up. But the vehemence with which some disabled people deny that they would choose to be nondisabled suggests that they would also (if they were sincere) reject this opportunity to make a conditional claim of genetic domination.

What if we asked the genetically disabled whether they would be willing to say that absent compensation, their disability does not put them at any *advantage* in pursuing their own conceptions of the good? Ackerman discusses in a footnote the question of whether a finding of genetic domination can be negated by someone who claims that a disabled genotype has "equivalent advantages" in pursuing that person's conception of the good. He tentatively concludes that even a claim of equivalent advantage would negate a finding of genetic domination, but notes: "There may be complexities lurking here that deserve further exploration."[24]

Even if Ackerman's tentative conclusion about equivalent advantage were reversed, it would not help much in providing compensation to the disabled. Again, some disabled people claim that they affirmatively prefer to be disabled, suggesting that they see their disability as a definite advantage in pursuing their conception of the good, not just an equivalent advantage.

In discussing Dworkin's theory, I suggested that it was "almost" the height of moral arbitrariness to have extreme variations in the compensation received by identically disabled people, not according to any decisions they actually make, but according to decisions they *would* make in a hypothetical insurance market because of different attitudes to risk. With Ackerman, we have now reached an even greater height of moral arbitrariness. Under Ackerman's system, one disabled person who sees his disabled genes as an advantage (or an equivalent advantage) can prevent all people with the same genetic disability from receiving any compensation. Moreover, one disabled person who sees disabled genes in *general* as an advantage (or an equivalent advantage) can prevent *all* disabled people, *whatever* their disability, from receiving any compensation. It does not matter if millions of other disabled people do not see their disabled genes as advantages, it does not matter how much disabled people could benefit from compensation, and it does not matter how little compensation would cost in terms of welfare reductions for others.

THE UNRAVELING OF ACKERMANIAN RESOURCE EGALITARIANISM?

The extreme tenuousness of any decision to compensate the disabled under Ackerman's system actually threatens to unravel the basic resource-egalitarian fabric of that system. If one person can negate a claim of genetic domination by affirming that the genes at issue are as good or better than other genes, why cannot one person negate a claim of resource domination in the same way? Suppose that one person has two grains of manna and another person has zero grains of manna. The person with no manna makes the supposedly Neutral claim for resource equality: "Since I'm at least as good as you are, I should get at least as much of the stuff we both desire."[25] Is this really a Neutral claim? Suppose the person with two grains finds some community, or even one person, whose conception of the good forbids people from accepting any manna as an initial resource endowment. Perhaps these people have taken a vow of poverty, or do not want to be entangled with the state, or believe that all resources should be earned by work, or whatever. If there is even one such person, the challenged holder of two grains can respond to his challenger, "Your claim for 'at least as much' manna is not a Neutral claim, because under a conception of the good held by our fellow citizens, it is better to receive *no* manna as an initial endowment than to receive an equal share." This argument would appear to be completely consistent with Ackerman's own statement that "So long as there is *some* conception of the good at which you are comparatively advantaged, you cannot verbalize your sense of grievance in a way that survives the conversational constraint imposed by Neutrality."[26]

Opponents of liberalism often claim that the vaunted neutrality of liberal theories is a sham. I am not much interested in such debates between liberals and their opponents. A nonneutral liberalism is good if it produces happiness; a neutral liberalism is bad if it produces unhappiness. Nevertheless, the foregoing discussion demonstrates that if Ackerman were to apply the same interpretation of Neutrality to resources that he applies to disability, he could not so easily claim that Neutrality results in equality of resources.

How Much Compensation?

Suppose that a claim for disability compensation by reason of genetic domination is successfully made under Ackerman's system. No citizen is prepared to say that the disabled genes in question would be an advantage, or even an equivalent advantage, in pursuing that citizen's own conception of the good. What is the nature and extent of the compensation to be provided? I will first consider this question in light of the Ackermanian theory of genetic domination just discussed; I will then evaluate Ackerman's own attempt to delineate the nature and extent of disability compensation.

One might expect that if any one citizen can prevent a finding of genetic domination, any one citizen can also cut off compensation, and in a similar way: by claiming that the compensation already provided has eliminated genetic domination under the citizen's own conception of the good. Suppose that there has been an uncontested finding of genetic domination. Compensation is being paid to those who suffer from genetic disabilities. Now one citizen demands an end to compensation. He says, "I agreed that the disabled genes at issue put people at a relative disadvantage in pursuing my conception of the good, but those same disabled genes *plus* the compensation that has already been paid no *longer* put people at a relative disadvantage; at this level of compensation, there is no more genetic domination." Under Ackerman's theory of genetic domination, it would seem that such an argument, if sincere, must cut off compensation.

If the theory of genetic domination is extended in this way, it could matter very much what kind of compensation or redistribution disabled people receive. Suppose that the genetic disability is one that limits movement. Society could spend vast sums increasing the locomotive ability of people thus disabled, through medical and environmental redistribution, without actually enabling them to move around as well as other people. No matter how much was spent on such efforts, then, it is possible that everyone (if they were honest) would say that the disabled still were at a relative disadvantage in pursuing each citizen's conception of the good. On the other hand, unconditional income redistribution might terminate genetic domination very quickly. While ten billion dollars per disabled person in medical redistribution might not be enough to terminate relative disadvantage in anyone's conception of the good, ten thousand dollars per disabled person in unconditional income redistribution might be enough: some citizens might say that a disabled person with an extra ten thousand dollars is now at a relative advantage, or at least no disadvantage, at pursuing those citizens' conception of the good.

If one attempts to limit disability compensation by extending Ackerman's theory of genetic domination, any limit appears radically indeterminate, just as the decision whether to compensate at all appears radically indeterminate. But this is not the approach Ackerman takes, at least not explicitly. His comments on the extent of disability compensation are undeveloped and somewhat contradictory. Sometimes he appears to concede that vast, almost unlimited sums might be required for disability compensation; at other times he appears to believe that such compensation can be kept within tolerable limits.

The matter is further complicated because Ackerman for the most part discusses the extent of disability compensation in the context of "second-best theory" rather than ideal theory. For Ackerman, "second-best theory" describes a situation in which the polity is committed to Neutral dialogue, but in which all ideal rights cannot be satisfied.[27] Under these circumstances, the governing Ackermanian principle is "equal sacrifice" of ideal rights.[28]

Ackerman discusses disability compensation most extensively in connection with an example involving genetic blindness:

> It is simply beyond our present technological capacity to remedy unequal sacrifice in some power domains. Genetic disadvantage provides straightforward examples. A child is born blind; assume that this defect qualifies him as a victim of genetic domination, and that the blindness is incurable under present medical technology. This means that the statesman cannot hope to root out genetic domination at its source. To fulfill the requirement of equivalent sacrifice, he will be obliged to compensate the blind citizen by giving him advantages in other power domains. Yet this makes a confrontation with the aggregation problem inevitable: how many educational, material, transactional advantages must the blind child receive before he is compensated for his initial disadvantage?[29]

Ackerman concludes that two types of compensation are necessary, "negative compensation" and "affirmative action." He first discusses negative compensation:

> The object here is to assure the victims of blindness that their initial disadvantage will not be exacerbated further by their treatment in other power domains. Thus, negative compensation requires that the blind child be provided an education *no less lib-*

eral than that provided others. . . . Nor can the demand for 'negative compensation' be satisfied by a
showing that per pupil expenditure upon blind
children is equal to that invested in more gifted citizens. The liberality of an education is not to be
measured by money spent but by insight gained. . . .
Nonetheless, a point must come where the states-
man must draw the line on further negative compensation and say that the (enormous) imperfec-
tions that remain in the blind child's education are
no greater than those that afflict other children.[30]

A successful program of negative compensation, Ackerman says, would "assur[e] the blind citizen that in each and
every power domain—other than genetic—he is asked to make
a sacrifice of ideal rights that is no greater than that required of
his fellows."[31] However, that is not enough, as the blind citizen
remains the victim of genetic domination. Therefore, we need
"affirmative action": A blind citizen "has the right to insist that
others make a *greater* sacrifice in nongenetic domains if overall equivalence is to be achieved."[32] Blind citizens must get
something extra in one of the nongenetic domains, such as liberal education, material wealth, and transactional flexibility.[33]

This discussion of compensation for the blind does not
come to grips with the question that faces all resource egalitarians once they compromise resource equality to allow for
redistribution to the disabled: does their system now require
vast expenditures to achieve only tiny benefits? I will first consider whether Ackerman's system requires such a result as a
matter of ideal theory, and will then consider whether Ackerman's concept of equal or equivalent sacrifice of ideal rights
sets an acceptable limit on redistribution to the disabled.

Note that in discussing the claims of blind people, Ackerman stipulates that blindness is "incurable" and that therefore genetic domination cannot be "root[ed] out" at its source.[34] What happens when tiny improvements *are* possible in the condition of genetically disabled people, but at vast expense? What happens when (as is probably the case with every genetic disability) vastly expensive medical research projects offer some probability, however small, of cure or improvement?

Ackerman's discussion implies that adequate compensation, under his theory, would in fact require vast expenditures to achieve tiny improvements in the condition of genetically disabled people. At a later point he asks whether a "comparable" education for a disabled person "requires the investment of enormous sums in an effort to teach him to control his own wheelchair," suggesting that such investment is indeed required.[35] But even this passage skirts the real issue, as the ability to control one's wheelchair might be an enormous benefit. The real issue that sets egalitarianism apart from utilitarianism is not whether adequate compensation requires enormous sums to achieve an enormous benefit, but whether adequate compensation requires enormous sums to achieve a tiny benefit—for example, tiny additional improvements in the ability of people to control their wheelchairs after they have reached a certain plateau.

Or consider the problem of intellectual disability. Ackerman says that the liberality of an education "is not to be measured by money spent but by insight gained."[36] This principle expresses the characteristic egalitarian insensitivity to cost. But while affording equal insight to the blind may not be an intolerable burden, what happens when we have to afford equal insight to children who are intellectually disabled? Suppose it is possible to obtain tiny increases in educational attainment by the intellectually disabled through the expenditure of vast sums. Ackerman's theory once again would appear to require such expenditures.

Intellectual disability also provides another example of the extreme oscillation to which resource-egalitarian theory is subject. Below a certain minimal threshold of dialogic competence, intellectually disabled people are not citizens at all, in Ackerman's view; they are not entitled to any resources. Ackerman gives the example of someone "whose brain is so damaged that he is unable to master the most primitive moral vocabulary, who can never identify himself as a being with his own purposes in the world, who stares in blank incomprehension when asked, 'Why should you get the manna rather than I?'"[37] Ackerman suggests that "*true* citizens may well vote to extend the protective cloak of citizenship to such unhappy creatures,"[38] but he believes that those who fail the test of minimal dialogic competence can make no claim based on justice. "The idiot human must base his claim on sympathy."[39] Thus, while society must apparently spend billions to educate intellectually disabled children who would (or perhaps could) rise slightly above the minimum dialogic threshold, society has no obligation at all to intellectually disabled people who fall below the threshold.

Moving from negative compensation to affirmative action, Ackerman avoids many difficulties for his theory by failing even to outline a standard by which to judge the adequacy of affirmative action. Someone who is disadvantaged genetically must be given something extra in other domains, but how much extra? Ackerman does not say. He implies that vagueness is unavoidable: "The precise identity of the power domain(s) in which victims of irremediable disadvantage are best compensated depends heavily on particular contexts and contestable judgments concerning the ways in which the blind's claim to equal respect can best be supported in the overall public dialogue."[40]

The utilitarian standard of redistribution to the disabled is that the disabled should be given additional resources to the extent they would benefit more from those resources than would nondisabled people. This standard may be very difficult to apply; there may be "contestable judgments." Similarly, any standard of egalitarian compensation may be difficult to apply. The problem is that Ackerman does not even offer any standard; he does not say what the "contestable judgments" should be about. Any standard Ackerman might offer (other than the utilitarian one) would be subject to the usual criticisms. If each disabled person must be made indifferent between her bundle of natural and material resources and the natural and material resources of nondisabled people, compensation would be virtually unlimited. If compensation must halt whenever one person decides the disabled are no longer at a relative disadvantage in pursuing that person's conception of the good, the disabled could be deprived of great benefits. And so on.

As a matter of ideal theory, Ackerman is no more successful at setting an intuitively acceptable limit to disability compensation than other egalitarian theorists who have tried to avoid utilitarian judgments. Let us now move from ideal theory to Ackerman's "second-best" theory. As noted, Ackerman's governing principle here is that if all ideal rights cannot be satisfied, there should be an equal or equivalent sacrifice of rights.

Ackerman distinguishes his theory from a maximin-egalitarian theory under which the disabled are the least-advantaged class. Unlike the proponents of such a theory, Ackerman would give consideration to the claims of people who are disadvantaged but are not the *least* advantaged: "There are millions of other people who are victimized by exploitation even though they do not qualify as 'worst-off.' Middle-class blacks and women *also* have legitimate grievances about the way they are subordinated by the power structure; and so, of course, do all people born to poverty."[41]

As suggested in Chapter 5, an egalitarian theory that is distributionally more moderate than maximin welfare egalitarianism *could* establish an intuitively acceptable limit to redistribution to the disabled—if it used a utilitarian standard to adjudicate the conflicting claims of the various classes and people who are deemed to be entitled to egalitarian concern. As between people who are *less* advantaged, resources could be distributed to those who would most benefit from those resources, even if those who would most benefit are not the *least* advantaged. We could say "equality" but do utility.

There is only a slight bit of evidence that Ackerman means to adopt such a utilitarian method of adjudicating between the claims of those who are exploited. At one point he notes that liberal statesmen may have to choose between a number of budgets that *all* arguably satisfy the principle of equal sacrifice, but in different ways. He then makes a cryptic reference to cost-effectiveness:

> [A] second round of contestable judgments is required where the statesman must trade off the value of additional investments in education against competing investments in transactional flexibility and other areas of structural concern.
>
> Now, as I warned earlier, I shall be saying very little about these 'particular' trade-offs between different forms of liberal investment—not because

these decisions are unimportant, but because so much depends on context. Thus, a small increase in investment may sometimes yield great returns in liberal education, while enormous expenditures will be worse than useless on other occasions.[42]

From a utilitarian perspective, this once again skirts the issue. The question is not whether we should spend a small amount of money to get a great return or instead spend an enormous amount of money to get a negative return; no one (I hope) would advocate the second alternative. The question is whether we should spend money to get a greater return instead of spending the same amount of money to get a lesser return. If Ackerman is saying that we should distribute resources among less advantaged claimants so as to get the most bang for our redistributive buck, he is taking a position that is similar at least to that of utilitarianism. His concept of benefit need not be precisely welfarist; he might say, for example, that we should distribute educational resources so as to maximize insight, rather than utility. Nevertheless, such an approach would coincide with utilitarianism in many cases and (as a result) would have some intuitive plausibility.

Is this what Ackerman means by "equal sacrifice of prima facie rights"? It is hard to tell. Suppose there were two genetic disabilities, A and B, both of which left people unable to walk. Disability A is far more easily treatable than disability B. Compared to a dollar spent on disability B, a dollar spent on disability A provides enormous benefits. If we spend X dollars on disability A, all victims of that disability will be almost completely cured; further expenditures on disability A will have no effect.

The utilitarian approach, of course, would be to spend every dollar up to X on disability A and to spend additional

money (if any) on disability B, even if it turns out that less or
no resources are devoted to disability B. Is there any version of
equal sacrifice that would mimic the utilitarian solution? Yes
there is, if we say that people's sacrifices should be as equal as
possible, in all cases, to the sacrifices made by those who have
sacrificed least. There are people who are not genetically disabled and who therefore have made no sacrifice in this domain. If we cure as much disability as we can, we will (under
this interpretation) be making the sacrifice of genetically disabled people as equal as possible to the sacrifice of those who
are not genetically disabled. Under this interpretation, equal
sacrifice is synonymous with minimum sacrifice, which is of
course a utilitarian concept.

It does not appear that Ackerman means minimum sacrifice when he says equal sacrifice. It seems more likely, in the
example just given, that Ackermanian equal sacrifice would
require us to distribute the vast majority of health-care resources to people with disability B, who get a comparatively
tiny benefit per dollar, and to distribute hardly anything to
people with disability A, who get a comparatively enormous
benefit per dollar. That way people with both disabilities would
travel the same distance (and the same percentage distance)
toward a complete cure. This is of course a counterintuitive
result, as we would be denying an almost-complete cure to
people with disability A for the sake of tiny improvements by
people with disability B.

Though Ackerman is vague on some points concerning
disability compensation, it appears that his theory combines
inadequate redistribution to the disabled and excessive redistribution to the disabled. There will be no redistribution to a
class of genetically disabled people if even one citizen affirms
that such people are advantaged (or equivalently advantaged)

in pursuing that citizen's conception of the good. There will be excessive redistribution to disabled people who can benefit only slightly from additional resources, at least unless Ackerman's principle of equal sacrifice is meant to incorporate a utilitarian distributive standard.

There is also the problem of disabilities that are accidental rather than congenital, which Ackerman basically ignores and which I have so far ignored in discussing his theory. If accidentally disabled people are entitled to no compensation, we once again have an example of extreme and morally arbitrary oscillation: billions for spina bifida, nothing for polio. If victims of accidental disability are considered to be "dominated" in the same way as victims of genetic disability, then the same criticisms, regarding insensitivity to relative benefit, apply to the theory's treatment of the accidentally disabled as apply to its treatment of the genetically disabled.

Van Parijsian Undominated Diversity

In his book *Real Freedom for All*,[43] Van Parijs endorses Ackerman's principle of undominated diversity as the proper measure of redistribution from the nondisabled to the disabled.[44] Redistribution would begin if everyone preferred to be nondisabled rather than to have a particular disability; redistribution would stop when one person could genuinely claim that the disability in question, *plus* redistribution thus far accomplished, was "at least as good as" being nondisabled.[45] Both genetic and accidental disabilities would be compensated.

Van Parijs acknowledges that this scheme provides no redistribution to a disabled person who is able to adapt her preferences so that she does not believe that her disabled state is inferior to a nondisabled state.[46] Van Parijs considers a number of proposals for allowing redistribution in the face of adaptive preferences.[47] Ultimately, however, he rejects all these proposals and reconciles himself to making the level of redistribution depend on adaptive preferences:

> Having an unusual pattern of preferences that happens to be (or has become) well suited to one's particular set of capacities and handicaps can then legitimately disqualify someone for compensation she would otherwise be entitled to. But what is wrong with this? One must, of course, make sure that the preferences are genuine, that they do not rest on delusion, and are consistent with full information and understanding. *This should take care of the cases in which 'penalizing' adaptive preferences is uncontroversially counterintuitive.* Beyond this, ignoring some people's preferences would amount to not giving them the equal respect they deserve.[48]

As noted above, however, undominated diversity also means that a few disabled people with adaptive preferences can prevent many *other* disabled people from receiving compensation. To me, this is an exceedingly counterintuitive result, especially if the many dissatisfied disabled people could benefit greatly from compensation, and if compensation would impose only minor burdens on the nondisabled. Van Parijs appears to be aware of this problem,[49] but he does not fully confront it.

Van Parijs also considers the possibility that undominated diversity would result in excessive redistribution. He notes that "some people may be so badly handicapped that even massive transfers from the rest of society would hardly make their situation more attractive, and would therefore still fail to meet the criterion [of undominated diversity]."[50] Here Van Parijs finally flinches; he allows considerations of relative benefit to play some role in his system. "It may be legitimate," he decides, "to stop [redistribution] because very large further transfers would only produce a hardly noticeable improvement in the beneficiary's situation."[51] This is a welcome and unusually forthright concession that some element of utilitarianism is indispensable if egalitarian theories are to avoid absurdity. Still, as argued in the next chapter, Van Parijs's concession does not go far enough. Thus, I would say that Van Parijs, like Ackerman, advocates a system that combines inadequate redistribution to the disabled with excessive redistribution to the disabled.

IX
Welfarism Weighted
or Unweighted?

Resource egalitarians have some difficulty incorporating utilitarianism into their distributive theories; they cannot accomplish the feat without some contortion. Welfare egalitarians have somewhat less difficulty, as they generally do not even pretend that the sole distributive principle should be equality of welfare.

The acknowledgment by welfare egalitarians that equality of welfare cannot serve as the sole distributive principle generally occurs in the context of a discussion of redistribution to the disabled. It is often evident from these discussions that welfare egalitarians include an element of utilitarianism in their theories: they are not prepared to impose a massive welfare loss on those who are better off in order to obtain a tiny welfare gain for those who are worse off. However, while the utilitarian elements in welfare-egalitarian theories are *almost* explicit, they are sometimes not *entirely* explicit.

Welfare egalitarians make their compromises with utilitarianism in two ways. Some are ethical pluralists: they simultaneously adhere to a number of different distributive principles, including welfare egalitarianism and utilitarianism. Other welfare egalitarians profess a kind of weighted welfarism; they believe that society should seek to increase the welfare of all its citizens, but should give extra weight to the welfare of those who are worse off. This view has now come to be known as prioritarianism.

The Ethical Pluralist Compromise
SEN

Amartya Sen is an ethical pluralist. Sen's central distributive principle is equality of capabilities to achieve functionings,[1] which can be viewed, I have said, as a kind of welfare egalitarianism. However, Sen believes that "aggregative considerations" are also relevant to distributive justice.[2]

Sen gives an example involving disability to show that "attainment equality" should not be the exclusive end of distributive policy: "When person A's potentials permit a maximal achievement of x, compared with a general maximal achievement of, say, $2x$ for all others (the difference may be related, for example, to some physical disability that person A has), a demand for equality as the only consideration would tend to have the effect of levelling down everyone else (without disabilities) to x."[3] The solution, Sen claims, is not to abandon the goal of "attainment equality" in the "capabilities" space, but to admit other considerations as well: "Equality would typically be one consideration among many, and this could be combined with *aggregative* considerations including *efficiency*. These latter influences would work against choosing 'low-level equality' and against pulling person 2 down to the low level of person 1 just for the sake of achieving equality of attainments."[4]

The example Sen considers here is not the difficult one for egalitarians. If a disabled person can reach only a low level of welfare, should everyone else be pulled down to that level as well? The question, as formulated, implies that pulling down everyone else will not help the disabled person *at all*. The tougher question for egalitarians, one that confronts them more directly with the need to incorporate an element of utilitarianism into their theories, is whether it would be right to reduce massively the welfare of nondisabled people in order to achieve an actual but tiny increase in the welfare of the disabled. One may infer from Sen's willingness to entertain "aggregative considerations including efficiency" that he would not approve of a massively welfare-inefficient transfer of resources to the disabled. But though a utilitarian element is probably present in Sen's theory, he does not take the last step in acknowledging it.

G. A. COHEN

G. A. Cohen's core distributive principle is equality of access to advantage,[5] which once again is a kind of welfare egalitarianism. Cohen presents this principle as a "weak equalisandum claim," a claim that people "should be as equal as possible . . . subject to whatever limitations need to be imposed in deference to other values."[6] Cohen mentions that one value which might limit equality is "keeping aggregate welfare high."[7] However, it is not clear to what extent he actually endorses the value of keeping aggregate welfare high, as the example he gives to illustrate this value is not at all convincing.

Cohen hypothesizes that some people may need extra resources to attain the same level of welfare because they are disabled: "They need twice the normal ration because half of such a double-share is required to overcome the illfare effects of a handicap from which they suffer. That half could be the cost of their renal dialysis."[8] Regarding these disabled victims of kidney disease who need extra resources to survive, Cohen states:

> There could . . . be an objection to servicing kidney failure (and similar) sufferers to the extent required to equalize welfare: the policy could be said—*is* often said—to have too depressive an effect on the welfare of everybody else in society. Yet, while that may be right, it hardly represents an *egalitarian* objection to equality of welfare. Keeping aggregate welfare high at the expense of kidney sufferers is not a way of distributing something more equally.[9]

This is an odd example by which to show how the value of keeping aggregate welfare high can counteract equality. While the monetary cost of renal dialysis is high, the benefit of renal dialysis is also very high: it keeps people alive who would otherwise die. In wealthy societies, such as Britain or the United States, it is hard to believe that utilitarianism would counsel against funding dialysis. Now it may be that social resources devoted to health care in a given society are too low, from a utilitarian perspective (as has long been the case in Britain). It may be that the cost of saving one life through dialysis is that many *other* people die from conditions that could be treated more cheaply. In that event health-care allocators would probably be taking the utilitarian course if they decided to save more lives instead of fewer.

Nevertheless, a far better example of how the value of keeping aggregate welfare high can limit the value of equality would be one in which a very expensive medical treatment does not provide *great* benefit to the disabled, such as keeping them alive, but instead provides only a very *slight* benefit to the disabled, or only a very slight chance of improvement. This is the more difficult case for egalitarians. It appears that Cohen, like Sen, would not advocate a massively welfare-inefficient transfer of resources to the disabled in such a case. However, like Sen, Cohen stops a little short of making this position completely explicit.

NORMAN DANIELS

Norman Daniels offers not a general theory of distributive justice, but a theory of "just health care."[10] Daniels's theory is quite complicated. I will focus here on the way in which it overlaps with both welfare egalitarianism and utilitarianism. Though Daniels is inspired by Rawls, his theory is actually closer to ethical pluralist welfare egalitarianism than to Rawlsian resource egalitarianism.[11] Like Sen, Daniels simultaneously espouses both an egalitarian distributive principle and a more utilitarian distributive principle.

Daniels believes that disease and disability are of moral concern because they impair "normal species functioning."[12] Impairments of normal species functioning, in turn, tend to reduce "an individual's share of the normal opportunity range for his society."[13]

These tenets are not in themselves egalitarian. Daniels is an egalitarian because he believes that health-care institutions should be "governed by a principle of fair equality of opportunity."[14] He offers a rough egalitarian priority rule for the allocation of health-care resources: "We should use impairment of the normal opportunity range as a fairly crude measure of the relative importance of health-care needs at the macro level. In general, it will be more important to prevent, cure, or compensate for those disease conditions which involve a greater curtailment of an individual's share of the normal opportunity range."[15] In other words, those who have suffered the greatest reduction in their opportunity range, as the result of health problems, should receive the highest priority in the allocation of health-care resources. I will refer to this principle as the Low Opportunity Priority Principle, or LOPP.[16]

If LOPP were allowed full sway, it would have extreme and unpalatable implications. Society would have to give priority to the treatment of the most severe health conditions, *even* if only tiny improvements in those conditions were possible. Death, for example, involves a pretty severe curtailment of an individual's share of the normal opportunity range. LOPP would require society to direct massive health-care resources to the prevention of premature death, even when life could only be prolonged a tiny amount, and even when the resources could instead be used to relieve a great amount of suffering caused by conditions short of death.

LOPP would also require society to provide tiny improvements in non-life-threatening conditions. Suppose that with limited resources society could either completely cure all paraplegics or could instead provide a smaller benefit to quadriplegics—say, enabling them to move their toes. Despite the great benefit that could be given to paraplegics and the comparatively small benefit that could be given to quadriplegics, LOPP would require that quadriplegia be treated before paraplegia, as quadriplegia involves a more severe curtailment of people's share of the normal opportunity range.

Daniels does not expressly endorse the unpalatable egalitarian implications of LOPP. He avoids endorsing these implications in several ways. First, he generally avoids discussing cases, such as those sketched above, in which society must decide whether to provide a tiny improvement to a severe condition or an enormous improvement to a less severe condition. Second, he hems his egalitarian principles with moderate qualifiers such as "in general" and "fairly crude measure."[17] This qualifying language suggests that Daniels would not take LOPP to its logical unpalatable conclusion. Third, and perhaps most important, Daniels puts forward a different principle that tends to counteract LOPP: the "Prudential Lifespan Account" of intergenerational justice.[18]

Daniels's Prudential Lifespan Account recalls (and predates) Dworkin's "prudent insurance" test for the allocation of health-care resources. In Daniels's theory, "prudent deliberators" behind a veil of ignorance must "choose principles governing the design of institutions that distribute *fair shares* of basic social goods over the lifespan."[19] Daniels is actually more perceptive than Dworkin in recognizing that his device bears some similarity to utilitarianism.[20]

Prudent deliberators behind the veil of ignorance surely would not provide a tiny improvement to a severe condition at the cost of forgoing an enormous improvement to a less severe condition. Accordingly, Daniels's Prudential Lifespan Account can lop off the more unpalatable implications of LOPP. Just as Sen's "aggregative considerations" counteract his egalitarianism in the space of "capabilities," so Daniels's Prudential Lifespan Account counteracts the implausible egalitarianism of LOPP.[21]

MARTHA NUSSBAUM

Martha Nussbaum believes that society should guarantee to each individual a threshold level of capabilities. Nussbaum takes the term "capabilities" from Sen, but she has a more specific view than Sen as to which capabilities are central to human welfare. She offers a list of ten "central human capabilities," a list that has evolved over time. According to Nussbaum, the central human capabilities include "being able to live to the end of a human life of normal length," "being able to have good health," "being able to use the senses," having "literacy and basic mathematical and scientific training," and "being able to form a conception of the good and to engage in critical reflection about the planning of one's life."[22]

Nussbaum does not say how she would make tradeoffs in attempting to provide people with the central human capabilities. This is a major gap in her theory, as such tradeoffs are assuredly necessary. Given the reality of disability and ill health, all the resources of a society could be devoted to just one of the central capabilities (life, health, senses, practical reason, etc.), without even raising everyone over a low threshold.

From a utilitarian perspective, the key question for Nussbaum, as for all welfare egalitarians (broadly defined), is whether she would provide tiny benefits to those who are worse off at the cost of denying enormous benefits to those who are somewhat better off. Because Nussbaum has a pluralist conception of welfare and attaches so much importance to the threshold level, this question in her case becomes three questions.

First, would Nussbaum provide a tiny benefit to someone below the threshold of a capability instead of providing enormous benefits to people above the threshold of that capability? Here, the answer, pretty clearly, is "yes."[23] In my view, and in the view of other utilitarians such as Peter Singer, even this partial commitment to welfare egalitarianism renders Nussbaum's theory implausible.[24]

Second, would Nussbaum provide a tiny benefit to someone below the threshold of a capability instead of providing enormous benefits to people who are also below the threshold of that capability, but who are at a somewhat higher level? Nussbaum does not explicitly answer this question, but it seems that she might take relative benefit into account in distributing resources below the capability threshold. This would introduce an element of utilitarianism into her theory, rendering it somewhat more plausible.

Third, would Nussbaum provide a tiny benefit to someone below the threshold of a capability instead of providing enormous benefits to people who are below the threshold of a *different* capability? Nussbaum realizes that tradeoffs need to be made between different capabilities.[25] She does not enunciate a general standard for making such tradeoffs, but it seems, once again, that she might take relative benefit into account.

While Nussbaum's theory shares some of the problems of other variants of welfare egalitarianism, she applies the theory with what seems like good utilitarian sense. In her book *Women and Human Development*,[26] Nussbaum describes manifest suffering by people in developing countries and the extra burdens faced by women in those countries. She advocates realistic measures to improve welfare in the developing world, focusing especially on the need for universal free primary education.

There is virtually no mention of disability in *Women and Human Development*.[27] In her article "Capabilities and Disabilities,"[28] Nussbaum does deal with the distribution of resources to the disabled. Here, however, the context is not developing countries, but special education policy in the United States. In the American context, Nussbaum endorses (as do I) the allocation of substantial resources for the education of the disabled.

As discussed in Chapter 4, priorities such as Nussbaum's make sense from a utilitarian perspective. Of course, some resources of developing countries should be allocated to special education in those countries (and some resources of rich countries should be allocated to special education in developing countries). Nevertheless, if one is concerned to produce the maximum increase in welfare with the limited resources available to developing countries, it makes sense to focus first on achieving universal free primary education in those countries.

The Prioritarian Compromise

Ethical pluralist egalitarians treat utilitarianism and welfare egalitarianism as two separate distributive principles, both of which may have moral force. Prioritarians, on the other hand, combine utilitarianism and welfare egalitarianism into one distributive principle. Prioritarians seek to maximize aggregate welfare, but they attach extra weight to the welfare of those who have less welfare.

A number of different terms have been used to describe this kind of weighted welfarist theory, including egalitarian welfarism,[29] extended humanitarianism,[30] weighted utilitarianism,[31] weighted beneficence,[32] prioritarianism,[33] the priority view,[34] and (among economists) a concave or nonlinear social welfare function.[35] For the most part, distributive theorists now seem to have settled on prioritarianism. Unfortunately, the two theorists who have done the most to popularize the term "prioritarianism" (Parfit and Arneson) do not completely agree on its meaning. Arneson would consider maximin welfare egalitarianism to be consistent with "an extreme version of prioritarianism."[36] In Parfit's usage, however, the priority of prioritarianism "is not . . . absolute. On [the prioritarian] view, benefits to the worse off could be morally outweighed by sufficiently great benefits to the better off."[37] I here follow Parfit, in order to maintain a distinction between welfare egalitarian views that do not contain an element of utilitarianism and prioritarian views that do contain an element of utilitarianism. Maximin welfare egalitarianism can limit itself to the egalitarian injunction: "Help those who are worse off." Prioritarianism must combine that injunction with the utilitarian injunction: "Help those who can most benefit."

For the remainder of this chapter I will argue against prioritarianism, which would give extra weight to the welfare of those who are worse off, and for an unweighted welfarism or (as it is usually called) utilitarianism. My argument will be tentative. I cannot confidently assert that it would never be right to give some extra weight to the welfare of those who have less welfare. I will try only to show that a plausible prioritarian theory must be close to utilitarianism, and that some common arguments in favor of prioritarianism have less force than might initially appear.

How are we to choose between utilitarianism and prioritarianism?[38] One way is to attempt to derive one of these two principles from a more fundamental moral principle, if any such exists. R. M. Hare thinks that utilitarianism, or something very close to it, can be derived from the principle that moral judgments must be universalizable and from the related principle that people should be treated with equal respect.[39] If one agrees with Hare on these matters, perhaps there is nothing else to say.

Another way of choosing between utilitarianism and prioritarianism is to submit the two principles, in abstract form, to the judgment of moral intuition. Thomas Nagel's endorsement of a version of prioritarianism is based, at least in part, on such an approach.[40] Yet another method is to pick the theory that is simpler. Peter Singer and other utilitarian bioethicists suggest that utilitarianism should be favored on this ground.[41]

But of course, the predominant approach in Anglo-American moral philosophy is to test theories against moral intuition by the use of examples. That, once again, is what I will do here. A major theme of my discussion will be the difficulty of coming up with examples that fairly and reliably pose the conflict between utilitarianism and prioritarianism.

SINGER EARTHQUAKE CASE

Consider again the Singer Earthquake Case, which made its last appearance in Chapter 5. After an earthquake, we come upon two victims, one more severely injured than the other:

> The more severely injured victim, A, has lost a leg and is in danger of losing a toe from her remaining leg; while the less severely injured victim, B, has an injury to her leg, but the limb can be saved. We have medical supplies for only one person. If we use them on the more severely injured victim the most we can do is save her toe, whereas if we use them on the less severely injured victim we can save her leg.[42]

This example is intended to demonstrate that it often seems right to distribute resources to people who will gain the most welfare from those resources, even if the people who will gain the most welfare are already better off.

Readers may have a number of different reactions and responses to the Singer Earthquake case. Some may say that it seems right to them to distribute the scarce medical resources to the worse-off victim who risks losing only a toe, not the better-off victim who risks losing a leg. Such a reaction would certainly reflect egalitarian intuitions, not utilitarian intuitions.

Other readers undoubtedly will share Singer's view, and mine, that here it seems right to help the victim who can most be helped, even though she is better off. Even so, a prioritarian might object, the Singer Earthquake case proves nothing in favor of utilitarianism and nothing against prioritarianism. As a prioritarian theory assigns *some* weight to the interests of the better-off, it necessarily follows that resources will sometimes be distributed to a better-off claimant, rather than to a worse-off claimant, when the better-off claimant would derive sufficiently greater benefit from those resources. The real significance of the Singer Earthquake Case, a prioritarian might argue, is to vindicate prioritarianism against a welfare egalitarianism that would grant absolute priority to the interests of the worse-off.

This prioritarian objection has some merit. An intuitive acceptance of distributing resources to the better-off victim in the original Singer Earthquake Case is not inconsistent with prioritarianism. At most, Singer's original example establishes an upper limit to the extra weight that a persuasive prioritarian theory can assign to the welfare of those who are worse off.

What if I were to add a little stipulation to the Singer Earthquake Case, a stipulated interpersonal comparison of welfare such as opponents of utilitarianism sometimes use in their own examples? As I have already presented three modifications of Singer's original example in Chapter 5, this will be Modified Singer Earthquake Case #4.

Modified Singer Earthquake Case #4

After an earthquake, we can help one of two victims. Victim A is more seriously injured; she has already lost a leg and she will also lose a toe on her remaining leg if we do not help her. Victim B is less seriously injured; she will lose a leg if we do not help her, but she has no other injury. You, the reader of this example, are to assume that the benefit to B of saving her leg will be only infinitesimally greater than the benefit to A of saving her toe.

Here, the facts are basically the same, but I have tacked on a stipulated interpersonal comparison of welfare (IPC). Given this stipulated IPC, I might argue, those who still believe it is right to distribute the scarce medical care to the victim who risks losing a leg must now accept utilitarianism in place of prioritarianism; they must acknowledge that resources should always be distributed to the people who can most benefit from them, even if the people who can most benefit are better off and even if the difference in benefit is infinitesimal.

Such a move would of course be illegitimate, for the reasons I explained in Chapter 2. I promised there that I would give an example of a stipulated IPC that could be used illegitimately to support utilitarianism, unlike most stipulated IPCs, which are used illegitimately to oppose utilitarianism. Modified Singer Earthquake Case #4 is that example. Although I have stipulated, in Case #4, that the benefit to B of saving her leg would be only infinitesimally greater than the benefit to A of saving her toe, this stipulation is not convincingly supported by the facts of the example; indeed, it is contrary to the facts of the example. Accordingly, we cannot be sure whether our intuitive reaction to the example as a whole is based on the facts, which point in one direction, or on the stipulated IPC, which points in the other direction.

So we cannot just stipulate away, in the Singer Earthquake Case, the enormous difference between the gain in welfare we can confer on victim A and the gain in welfare we can confer on victim B. Let us therefore try to modify the facts of the Singer Earthquake Case so that the benefit to the better-off victim is not so much greater than the benefit to the worse-off victim.

Modified Singer Earthquake Case #5

After an earthquake, we can help one of two victims. Victim A is more seriously injured; she has already lost a leg and she will also lose a little finger if we do not help her. Victim B is less seriously injured; she will lose a thumb if we do not help her, but she has no other injury.

Here it still seems to me that we should help B, even though she is better off, because she is likely to suffer more from losing a thumb than victim A is likely to suffer from losing a little finger. In this example, the difference in benefit is much smaller than in the original Singer Earthquake Case. If we think, here, that we should still help the victim who is better off, we are closer to a rejection of prioritarianism.

In assessing our reactions to Modified Singer Earthquake Case #5 (leg plus little finger versus thumb), we should remember that if victim A has already lost a leg, she is likely to become more reliant on her arms and hands than she would otherwise be. Therefore, the loss of a finger might be more damaging to victim A than to someone who had not lost a leg. My reaction to Case #5 is based on a layman's assumption that though the loss of a leg may make victim A more reliant on her hands, she would still be hurt less by the subsequent loss of her little finger than B would be hurt by the loss of her thumb. If medical knowledge indicated that the loss of a little finger would be very harmful to someone who had lost a leg, my intuitive verdict on Case #5 might change, but so, of course, might the utilitarian approach to those cases.

Let me now try to attack the problem from the other direction by constructing, if possible, an example in which it is convincing that a person with more welfare would get the exact *same* benefit from a scarce resource as a person with less welfare. As Rawls notes, no less a utilitarian than Henry Sidgwick believed that when the same benefit can be conferred either on people who are worse off or on people who are better off, a more equal distribution of utility should be preferred.[43] Sidgwick thought that this tie-breaking rule followed from Bentham's dictum "everybody to count for one, and nobody for more than one."[44] I will refer to Sidgwick's position as the Sidgwickian Concession to egalitarianism. Sidgwick's position can also be seen as the prioritarian view closest to utilitarianism.

Suppose we can construct an example in which it is convincing that a better-off claimant and worse-off claimant would receive exactly the same benefit from scarce resources. If we think, faced with such an example, that the resource should be distributed to the person with less welfare, we at least will have taken one step away from utilitarianism and toward prioritarianism. On the other hand, if we feel no intuitive pull to distribute the scarce resource to the person with less welfare, we may support an uncompromising utilitarianism that concedes nothing at all to egalitarianism.

Modified Singer Earthquake Case #6

After an earthquake, we can help one of two victims. Victim A is more seriously injured; she has already lost a leg and will lose a thumb if we do not help her. Victim B is less seriously injured; she will also lose a thumb if we do not help her, but she has no other injury.

Here, I definitely feel we should help the worse-off victim. This reaction (for those who share it) might seem to represent a clear rejection of uncompromising utilitarianism in favor of at least some egalitarian preference for the worse off. However, the example is probably not a fair test. Although I tried to equalize the benefit to be received by the two victims, I doubt that I succeeded. There are two reasons why victim A is more likely to be hurt by the loss of a thumb than victim B.

One reason has already been discussed. The functional effect of losing a thumb would probably be greater if one has already lost a leg. The loss of a leg would probably make someone more reliant on her arms and hands—to operate a wheelchair, to use crutches, to attach and remove a prosthesis, and so forth.

More generally, a misfortune in any one domain is likely to affect the impact of any subsequent misfortune in the same domain. Sometimes a prior misfortune may make the impact of a subsequent misfortune less than it otherwise would have been. For example: a concert pianist with frostbite may be less affected by the second finger she loses than by the first. In most cases, however, as in Modified Singer Earthquake Case #6 (leg plus thumb versus thumb), a prior misfortune would likely increase the functional severity of a subsequent misfortune.

Another reason why Modified Singer Earthquake Case #6 is probably not an equal-benefit case is that equal functional damage does not mean equal hedonic damage. Suppose we were able to assume that victim A and victim B would suffer the exact same loss of function from losing a thumb, even though victim A has already lost a leg. I would still think that the loss of a thumb would harm victim A more than victim B. Putting myself in B's position, I think I would be better able to accept the loss; putting myself in A's position, I think the loss of a thumb, coming on top of the loss of a leg, would have a more severe effect on my happiness.

It is widely accepted that money has diminishing marginal utility. I am suggesting the more general principle that for many people, at least, fortune has diminishing marginal utility: those who are less fortunate generally suffer more from additional bad fortune, and generally benefit more from good fortune, than those who are more fortunate.

Now different people may have different reactions to successive misfortunes. With respect to Modified Singer Earthquake Case #6, some may think that losing a thumb would have *less* of an effect on them if they had already lost a leg. Perhaps they would be psychologically adapted to the loss of body parts after loss of a leg. Or perhaps they would be so depressed by having lost a leg that they would hardly notice the additional misfortune of losing a thumb (though I doubt both of these scenarios).

Others may think that losing a thumb would have exactly the *same* effect on them whether or not they had lost a leg, as long as the functional damage was the same. For such people, examples such as Modified Singer Earthquake Case #6 might serve as a fair test of the Sidgwickian Concession to egalitarianism; it cannot so serve for me, even if I were able to assume equal functional damage.

The foregoing considerations illustrate the difficulty of constructing a truly convincing equal-benefit case. The mere fact that one of the claimants is worse off implies that an *outwardly* identical loss or gain will not be hedonically identical. Sometimes the gain or loss might have a smaller effect on the worse-off claimant's welfare; more often, I believe, it will have a larger effect on the worse-off claimant's welfare.

For the same reasons, of course, it is difficult to construct a case in which the better-off claimant would gain only *slightly* more welfare from a scarce resource than the worse-off claimant. If we cannot be sure where the equal-benefit point is located, we cannot be sure that we have moved only slightly away from that point in a given direction.[45]

SCANLON PAIN RELIEF CASE

The various versions of the Singer Earthquake Case that we have considered suggest (to me, at any rate) that while prioritarianism cannot be ruled out, a plausible prioritarian theory must be close to utilitarianism. Of course, this is only one type of example. Other examples might be adduced, and have been adduced, to support a prioritarian view. I will now review one such example, by T. M. Scanlon. This example will demonstrate, yet again, how difficult it is to pose the choice between utilitarianism and prioritarianism.

Scanlon believes that his contractualist approach to morality yields a kind of prioritarianism. In his book *What We Owe to Each Other*,[46] he attempts to construct an example in

which a better-off person would benefit *more* from a scarce resource, but in which it seems right to distribute the resource to
a worse-off person who would benefit less:

> Consider, for example, a case in which we can pre-
> vent A from suffering a month of very severe pain
> or prevent B from suffering similar pain for two
> months. Supposing that it would be wrong to help
> A rather than B in this case, it does seem to make a
> difference if we add that even if we help A, she will
> still suffer this pain for the next five years, whereas
> B will be free from pain after two months, whether
> we help him or not. So there is generic reason, from
> A's standpoint, to reject a principle that directs one
> in such cases always to help the person in B's situa-
> tion, the one to whom one can bring the greater
> immediate benefit.[47]

It is not completely clear, at this point in Scanlon's argument, whether Scanlon is saying we should help A rather than
B in the case where A faces five years of severe pain, or merely
that A's claim is stronger in that case. However, Scanlon then
goes on to claim that while A might benefit more from a pain-
free month in the case where she faces five years of pain than
in the case where she does not, the benefit to A in either case
would be less than the benefit to B:

> One could argue that this is not really a case of tak-
> ing a person's level of well-being, as distinct from
> the difference one can make to her, into account,
> since the fact that A will be in pain for so long makes
> one month's freedom from pain a greater benefit to
> her than it would be to B. But while A's bleak future

may indeed make a pain-free month more valuable
than it otherwise would be, it is still doubtful that it
makes one month a greater boon than *two* months
is for B. So it is plausible to claim that the way in
which A's situation is worse strengthens her claim
to have *something* done about her pain, even if it is
less than could be done for someone else.[48]

Now it does seem that Scanlon thinks we should help A
instead of B; otherwise, there would be no reason to claim that
the benefit to B would be greater even in the five-year case.

In considering the Scanlon Pain Relief Case, I wonder
whether A knows that if we give her a month of pain relief, it
will be her last pain-free month for the next five years. If A is
aware of the situation, my reaction to the example is double
uncertainty. I am not sure who should be helped, and I am also
not sure who would benefit more from help.

If A is not aware of the situation, then I am indeed convinced that B would benefit more from two pain-free months
than A would benefit from one pain-free month, as Scanlon
suggests. In that situation, however, it does not seem to me that
we should help A; it seems right instead to help B, who could
benefit more.

Of course, these reactions to the Scanlon Pain Relief Case
may not be shared by others. I would emphasize, however, that
they are shared, at least to a minor extent, by Scanlon himself.
As the above-quoted passages from his book illustrate, Scanlon is somewhat tentative in his conclusion that B would benefit more from two pain-free months than A would benefit
from one pain-free month, where A will suffer pain for the next
five years. And he is also somewhat tentative in his intuitive
conclusion that we should give A one month of relief from pain
instead of giving B two months of relief.

This, I think, illustrates a common dynamic in examples intended to justify prioritarianism. If the example is constructed in such a way as to elicit a judgment that we should help the worse-off claimant, it will not be entirely clear that the worse-off claimant really would benefit less from our help. On the other hand, if the example is constructed so as to make it entirely clear that the worse-off candidate really would benefit less from our help, the example will no longer reliably yield the judgment that we should help the worse-off claimant.

In constructing his example, Scanlon took some pains (no pun intended) to consider whether the facts of the example indeed illustrated that B, the better-off claimant, would benefit more from help than would A. It may be wondered: Why bother? Why not just instruct the reader to assume that B would benefit more and go on to consider whether it nevertheless seems right to help A instead? As previously discussed, such a move would be illegitimate, whether it is used in favor of utilitarianism or (as is usually the case) against utilitarianism.[49] If the facts of an example suggest that one claimant would benefit more from help, but we tack on a bald stipulation to the contrary, we cannot be sure whether our intuitions are responding to the facts or to the stipulation. The point of an example is to exemplify. If our example does not exemplify the features we want the reader to assume, it hardly makes sense to use an example at all. We might just as well present, for direct intuitive evaluation, whatever principle we are trying to evaluate.

TWO PATIENTS, TWELVE PILLS

There are other ways in which we can go wrong in testing utilitarianism against prioritarianism. One tempting mistake, briefly adverted to above, is to ignore diminishing marginal utility. Another tempting mistake is to confuse things by throwing marginal egalitarianism into the mix. Both these mistakes can unfairly bias the test against utilitarianism.

Suppose there are two medical patients who suffer from constant severe pain, patient A and patient B. Unless they are treated, their pain will last for 1 month. We have 12 pills of a scarce pain-relief drug that will provide some relief to each patient. Patient B will get more pain relief from the drug; with each pill, he will be relieved of 2 hours of pain per day. Patient A will get less pain relief; with each pill, he will be relieved of only 1 hour of pain per day. How should we distribute the pills between the two patients?

In this example, it might be thought that the utilitarian solution is to provide all the pills to patient B, so that he receives complete pain relief (24 hours per day) and patient A receives zero pain relief. It might further be thought that if we reject the utilitarian solution, we are endorsing some welfarist theory, such as prioritarianism, that is more egalitarian than utilitarianism. Neither of these suppositions is necessarily correct.

First, pain relief may have diminishing marginal utility. It may be a greater benefit to be relieved of 1 hour of pain, from 24 hours of pain per day, than to be relieved of 2 hours of pain, from 10 hours of pain per day. So if we decide that it would be wrong to maximize hours of pain relief, we are not necessarily rejecting utilitarianism.[50]

Second, this example pits utilitarianism not only against prioritarianism, but also against marginal egalitarianism. As demonstrated in Chapter 5, marginal egalitarianism is not always aligned with prioritarianism against utilitarianism; there can be cases in which marginal egalitarianism is aligned with utilitarianism against prioritarianism. If we think, in the above example, that medical supplies should be divided equally, we do not necessarily favor prioritarianism over utilitarianism;

we may simply be responding to the intuitive appeal of marginal egalitarianism.[51]

In Chapter 4, I offered an example ("Poor Two-Disability Society") that was biased against utilitarianism in the ways just discussed. Poor Two-Disability Society was also biased against utilitarianism in another way: in that example, if those who benefited less than others from medical resources did not receive any help, they might feel condemned to be second-class citizens for the rest of their lives, which would be a source of great disutility. But in Poor Two-Disability Society, there was also a far greater difference in benefit than in the example just discussed about dividing twelve pills between two patients. In Poor Two-Disability Society, those who benefited more than others from medical resources received not twice as much pain relief at any given cost, but 240 times as much. This enormous difference in benefit was enough, in my view, to wash away completely all other considerations.[52] But in testing utilitarianism against prioritarianism, we cannot use examples that feature an enormous difference in benefit. We must use examples in which the difference in benefit is fairly small, and so we must pay attention to considerations like diminishing marginal utility and the alignment of marginal egalitarianism.

THE "DISTRIBUTION" OF WELFARE

Let us now step back and take up a general consideration bearing on the contest between utilitarianism and prioritarianism, which will, however, lead us back to a discussion of what kind of examples are proper in representing that contest. Many critics of utilitarianism think it wrong that utilitarianism is unconcerned with the distribution of welfare, except perhaps (as in the case of Sidgwick) to break ties. To a utilitarian, a slight increase in the sum of welfare can justify a wildly uneven distribution of welfare. But shouldn't we care both about maximizing welfare and about equalizing welfare? And shouldn't we, therefore, sometimes prefer a smaller amount of welfare that is more evenly distributed to a larger amount of welfare that is less evenly distributed?

If the question is put in these terms, it does seem a defect of utilitarianism that it is unconcerned with the distribution of welfare. I would argue, however, that a question phrased in these terms is somewhat deceptive. As William Shaw observes, welfare itself is never distributed; resources are distributed.[53] To speak of the distribution of welfare is to speak of welfare as if it were a resource. This kind of phrasing, I would argue, evokes our moral intuitions about the distribution of resources, including our awareness that resources have diminishing marginal utility.

The utilitarian economist Yew-Kwang Ng believes that prioritarianism in general is the product of what he calls "utility illusion."[54] For utilitarian reasons, we must give less weight to the marginal *income* of the rich. If we then give less weight to the welfare or utility of the rich, we have engaged in a kind of double-discounting we did not really intend.[55] I would not go so far as Ng in discrediting all egalitarian deviations from utilitarianism as the product of illusion or confusion. I do think, however, that speaking of the distribution of welfare does produce a type of "utility illusion" by picturing welfare as a resource.[56]

Welfare Numbers

Examples involving the distribution of welfare often include hypothetical numbers that supposedly denote welfare levels. As James Griffin argues, we should be wary of unrealistic numbers: for example, it is not credible that we can distribute a given amount of resources so as to reach a "welfare distribution" between two people of either (50, 50) or (100, 1).[57] But even realistic numbers, I believe, are deceptive, as they once again treat welfare as a resource and evoke intuitions about resources. In addition, examples involving numbers can evoke intuitions that are not moral at all, but rather aesthetic.

Suppose there are two classes in society, A and B. We must choose between two social policies. One policy will result in the welfare distribution (30, 15), and the other policy will result in the welfare distribution (10, 10), where the first number represents the welfare level of class A and the second number represents the welfare level of class B.

In this example I am initially undecided. Though I lean toward the distribution (30, 15), I feel a definite intuitive pull toward the distribution (10, 10).[58] The initial appeal of (10, 10) as an alternative to (30, 15) vanishes, however, when I try to translate the numbers into reality, when I reflect on the horrible loss of potential welfare that every single person in society would suffer if the distribution (10, 10) were somehow imposed on them. I conclude that the initial appeal of (10, 10) is due, at least in my case, to one or both of two distorting factors. First, I may be reacting to the numbers as if they actually represented wealth and not (as stipulated) welfare. A society in which everyone was poorer but all had equal wealth could conceivably be happier than a society in which everyone was richer but wealth was unequal. Second, I may be drawn to the distribution (10, 10) for aesthetic rather than moral reasons. If either of these distorting phenomena is present, of course, the example cannot reliably test moral intuition.

It is difficult to specify a case in which an interpersonal welfare comparison is based on facts rather than bald stipulation, and in which the facts convincingly demonstrate that a better-off claimant would gain only slightly more welfare from a scarce resource than a worse-off claimant. Therefore, it is difficult to choose between utilitarianism and prioritarianism.[59] I tentatively support the utilitarian approach because (1) I can imagine a lot of cases, such as the Singer Earthquake Case, where a distributive decision would clearly depart from utilitarianism in the direction of egalitarianism, and would clearly seem wrong; and (2) I can think of no case where a distributive decision would clearly depart from utilitarianism in the direction of egalitarianism, and would clearly seem right.

X
Intuition about Aggregation

U p to now I have not sharply confronted an aspect of distributive justice that poses some problems for utilitarianism. It is sometimes thought that utilitarianism produces counterintuitive results in cases involving aggregation.[1] Suppose that we can provide many people with smaller benefits or can instead provide a few people with larger benefits. Utilitarianism would aggregate the benefits to be received by each group. If the many smaller benefits sum to more than the few larger benefits, utilitarianism would tell us to help the many rather than the few. Some believe that this is wrong, or that it could be wrong.[2]

There is another kind of case involving aggregation that is not as controversial. Suppose that we can confer a benefit on each member of a large group of people or can instead confer the *same* benefit on each member of a smaller group. Here, aggregation does not seem counterintuitive at all to most people; it seems right, absent special considerations, to benefit more people rather than fewer people.[3]

In this chapter I focus on the first, more controversial kind of aggregation case, not the second, less controversial kind.[4] For the most part, I use the term "aggregation" to refer to the aggregation of smaller benefits, about which many theorists are doubtful, not the aggregation of equal benefits that most theorists accept. I would also emphasize that the term "aggregation" does not itself imply a decision to help the many rather than the few. We must first conclude that the many smaller benefits really do sum to more than the few larger benefits.

I reject the view that utilitarianism routinely produces counterintuitive results in cases involving aggregation. While the utilitarian course often seems *right* in cases involving aggregation, it rarely seems wrong. When we think it wrong to help the many, I contend, we are generally not convinced that helping the many is the utilitarian course.

I have stressed the place in utilitarianism of the greater-benefit criterion: resources should be distributed to the people who will benefit most from those resources. The issue of aggregation points up an aspect of the greater-benefit criterion that is not precisely ambiguous, but that I have not explored until this chapter. Sometimes a few people will get the greatest benefit from resources *per person,* but many other people will get the greatest benefit *in aggregate.* Utilitarianism would distribute resources (absent secondary considerations) to people who will get the greatest benefit in aggregate. An opponent of aggregation might distribute resources to people who will get the greatest benefit per person; such a position might be called innumerate utilitarianism.

At the end of this chapter, I discuss the way in which aggregation affects the relationship between utilitarianism and egalitarianism. Sometimes aggregation leads utilitarianism to take a position consistent with egalitarianism, and sometimes aggregation causes utilitarianism to take a position opposed to egalitarianism. Aggregation also permits utilitarianism to be more respectful of liberty than a thoroughgoing egalitarian theory can hope to be.

Cases in Which the Result
of Aggregation Seems Right

It is easy to imagine cases in which it seems *right* to help the many rather than the few, based on an aggregation of lesser benefits that the many stand to gain. Scanlon, who is suspicious of aggregation, discusses an example in which we can decide either to save one person's life or to save a million people from blindness or complete paralysis.[5] Scanlon does not give an unequivocal answer as to whether aggregation would be right in such a case, but he does freely concede that to many people, aggregation would *seem* right and a refusal to aggregate would seem wrong.[6] To me, and I trust to many others as well, it would seem clearly right to save just one hundred people from blindness, or from becoming quadriplegics, or from becoming paraplegics, even at the cost of not saving one other person from immediate death.

Does an intuitive endorsement of the decision to help the many, in cases such as these, reflect an intuitive judgment that the decision to aggregate is morally correct? It does indeed reflect such a judgment, but only if we are certain that the benefit to be received by each of the many is in fact smaller, on a one-to-one basis, than the benefit to be received by each of the few. In most cases discussed under the rubric of aggregation, we are unlikely to doubt that the benefit to be received by each of the many is smaller. Scanlon's example, however, is a partial exception, at least for me. I am not completely convinced that being saved from complete paralysis is a smaller benefit than being saved from death. It seems to me that complete paralysis might in some sense be a fate worse than death, even though I probably would not choose death over complete paralysis if those were the only alternatives.

Because I am not completely convinced that being saved from complete paralysis is a smaller benefit than being saved from death, my view that it is better to save one hundred people from complete paralysis than to save one person from death does not necessarily reflect an endorsement of aggregation, in the sense in which I here use the term, that is, the aggregation of smaller benefits. On the other hand, I have no doubt that being saved from paraplegia or blindness is a smaller benefit than being saved from death. Therefore, my view that it is better to save one hundred people from blindness or paraplegia than it is to save one person from death does indeed reflect an endorsement of aggregation in the case presented.

There are many cases in which helping the many seems correct, and in which it is clear that the benefit to be received by each of the many is in fact smaller, on a one-to-one basis, than the benefit to be received by each of the few. Therefore, we can conclude that a decision to aggregate often seems right, and that an uncompromising *refusal* to aggregate will often produce counterintuitive results.

Cases in Which the Result of Aggregation Seems Wrong

In some cases, the purported result of aggregation does not seem clearly right; it seems clearly wrong. Does an intuitive rejection of the purported result of aggregation in such cases reflect an intuitive judgment that the *decision* to aggregate is wrong? It could reflect such a judgment, but only if we are convinced that aggregation has been done correctly, that the many small benefits do in fact sum to more than the few large benefits. This point is fairly obvious, but seems often to be neglected by those who claim that utilitarianism produces counterintuitive results.

Consider a much-publicized real example. In Oregon's abortive experiment with Medicaid rationing, an early analysis of the costs and benefits of various medical procedures resulted in a priority ranking in which an appendectomy received less priority than a procedure for capping teeth.[7] Health-care allocators in Oregon rejected this ranking. They found it counterintuitive, as would most people.

The rationing of medical resources between low-cost, low-benefit procedures and high-cost, high-benefit procedures is a paradigm example of aggregation in the real world. In philosophers' examples, we typically are forced to decide between providing many small benefits or a few large benefits because of some concatenation of freakish accidents. I do not mean to proclaim philosophers' examples worthless; I use them myself, throughout this book. Nevertheless, it may be well to remember that in the real world, if we must choose between providing small benefits to a large group of people or large benefits to a small group of people, it is generally because the small benefits are cheaper; more of them can be provided at a given cost.

When health-care allocators in Oregon initially ranked a procedure for capping teeth above an appendectomy, they aggregated and arrived at a counterintuitive result. Does the counterintuitiveness of this result reflect a moral intuition that aggregation is wrong in principle? I think not. To me, the counterintuitiveness of ranking a procedure for capping teeth above an appendectomy seems wholly driven by the hedonic intuition that a given amount of money spent on capping teeth cannot possibly provide more benefits to people than the same amount of money spent on appendectomies. I reject the ranking because I think the initial analysis must have made some mistake in quantifying and aggregating benefits; in other words, I reject the ranking because it seems clearly to be *inconsistent* with utilitarianism. Others who reject the initial Oregon ranking might think that for them, such an intuitive reaction also (or even instead) reflects a view about the propriety of aggregation in general. That is possible, but it is hard to be sure. The only way to be sure that the counterintuitiveness of a purported result of aggregation reflects a moral intuition against aggregation is if we are convinced that the many smaller benefits really do sum to more than the few larger benefits. The verdict of moral intuition cannot be clear unless the verdict of hedonic intuition is clear.

For most of us, I believe, there are few if any cases in which we are convinced *both* that the result of aggregation is morally wrong *and* that aggregation has been done properly. When we are convinced that the result of aggregation is wrong, we are likely to be unsure, at best, whether the many smaller benefits really do sum to more than the few larger benefits.

Scanlon offers an example involving a televised World Cup match to demonstrate that aggregation can seem wrong:

> Suppose that Jones has suffered an accident in the transmitter room of a television station. Electrical equipment has fallen on his arm, and we cannot rescue him without turning off the transmitter for fifteen minutes. A World Cup match is in progress, watched by many people, and it will not be over for an hour. Jones's injury will not get any worse if we wait, but his hand has been mashed and he is re-

ceiving extremely painful electrical shocks. Should we rescue him now or wait until the match is over?[8]

In this example, I share Scanlon's view that the technician should be rescued immediately, even at the cost of interrupting the World Cup broadcast. However, I deny that this intuitive reaction represents a judgment that aggregation would be wrong in this case. I am not at all convinced that the disappointment or annoyance that millions of football fans might experience, as a result of an interrupted broadcast, would sum to more than the suffering the technician would experience if he were not rescued.[9] Therefore, I am not at all sure that aggregation would lead us to delay rescuing the technician.

What is more, Scanlon himself (once again) does not appear to be sure that aggregation would lead us to delay rescuing the technician. He does not actually claim that the disappointment of millions of football fans would sum to more than the suffering of the one technician. What Scanlon claims is that the technician should be rescued immediately, and that this conclusion does not "depend on how many people are watching—whether it is one million or five million or a hundred million."[10] But this is just a statement of the position against aggregation; Scanlon has not given an example showing the counterintuitiveness of aggregation unless he is prepared to claim that the disappointment of the fans, at some large audience size, actually would sum to more than the suffering of the technician.

Consider another example that purports to demonstrate the counterintuitiveness of aggregation. Alastair Norcross claims that consequentialism plus aggregation leads to a conclusion he calls Life for Headaches: if there is a sufficiently vast number of people who are experiencing fairly minor headaches, and the headaches will continue for one more hour without our intervention, it would be right to kill one innocent person in order to relieve the headaches.[11] Norcross actually accepts and advocates Life for Headaches, but he freely and somewhat gleefully concedes that this conclusion is counterintuitive.

However, Norcross does not specify, in this example, any number of headaches that he claims would sum to more than the disvalue of one death; he merely claims that there must *be* some such number. Let us suppose that it is every person on the planet who is suffering a fairly minor headache that will continue for one hour without our help. In addition, let us change Norcross's example so that we do not even have to kill one person to relieve the headaches; we merely have to forgo saving the one person's life. Here I am not convinced that six and a half billion fairly minor one-hour headaches would sum to more than one human death. Therefore, while I agree that it would seem wrong not to save the one person's life, the example once again does not suggest to me that aggregation would be wrong; aggregation, correctly done, might lead us to take the course that seems intuitively correct: saving the one person's life.

At this point I might try to imagine a world with an enormously greater population, or additional planets full of minor headaches, as Norcross evidently intends. But as the exercise itself gives me a headache, I will try to bring this discussion to a point. It is very easy for me to imagine cases in which it seems right to help the many rather than the few, *and* in which I am convinced that the benefit to be received by each of the many is in fact smaller, on a one-to-one basis, than the benefit to be received by each of the few. Therefore, it is very easy for me to imagine cases in which the decision to aggregate seems right. By contrast, it is very difficult for me to imagine cases in which it seems *wrong* to help the many rather than the few, *and* in which I am convinced that the benefits to be received by the many really do sum to more than the benefits to be received by the few. Therefore, it is very difficult for me to imagine cases in which the decision to aggregate seems wrong.

Moral intuition about cases is not uniform, and hedonic intuition may also not be uniform. Some may be completely convinced, in a given case, both that the result of aggregation is morally wrong and that the many small benefits really do sum to more than the few large benefits. However, I doubt that my hedonic intuitions differ that much from those of theorists who have claimed that utilitarianism produces counterintuitive results in cases involving aggregation. As noted, such theorists seem strikingly unwilling to specify a case in which they not only claim that the result of aggregation seems wrong, but also claim that aggregation has been done properly.

Egalitarianism, Aggregation, and Rights

Egalitarians are often suspicious of aggregation, and it might superficially seem that opposition to aggregation is an egalitarian position. In fact, aggregation sometimes leads utilitarianism to take a position consistent with egalitarianism. Suppose that there are many disabled people who are worse off and a few disabled people who are better off. With limited resources, society can either provide a large and expensive benefit to each disabled person who is better off or can instead use the same resources to provide a smaller and less expensive benefit to each disabled person who is worse off. If the many small benefits sum to more than the few large benefits, utilitarianism would support helping the many worse-off disabled people instead of the few better-off disabled people. This would also be the egalitarian position, but it would not be the position of someone who always rejects aggregation, who thinks we should always provide larger benefits to the few instead of providing smaller benefits to the many (a position I have referred to as innumerate utilitarianism).

Where the many who could receive smaller benefits are better off than the few who could receive larger benefits, aggregation does lead utilitarianism to take positions contrary to egalitarianism. As suggested, the utilitarian course often seems right in such cases. It seems right, for example, that we should save 100 people from paraplegia instead of saving one person from quadriplegia.

But the true extent of egalitarian implausibility is illustrated by another kind of aggregation case. Even if the benefit to each of the many is greater than the benefit to each of the few, egalitarianism will still favor the few if the few are worse off.

Suppose that there are 100 paraplegics and one quadriplegic. With limited resources, we can either (1) cure all the paraplegics completely, or (2) enable the one quadriplegic to move his toes. Welfare egalitarianism would tell us to help the one quadriplegic because he is worse off. This welfare-egalitarian course would seem wrong even if there were an equal number of paraplegics and quadriplegics; it seems spectacularly wrong if there are 100 paraplegics, all of whom must forgo a complete cure.

AGGREGATION, THE DEFENDER OF LIBERTY

The topic of aggregation is connected in interesting ways to the topic of rights. In part because of its commitment to aggregation, utilitarianism is better able than egalitarianism to protect rights that people typically feel they should have. I have already argued in Chapter 5 (and will argue further in Chapter 11) that utilitarianism can better support a right to bodily integrity than can egalitarianism. The same can be said about most rights that people feel they should have. Utilitarianism takes into account and aggregates the insecurity people feel if important interests are not respected, the costs people undergo in order to resist what they see as a violation of their rights, and the costs that government must pay in order to overcome that resistance. A pure egalitarianism cannot take any of these matters into account as long as those who are worse off, in welfare or resources, benefit from the violation of rights.

As I have previously suggested, a high priority for egalitarianism—perhaps the highest priority—should be the prevention of premature death. Someone who dies young is worse off than others, and young people who die by violence are especially badly off. If a police state can reduce violent deaths, a police state may be the system favored by egalitarianism. Because of its commitment to aggregation, utilitarianism is better able to avoid endorsing a police state. Utilitarianism would certainly consider it a great benefit if one person could be saved from violent death. But utilitarianism would also aggregate the denial of liberty that millions would suffer under a police state. As Richard Tuck has argued, the loss of liberty by millions may aggregate to more than the disutility of a few deaths.[12]

Another problematic area for egalitarians is voting rights. Suppose we have identified the worst-off class. As egalitarians, our task would be to organize society for their maximum benefit. But those who are better off will predictably resist this maximin-egalitarian approach. What better way to overcome this resistance and insure high priority for the worst-off class than by limiting the franchise to that class or its representatives?[13] A logical egalitarian political system is one in which those who are better off do not get to vote at all. Similarly, prioritarians—those who mix utilitarianism and welfare egalitarianism—should logically support a system in which those who have least welfare get extra votes. Of the theories under consideration, utilitarianism is the only one that can even potentially support a system of one person, one vote.

THE ILLIBERAL AND APOLITICAL IN RAWLS'S POLITICAL LIBERALISM

As egalitarianism is less able to justify liberty and democracy than is utilitarianism, egalitarians often accept a separate principle, such as Rawls's liberty principle, that constrains the search for equality. In theory, utilitarianism could accommodate a liberty constraint just as well (or as poorly) as egalitarianism. But utilitarianism has less need of such a constraint.

A liberal egalitarian might concede my point that pure egalitarianism is less hospitable to liberty and democracy than pure utilitarianism. Nonetheless, the liberal egalitarian might argue, Rawls and other egalitarians do give liberty a fundamental place in their theories, while most utilitarians do not give liberty a fundamental place. In Rawls's case, it might be argued, liberty is a more important value than equality, as the liberty principle is prior to the difference principle.

Such a liberal egalitarian argument misconceives the place of liberty in Rawls's system. Liberty is indeed prior to the difference principle, but it is not prior to the maximin rule for choice in the original position, which is itself an egalitarian principle. Maximin, it will be remembered, requires us to choose the set of principles that yield the most tolerable worst-off condition. If we take seriously the structure of Rawls's theory, his commitment to the maximin rule is prior to his commitment to the liberty principle; maximin is used to derive the liberty principle. Therefore, as Tuck has suggested, the place of liberty in Rawls's system is far less secure than many assume.[14] All of the illiberal implications of pure egalitarianism are also implications of the maximin rule. Since we cannot exercise Rawls's two "moral powers" if we are dead, any infringement of liberty that can minimize premature death has a strong claim to justification under the maximin rule.

Quite apart from the shaky foundation of Rawls's liberty principle, there is a deeply illiberal aspect to his doctrine of public reason, which holds that political argument should appeal to shared principles. Rawls seeks, through the doctrine of public reason, to maintain a consensus on shared principles of political justice. This ambition generates a repressive impulse to censor political argument, an impulse that is at war with the liberty principle (though the liberty principle does win the war).[15]

I will not attempt here to prove the illiberalism of Rawls's doctrine of public reason. Even were I to succeed in such an attempt, I could not claim that the illiberalism of public reason is a result of Rawls's egalitarianism. It is, rather, a result of his utopian contractarianism. Rawls seriously hopes to achieve and maintain a society-wide agreement on principles of justice governing now-controversial areas of politics and economics. In his more ambitious moments, Rawls hopes that people outside the least-advantaged class will as a rule forbear from voting their own economic interest, and will instead vote to maximize the fortunes of the least-advantaged class. Other egalitarian theorists do not entertain such apolitical hopes, and therefore do not have the illiberal impulse to rule out of bounds certain modes of political argument.

ILLIBERAL UTILITARIANISM?

As I have said, aggregation allows utilitarianism to protect liberty better than egalitarianism can hope to do. Some egalitarian critics of utilitarianism, including Rawls, believe that aggregation does have some illiberal implications. Rawls actually claims that political and religious liberty would be in danger in a utilitarian system. He writes of a "possible balance of social advantages to a sizable majority from limiting the political liberties and religious freedoms of small and weak minorities."[16]

This is in effect an aggregation argument. Rawls implicitly acknowledges that the joy any one member of the majority might feel at oppressing a hated minority would not be greater than the suffering of any one member of the oppressed minority. But he claims that the joy of the oppressors, aggregated together, can exceed the suffering of the oppressed minority.

I doubt that the joy of oppressors really ever does aggregate to more than the suffering of the oppressed. But in any event, we know from history that people can learn toleration. Are the British any less happy now that they do not persecute Catholics? Are the French any less happy now that they do not persecute Protestants? I don't think so. Since the majority can be just as happy in a tolerant regime as in an oppressive regime, the joy of oppressors has no weight at all in a long-term utilitarian analysis, and the suffering of an oppressed minority is a net loss, impermissible from a utilitarian perspective.

"Greatest Happiness of the Greatest Number"

Before concluding this chapter, I must do my part to dispel a persistent confusion. I have been surprised to hear, from very intelligent people, the suggestion that utilitarianism cannot possibly justify any help to the disabled. Why not? Because the disabled are a minority, and utilitarianism seeks the "greatest happiness of the greatest number."

Previous utilitarian writers, such as Griffin, Shaw, and Geoffrey Scarre, have made great efforts to explain that the phrase "greatest happiness of the greatest number" is confusing and inexact; that it does not properly represent utilitarianism; and that while Bentham used the phrase for a time, he ultimately abandoned it in favor of "the greatest happiness."[17] The phrase "greatest happiness of the greatest number" refers to two different goals: the greatest happiness and the happiness of the greatest number. Sometimes these goals coincide; sometimes we aggregate the happiness of the greatest number and find that it is also the greatest happiness. But when the two goals diverge, utilitarianism pursues the greatest happiness, not the happiness of the greatest number.

Suppose that we could give ice cream cones to 100 well-fed people, each of whom would like an ice cream cone. Alternatively, we could relieve 50 other people from horrible pain. Would utilitarianism tell us to give ice cream cones to the 100, in order to promote the happiness of the greatest number? No; utilitarianism would tell us to relieve the 50 from horrible pain, in order to promote the greatest happiness.

At one time, I thought all this was obvious. No one, I thought, could possibly be confused by the phrase "greatest happiness of the greatest number" into thinking that utilitarianism seeks not the greatest happiness, but the happiness of the greatest number. Now I know better: despite the best efforts of generations of utilitarian writers, that unfortunate phrase continues to sow confusion.

I am not quite done with aggregation. In the next chapter I will consider issues involving the aggregation of life years. In that context, familiar patterns appear in a somewhat different light.

XI
Distribution of Life

In this chapter I discuss utilitarian and egalitarian approaches to the distribution of scarce life-saving medical resources (hereinafter the distribution of life). Utilitarianism faces more problems here than in other areas. Nevertheless, a version of utilitarianism is still more attractive than egalitarian alternatives.[1]

In most distributive contexts, I have argued, utilitarianism has considerable intuitive appeal. Its sensitivity to relative benefit allows it to strike the right balance in helping the disabled. By contrast, egalitarian theories that are insensitive to relative benefit have to be modified in the direction of utilitarianism in order to gain intuitive appeal. They must find some way of distributing additional resources to the disabled when the disabled would benefit greatly from those resources, and they must find some way of stopping redistribution to the disabled when the disabled would no longer benefit much from additional resources.

Unfortunately, the same sensitivity to relative benefit that makes utilitarianism an appealing approach to most distributive problems appears to make utilitarianism a counterintuitive and unappealing approach to the distribution of life. If the disabled have on average less welfare than nondisabled people, it seems to follow that the disabled benefit less from life than do nondisabled people. Utilitarianism would therefore place a lower value on disabled life than on nondisabled life, and if a choice had to be made between saving the lives of disabled people and saving the lives of nondisabled people, utilitarianism would counsel us to give less preference to the disabled. So, for example, disabled people would receive less preference, in the distribution of life-saving organ transplants, than nondisabled people.

Moreover, the utilitarian preference *against* disabled people in the distribution of life would appear to be exactly proportional to the utilitarian preference in *favor* of disabled people in the general distribution of resources. The assumption that the disabled have less welfare than they would have if not disabled gives disabled people a strong claim on resources under utilitarianism: if resources can be used to cure or even ameliorate their disability, they could benefit greatly from those resources. But the closely related assumption that the disabled have on average less welfare than nondisabled people appears to put the disabled at an equally great disadvantage in the distribution of life. However morally urgent it might be to cure a given disabled person, increasing her welfare, it would seem that the same moral urgency must attach to a decision to preserve the life of a nondisabled person in *preference* to that disabled person, assuming that only one of them could survive.

This problematic seesaw also moves in the other direction. Suppose we say that the view of disabled people as miserable is based on a superficial and discredited psychology. As discussed in Chapter 3, many psychologists believe that people have a great capability for hedonic adaptation to adverse situations, including disability.[2] Therefore, it would arguably be a mistake to think, for example, that much welfare could be gained by preserving the life of an ambulatory person in preference to the life of a paraplegic. All well and good, but the apparent implication of such an argument is also that a paraplegic would not benefit very much if she were cured of paralysis, and that she would benefit even less from assistance that fell short of a complete cure.

To speak of the distribution of life between disabled people and nondisabled people is actually somewhat inaccurate. If someone has a life-threatening medical condition, that person is disabled, whether or not she also has, in addition, another disability. So the "nondisabled" candidate for life-saving medical care is, herself, disabled. It might be more accurate to speak of the distribution of life between the disabled and the doubly disabled, but I will use the disabled/nondisabled terminology as shorthand.

In Chapter 4, I observed that utilitarians are far more concerned with increment interpersonal comparisons than with level IPCs; they are far more concerned with how much a person can benefit from additional resources than with how badly off the person is. I confronted, in Chapter 4, a common and fallacious assumption of egalitarian critics of utilitarianism: the assumption that if the disabled have less welfare (a level IPC), they also benefit less from additional resources (an increment IPC). I demonstrated that, in general, the opposite is more likely true: if the disabled have less welfare, that represents an opportunity to increase their welfare by devoting additional resources to them.

In the distribution of life, however, it seems that the egalitarian critique of utilitarianism is vindicated. Since the benefit that people get from continued life depends on their level of welfare, it seems that the distribution of life is one area where the level IPC of lower welfare does imply the increment IPC of less benefit from additional resources.

In their book *The Allocation of Health Care Resources*,[3] utilitarian bioethicists John McKie, Jeff Richardson, Peter Singer, and Helga Kuhse accept the view that utilitarianism requires health-care allocators to discriminate against the disabled in the distribution of life. Singer et al. defend such discrimination as a proper result of the health-care allocation theory that seeks to maximize quality-adjusted life years (QALYs), and they support the QALY-maximization theory as an application of utilitarianism to the field of health-care allocation.[4]

Discrimination against the disabled in the allocation of life-saving resources has been termed "double jeopardy."[5] Many people find the idea of imposing such double jeopardy on the disabled to be counterintuitive, and I do also. In this chapter I seek to articulate a utilitarian theory that can avoid discriminating against the disabled in the distribution of life. Some of my arguments go to the practical difficulties of instituting double jeopardy, while others constitute more principled objections. My most fundamental objection to double jeopardy is that the maximization of happiness among people who are alive is morally more important than the preservation in life of those people who are happiest. While double jeopardy would preserve the lives of happier people, it would make existing people less happy overall.

If I oppose the allocation of life-saving medical care so as to maximize QALYs, I may justly be asked on what alternative basis I would allocate such care. My somewhat tentative view is that life-saving medical care should in general be allocated so as to maximize life expectancy, at least when life expectancy is based on age or on certain medical factors. I would therefore accept one part of the QALY-maximization approach and reject the other part. Instead of maximizing quality-adjusted life years, I would in general maximize life years. A life-expectancy approach has problems of its own, as discussed below. Nevertheless, it is more appealing than the alternatives, especially if it is understood as an articulation of utilitarianism, not a replacement.

The most prominent setting for the distribution of life in wealthy countries is organ transplantation. As I discuss possible criteria for the distribution of life, I will sometimes comment on the extent to which these criteria are actually used in the distribution of life-saving organs in the United States.

Basics of QALY Maximization

It may be useful first to review the concept of QALYs and the theory of QALY maximization. Under the QALY scheme, normal health is assigned a utility of 1.0 and death is assigned a utility of 0.0. Sub-optimal health conditions are assigned utilities of between 0.0 and 1.0, though in rare cases a utility of less than 0.0 may be assigned, signifying a condition worse than death.

A number of approaches have been devised for assigning utilities to health states, and these are all lucidly described by Singer et al.[6] The two approaches that Singer et al. appear most to favor (and that seem most consistent with preference utilitarianism) are the standard gamble and time trade-off approaches. Under both of these approaches, survey subjects answer hypothetical questions in which they must trade off life and health. Subjects may be members of the general population, medical patients who are in one of the health states being valuated, or medical patients who are in a sub-optimal health state other than the health state being valuated.

Under the standard gamble approach, researchers seek to find the point at which subjects are indifferent between two options. One option gives subjects a normal life expectancy, but in a reduced health state—for example, paraplegia. The second option gives subjects a probability p of normal life expectancy at *normal* health and a probability $(1 - p)$ of instant death. Researchers vary p until subjects are indifferent between the two options. When a subject is indifferent between the two options, p represents the utility that he has assigned to the reduced health state. Suppose, for example, that a subject is indifferent between (1) normal life expectancy as a paraplegic and (2) a probability .75 of normal life expectancy at full health and a probability .25 of instant death. He would then have assigned the paraplegic health state a utility of .75.

Under the time trade-off approach, subjects once again choose between two options: reduced health for a longer lifespan or normal health for a shorter lifespan expressed as a fraction t times the longer lifespan. Researchers vary t until subjects are indifferent between the two options. When a subject is indifferent between the two options, t represents the utility he has assigned to the reduced health state. Suppose, for example, that a subject is indifferent between (1) living 20 years as a paraplegic and (2) living 3/4 as long, or 15 years, in full health. He would once again have assigned the paraplegic health state a utility of 3/4 or .75.

After subjects select utilities for states of reduced health, researchers average those individual utilities to reach a social utility. The social utility of a state of reduced health represents the reduced value of life in that state. So if the value of one year of life at full health is 1.0 and the utility of paraplegia is .75, the value of one year of life as a paraplegic is .75, the value of two years of life as a paraplegic is 1.5, and so on. The value of a year of life at reduced health has been adjusted downward to reflect a lower quality of life—hence the term "Quality-Adjusted Life Year" or QALY.

Under the QALY-maximization approach, health-care resources are allocated so as to maximize QALYs, sometimes within an explicit budget constraint. As Singer et al. observe, QALY maximization is an application of preference utilitarianism (some might say: an *attempt* to apply preference utilitarianism) in the domain of health-care allocation. Individuals prefer longer life to shorter life, and they prefer a higher quality of life to a lower quality of life. QALY maximization blends these two preferences, using the weights that individuals themselves assign to them, and then maximizes the resulting metric: a quality-adjusted life year.

We can now reformulate the seesaw problem described above in terms of QALYs. Suppose that paraplegia has been assigned a utility of .75. Then the gain in QALYs from curing any one person of paraplegia would be the increase in utility from .75 to 1.0 (.25), times years of life expectancy. So, for example, 5 QALYs would be gained by curing a paraplegic who is expected to live for another 20 years. This seems a substantial gain in QALYs, reflecting the considerable importance a utilitarian distributive policy would attach to curing paraplegia.

Unfortunately, the exact same number of QALYs per year of life expectancy would be gained by selecting *against* a paraplegic and in favor of an ambulatory person in normal health (hereinafter an "ambulatory") for life-saving medical care, if the life-saving care could be provided to only one of them. Suppose, for example, that the two candidates for scarce life-saving treatment are a paraplegic and an ambulatory, both of whom would die immediately without treatment and would live 20 additional years after receiving treatment. The principle of QALY maximization would direct us to give the scarce treatment to the ambulatory. By doing so we would achieve a gain of 5 QALYs, exactly the same gain in QALYs we would achieve if we completely cured one paraplegic who would live for an additional 20 years.

Suppose now we believe that the .75 utility puts too low a value on the life of paraplegics; the estimated utility of paraplegic life should be raised, for example to .9. All well and good, but we will simultaneously reduce the social importance of curing paraplegia from .25 QALYs per year of life expectancy to .1 QALYs per year of life expectancy, and we will correspondingly reduce the social importance of aiding paraplegics in ways that fall short of a complete cure.

Practical Objections

Is there a way of avoiding "double jeopardy" for the disabled without abandoning utilitarianism? I will first list some utilitarian objections to QALY maximization with double jeopardy that are largely practical, and that do not constitute my main argument against double jeopardy. I suspect that many readers will be impatient with these objections, believing that they cannot possibly explain the wrongness of double jeopardy. As I share this view, I will try to be brief. However, I will also try to be complete, as some readers may think that the following practical objections *do* explain why double jeopardy seems wrong.

1. The utilities assigned to disabled health states are too low, as they are often based on the hypothet-

ical preferences of *non*disabled people. Studies show that nondisabled people tend to assign lower utilities to disabled health states than do disabled people, though this pattern is not universal.[7]

2. Because the utilities assigned to disabled health states are too low, a policy of QALY maximization with double jeopardy could actually result in a *loss* of QALYs, as compared to a simple policy of life-year maximization. This could occur because the QALY-maximization approach does not just discriminate against disabled people and in favor of nondisabled people; it discriminates against *younger* disabled people and in favor of *older* nondisabled people. A younger disabled person could lose out to an older nondisabled person in the competition for life-saving treatment if the greater life expectancy of the disabled person was more than offset by her supposedly lower quality of life. But if the utilities assigned to disabled health states are inaccurately low, the apparent gain in QALYs achieved by double jeopardy may actually be a loss of QALYs.

Suppose that the official utility for blindness is .5 (higher than some actual estimates),[8] but that the "correct" utility is .75. There are two candidates for life-saving treatment: a 35-year-old blind person and a 50-year-old sighted person. Assuming for the sake of simplicity that both could be expected to live to age 75 with treatment and would die immediately without treatment, health-care allocators under a policy of double jeopardy would give the treatment to the sighted person, for an apparent gain of 5 QALYs.[9] In fact, however, this application of double jeopardy would result in an actual *loss* of 5 QALYs, because of the inaccurately low utility.[10] So if the utilities assigned to disabled health states are too low, a policy of life-year maximization might actually do better at maximizing QALYs than a policy of QALY maximization.

3. As QALY maximization discriminates against the younger disabled and in favor of the older nondisabled, the victims of double jeopardy may be more likely than its beneficiaries to have young children. Further, the victims of double jeopardy may be more likely than its beneficiaries to be children themselves, or young adults with living parents.

   It is often thought that, in general, the loved ones of those who die at a younger age suffer more than the loved ones of those who die at an older age.[11] If this is true, it is possible that any QALYs gained through a policy of double jeopardy would be offset by the increased suffering a policy of double jeopardy would impose on the loved ones of its victims, as opposed again to a simple policy of life-year maximization.

4. Differences in quality of life between competing candidates for treatment are likely to be much smaller than differences in life expectancy. If, for example, we distributed treatment randomly, we could easily end up distributing it to a candidate who could gain 6 additional months of life, instead of a candidate who could gain 10 additional

years of life. Here one candidate can achieve a gain in life years that is 20 times as great as the other candidate. It is unlikely that we would ever see a situation in which we were convinced that one candidate for treatment had a quality of life 20 times as great as another; we might well never see a situation in which we were convinced that one candidate's quality of life was even twice as great as another's.

5. While it is relatively easy to determine how old a person is and to collect some other information relevant to life expectancy, it is too difficult to collect the information necessary to make accurate quality-of-life assessments. Suppose a paraplegic is selected against for a heart transplant. Shouldn't she be able to inquire whether the successful candidate has in the past suffered from a mental illness and has perhaps attempted suicide? Maybe a searching review of the medical history of the successful candidate would reveal that he actually has a lower quality of life than she does, based on indicia that are not as obvious as paraplegia. Indeed, one may wonder why disability should be the only quality-of-life factor considered relevant to the allocation of life-saving treatment. What about beauty, or intelligence, or wealth, or status? Commenting on an earlier incarnation of this chapter, Roger Gottlieb suggested (facetiously) that as academic status is positively correlated with happiness, we should have a rule of "no transplants for adjuncts."

As I say, these are largely practical objections. Perhaps they can be refuted or, if they are legitimate, perhaps a QALY-maximization scheme can be devised that would obviate them. For example, utilities might be based on the preferences of disabled people or, where that is not possible, might be adjusted upwards; extra preference might be given to disabled candidates for life-saving treatment who are parents of young children or are children themselves; and so on.

Indirect Effect of Double Jeopardy

I do not rely on the practical objections just listed; I assume that the defenders of QALY maximization can successfully meet them. I pass instead to what I consider a more principled objection: the effect that a policy of QALY maximization would have on the general disabled community. A policy of double jeopardy would cause resentment, fear, anger, and a diminished sense of self-worth among many disabled people. Far more disabled people would be affected in this way than would actually become direct victims of the policy.

In one of his articles attacking double jeopardy, John Harris makes a very effective utilitarian argument along these lines that unfortunately—because he is not a utilitarian—he does not take to its logical conclusion:

> Where people live in a community that values individuals differentially according to the success of their lives and its quality and predicted length of un-elapsed time, this is highly likely to have a disastrous effect on their sense of personal worth and their sense of security. Where people are frightened

not only of suffering injury or illness, or of possessing genes which will likely shorten their life expectancy, or are already coping with the deleterious
effects of these; but are also frightened of the effect
that others' knowledge of these disadvantages will
have on their standing in the community, their access to other dimensions of its care, including health
care, and to rescue and other services, then this is
surely likely to have a divisive and corrosive effect
on the sense of community. This is also part of what
is wrong with what I have called double jeopardy.[12]

Having convincingly argued that a policy of double jeopardy would cause misery among many disabled people, not
just among unsuccessful candidates for treatment, Harris
could have concluded that such a policy would do more harm
than good to the well-being of people. Instead, he concludes
that the misery caused by double jeopardy would in turn harm
the "sense of community." From a utilitarian perspective, this
is like saying that a patient has died, so unfortunately he cannot take his medicine. Misery, not a loss of "community," is the
ultimate utilitarian objection to any objectionable policy.

While Harris could be more effective (from a utilitarian
perspective) in driving home his point about the indirect effects
of double jeopardy, Singer et al. do not appear to appreciate
the full force of the point. Responding to the passage from
Harris just quoted, Singer et al. write: "If it could be shown that
allocating health care according to the QALY method would,
in some particular case, have a 'divisive and corrosive effect on
the sense of community' (sufficient to outweigh any benefits
its application might be expected to have), then we would be
prepared to restrict its application in that case."[13] If Singer et

al. are referring to a *policy* of double jeopardy as one "case" of QALY maximization, their comment is appropriate. But if, as seems likely, they are focusing on individual *applications* of a policy of double jeopardy, they miss the point. It is not just any particular application of double jeopardy that would cause unhappiness among disabled people in general; it is the policy of double jeopardy itself.

I would add one thought to Harris's convincing description of the negative indirect effect that a policy of double jeopardy would have on the disabled. Disability tends to reduce welfare, but the extent to which disability reduces welfare is mutable. People can achieve hedonic adaptation to a greater or lesser extent. The message that enlightened societies currently send to the disabled is that they can be happy—just as happy, in most cases, as people who are not disabled. This message undoubtedly aids in hedonic adaptation. If we were to adopt a policy of double jeopardy, on the theory that disabled people are in general less happy than nondisabled people, we could to some extent disrupt hedonic adaptation. We could cause, to some extent, the very unhappiness we assume now exists. I believe Singer et al. are too sanguine about the effect a policy of double jeopardy would have on the happiness of the general disabled community.

In assessing the indirect effects of double jeopardy, we must not neglect to consider its indirect effects on people who are not disabled. Might a policy of double jeopardy have positive indirect effects on nondisabled people sufficient to outweigh the negative indirect effects on the disabled? Considering first the general population of people who have no substantial disability and *also* have no reason to believe they will need scarce life-saving treatment, I do not think they will derive any significant benefit from a policy of double jeopardy. Speaking as a member of this group, I certainly find no reassurance in the thought that in the unlikely event I should be a candidate for scarce life-saving treatment, and in the unlikely event that a competing candidate is severely disabled, I will be chosen for treatment. Moreover, members of the general nondisabled population must realize that they might become disabled (for example, paraplegic) before they develop the need for scarce life-saving treatment (for example, a heart transplant). Everyone is a potential victim of double jeopardy, and I would not be surprised if anxiety over being a potential victim of double jeopardy were greater even in the general healthy population than reassurance over being a potential beneficiary of double jeopardy, however irrational that might be.

The reassurance of being a potential beneficiary of double jeopardy might be greater among people who have reason to believe they will need scarce life-saving treatment but are otherwise not disabled. Nevertheless, I don't think that the possible indirect benefit of double jeopardy to such people would come close to matching the indirect harm a policy of double jeopardy would cause. Obviously, there is a great deal of speculation in these assessments; others may disagree.

Opponents of utilitarianism often claim that utilitarians invent contrived reasons to take positions that seem intuitively correct but that also seem, at first sight, to be inconsistent with utilitarianism. Have I engaged in such a dodge? Have I constructed an artificial utilitarian case against double jeopardy that does not really explain why double jeopardy is wrong? My argument about the indirect effects of double jeopardy might be caricatured, not entirely unfairly, as one that claims double jeopardy is wrong because it would be resented, instead of acknowledging that (as many believe) double jeopardy would be resented because it is wrong.

In listing what I called the practical utilitarian objections to double jeopardy, I was willing to concede that those objections did not explain why double jeopardy seems intuitively wrong. Here I am not willing to make the same concession. I am, however, willing to make a different concession. There may be a further reason why double jeopardy seems wrong, one that requires an elaboration of utilitarianism. In order to rule out double jeopardy on utilitarian grounds, it might be necessary to distinguish between two kinds of utility.

I have noted that in my view, double jeopardy would create enough unhappiness among disabled people to outweigh, morally, the gain in QALYs it might achieve. But the two kinds of utility in this calculation are different, or could be considered different. On one side we are making existing people less happy, by causing fear, resentment, diminished self-worth, etc.; on the other side, we are preserving the existence of people who are happier.

I have assumed that we should make existing people as happy as possible; call this proposition P1. I have also assumed, in common with the defenders of double jeopardy and in opposition to its opponents, that if we cannot preserve the existence of all persons, we should preserve the people who are happiest; call this proposition P2. I have concluded that a policy of double jeopardy would be wrong, even though it would preserve the existence of happier people, because it would also make many existing people less happy.

So far, so good. It may be doubted, however, whether I am using the same scale to weigh the net gain under P2 (preserving happy people) and the net loss under P1 (making existing people unhappy). Arguably, the net loss under P1 would only outweigh the net gain under P2 if P1-type consequences (net happiness among existing people) were counted more heavily than P2-type consequences (preserving happier people). That is possible; it may be that double jeopardy can be avoided, on utilitarian grounds, only if we believe that it is more important to make existing people happy than to preserve in existence those people who are happiest.

This distinction between kinds of utility, then, is the most fundamental (but still tentative) solution I would offer to the paradox that utilitarianism seems to strike the right balance in the distribution of non-life-saving resources, but seems to strike the wrong balance in the distribution of life. In the distribution of non-life-saving resources, we are only concerned with P1-type utility: increasing the welfare of existing people. In the distribution of life, we are still concerned in part with P1-type utility, but are also concerned with P2-type utility: preserving those people who have the most welfare. Singer et al. equate P1-type utility and P2-type utility, and that is why they support double jeopardy. I oppose double jeopardy because I believe P1-type utility is morally more important than P2-type utility, because I believe that it is more important to make existing people happy than to preserve in existence those people who are happiest.[14]

Life-Year Maximization and Utilitarianism

I have argued that a life-year maximization approach to the distribution of life can be based on utilitarianism. Some may reject this conclusion; they may believe that utilitarianism cannot lead to life-year maximization, but must instead lead to QALY maximization and double jeopardy. Certainly QALY maximization is a more straightforward application of utilitarianism to the distribution of life.

Those who doubt that life-year maximization can be derived from utilitarianism could still endorse life-year maximization. They could view life-year maximization as a freestanding distributive theory rather than as part of a utilitarian theory. They could believe that we should distribute life to those who will most benefit from life, and that the morally relevant sense of "benefit" here is simply life years.[15]

That, however, is not my view. I persist in advocating life-year maximization on utilitarian grounds. Therefore, while I consider life expectancy to be the most important criterion for the distribution of life, I might in some cases be willing to depart from a pure life-expectancy approach, if there are good utilitarian reasons to do so.

LIFE EXPECTANCY BASED ON WHAT?

Life expectancy is a prediction that can be based on a number of different factors. It seems right to consider some factors in distributing life-saving treatment, but wrong to consider other factors. To me, it seems right to consider age and certain medical factors. It seems wrong, in general, to consider factors such as race, gender, and wealth.

I will not attempt to specify completely what life-expectancy factors should be considered in the distribution of life, or whether all those factors should have equal weight. Any attempt to specify a complete theory of life-year maximization may run into paradox.[16] For example, it seems right to consider that a candidate for scarce treatment has a comorbid condition that reduces her post-treatment life expectancy, that is, some life-shortening medical condition other than the condition requiring scarce treatment. But it does not seem entirely right to consider that a candidate has unfortunate genes that merely *predispose* her to contract cancer, for example, even if those genes substantially reduce her post-treatment life expectancy.

Or suppose that one candidate has a slightly longer post-treatment life expectancy based on admissible factors, but another candidate has a slightly longer post-treatment life expectancy based on all known factors. We may decide to distribute scarce treatment to the first candidate. But how can we say we are doing so to maximize life years, if we actually think the second candidate would gain more life years from treatment? (I assume, unless otherwise specified, that the difference in post-treatment life expectancy between two candidates is the same as the difference in life years they could gain from treatment.)

Yet another way in which our intuitions about life expectancy may be tested is if one of the inadmissible factors is a significant predictor of successful treatment. We can imagine cases in which the correlation is disturbingly high. Suppose, for example, an epidemic fatal disease. We have a scarce treatment that is 100 percent effective for whites who contract the disease: all whites given the treatment are completely cured. Unfortunately, the treatment is not very effective for blacks who contract the disease: 20 percent of blacks given the treatment are completely cured, but 80 percent of blacks given the treatment die anyway. In this extreme case, I would think it wrong to give blacks equal priority in distribution of the scarce treatment; whites should be given almost complete priority, as the cost of curing one black person is that five white people must die. And of course, if the situation were reversed, blacks should be given almost complete priority.[17]

In the usual, less extreme non-imaginary case, I would oppose taking into account factors such as race, gender, and wealth, even if they predict successful treatment to some extent. This is not because differences in life expectancy are morally irrelevant in such cases; they are often relevant, but there are countervailing moral reasons (I would say: utilitarian reasons) to avoid discrimination.

It may be possible to corral all our intuitive judgments about life expectancy into a completely coherent theory, or it may not. As I say, I do not claim to present a complete theory here. I acknowledge the problems and paradoxes of life-year maximization, but I nevertheless contend that it is more appealing than the egalitarian alternatives discussed below.

LIFE EXPECTANCY AS A FACTOR IN THE DISTRIBUTION OF ORGANS FOR TRANSPLANT

In the United States, the allocation of organs for transplant is governed by a number of different factors. Those factors directly related to life expectancy are probably the most important.

In order to become a candidate for receiving a transplant from a cadaveric donor, patients have to be listed by a transplant center. A large part of the allocation process occurs at this stage. Many patients do not make it onto the list because they are too old or because they have comorbid conditions that would reduce life expectancy.[18] For example, the recipient of the first self-contained battery-powered artificial heart had been rejected as a candidate for a human heart transplant "because he had kidney failure and abnormally high blood pressure in blood vessels in his lungs, which made a transplant unlikely to succeed."[19]

The allocation of organs among patients who make it onto the list is governed by detailed policies of the United Network for Organ Sharing (UNOS).[20] These policies differ by organ and change over time. One of the most important factors in the allocation of all life-saving organs is blood-type matching, which is directly related to life expectancy.[21] Other allocation criteria in UNOS policies are related to life expectancy to some extent.[22] However, the system is not completely consistent with a life-expectancy approach, as further discussed below.

EFFECT ON OTHERS

In theory, utilitarians who have the task of distributing life would want to consider the extent to which the survival or death of candidates for treatment would benefit or hurt people other than the candidates themselves. Utilitarians may think, for example, that a mother with young children should receive some preference in the allocation of life-saving treatment, because of the suffering that the mother's death would cause her children. Utilitarians may think that a doctor should receive preference in the allocation of life-saving treatment, if the doctor's situation is such that her death would mean death or pain for others as well.

In theory, these considerations do not seem improper to me. Nevertheless, health-care allocators are reluctant to take account of benefits and burdens to people other than candidates for treatment. No one wants to repeat the fiasco of the Seattle "God committee," which in the 1960s allocated scarce dialysis based on factors such as supposed social worth. As Robert Veatch observes, this effort produced such chaos and controversy as to make it seem objectionable on utilitarian as well as non-utilitarian grounds.[23] Even a narrower focus on the effects that death would have on loved ones may be impractical.

But if we cannot directly consider the effect of death on loved ones, we can still consider which of the available allocation criteria may *tend* to produce the best consequences for the loved ones of candidates for treatment. Arguably, the maximization of life years actually tends to produce better consequences for loved ones than competing criteria (some of which are described below). The more years of life we can give to a candidate for treatment, the more years *with* that person we can give to her loved ones. In practice, therefore, effects on loved ones may not be a utilitarian reason to depart from life-year maximization, but instead an independent utilitarian reason to support that approach.

Another possible issue regarding effect on others is whether life-year maximization might have a negative indirect effect, similar to the effect that a policy of anti-disabled discrimination would have on the general disabled community.[24] This could depend on what factors are taken into account in determining life expectancy. If only medical factors and age are considered, it is unlikely that life-year maximization will have a very harmful indirect effect. As noted, American transplant centers have routinely used age and comorbidity as allocation factors. These practices have provoked little protest, especially if one considers how fiercely representatives of the elderly protect their interests in other contexts. By contrast, Stanford University Medical Center raised a firestorm of protest when in 1995 it initially refused to list a woman with Down syndrome for a heart-lung transplant. Doctors had feared that the intellectually disabled woman would not be able to follow "the complicated regimen of post-transplant drugs."[25] However, protests led Stanford to change its position and list the woman as a candidate for a heart-lung transplant, which she did then receive.

Egalitarianism and the Distribution of Life

While I am tentative in specifying a utilitarian theory for the distribution of life, I am less tentative in rejecting egalitarian approaches. In this section I discuss four prominent egalitarian criteria for the allocation of life-saving medical resources: allocation by age, allocation by imminence of death, allocation by waiting time, and random allocation. Allocation by age gives preference to those who are worse off in having lived fewer years. Allocation by imminence of death gives preference to those who are worse off in that they will die sooner without treatment. Allocation by waiting time gives preference to those who are worse off in that they have waited longer for treatment. Random allocation gives each person an equal chance to receive life-saving medical resources.

Just as life-year maximization can be seen as either a freestanding distributive theory or part of a utilitarian theory, so age and imminence can be seen as either freestanding distributive criteria or part of a welfare-egalitarian theory. Random allocation, in turn, can be seen as an application of marginal egalitarianism to the distribution of life. At the end of this section, I also consider possible resource-egalitarian approaches to the distribution of life. None of these resource-egalitarian approaches has attracted significant support.

In the distribution of life-saving medical resources, many theorists advocate a mixed view, one that combines life expectancy and some or all egalitarian criteria. I contend that in any such mix, life expectancy should be the major ingredient.

AGE

One egalitarian approach to the distribution of life-saving medical resources is to allocate by age: younger candidates for treatment get priority over older candidates. We distribute life to those who have had the least life. As age is an element in life expectancy, allocation by age will often be consistent with life-year maximization. However, the two allocation criteria can diverge. For example, a younger candidate may have a much shorter post-treatment life expectancy than an older candidate because the younger candidate has a comorbid condition (such as cancer) in addition to the condition requiring scarce life-saving treatment (such as heart failure requiring a heart transplant). An age-based approach would tell us to give treatment to a 20-year-old who could gain only 1 year from treatment in preference to a 30-year-old who could gain 10 years from treatment.

Even apart from its partial convergence with the life expectancy approach, allocation by age can arguably claim support from some broader utilitarian considerations. F. M. Kamm has examined the notion that years of life have diminishing marginal utility (DMU), so that each successive year contributes less to a person's welfare than the previous year.[26] If life has DMU, a younger patient with a shorter post-treatment life expectancy might gain more from treatment, in utility or welfare, than an older patient with a longer post-treatment life expectancy. Utilitarianism might therefore tell us to distribute treatment to the younger patient, despite her shorter life expectancy.

Does the marginal utility of life diminish very much as we get older? Kamm thinks not.[27] As to this issue, one's conception of utility or welfare may be determinative. Under a hedonic view, in which utility is seen as a positive mental state or experience, age may make little difference to the marginal utility of life, at least over the large middle range of years. We may be just as happy in our sixtieth year as in our twentieth year, or even happier. Age may also make little difference under some preference-based views, in which utility is seen as the satisfaction of preferences or informed preferences. We may have more of our preferences satisfied in our sixtieth year than in our twentieth year. However, under a view of utility as satisfaction with one's life as a whole, age may make a bigger difference. Looking backward, we may say that if we had not made it from 20 to 21, our life satisfaction would have been reduced substantially more than if we had not made it from 60 to 61.[28]

Even if we do not think that life has DMU over the whole age range, we may think the years beyond some late age contribute less to welfare than earlier years. At the other extreme, we may think that very young years contribute less to welfare than older years—perhaps, as John Broome suggests, because people have little psychological connectedness with their very young selves.[29] In assessing the burden of disease and the cost-effectiveness of health interventions, the World Bank and World Health Organization use a complicated measure called the Disability-Adjusted Life Year (DALY). One difference between the DALY measure and the simpler QALY measure discussed above is that the DALY measure discounts years in childhood and old age.[30]

Another utilitarian consideration that may be used to judge between life expectancy and age is how the two criteria would differ in their effects on the loved ones of candidates for treatment. As noted, it is often thought that the loved ones of those who die young suffer more, in general, than the loved ones of those who die old. I agree with this general observation. However, if a younger candidate for treatment has a shorter post-treatment life expectancy than an older candidate, it is likely that the younger candidate will die young in any event, no matter what we do. Treatment may prolong the younger candidate's life a little, but his family will still experience the added suffering of a young family member's death. On the other hand, if the older candidate has a substantially longer post-treatment life expectancy, he may not die until an age when death is more expected and family members are more reconciled to it. On balance, I would say that the life expectancy approach probably tends more to minimize the suffering of loved ones than age-based allocation.

As with life-year maximization, allocation by age might be advocated as a fundamental moral criterion. It might be argued that we should distribute life-saving resources to the people who are worst off, and that the only morally relevant sense of "worst off" here is age. Harris and Michael Lockwood have referred to a view of this kind as the "fair innings" view.[31] Lockwood has expressed sympathy for the fair innings view:

> The thought here, which seems to me absolutely correct, is that an older person seeking [treatment] . . . has already by definition lived for longer than a younger person. To treat the older person, letting the younger person die, would thus be inherently inequitable in terms of years of life lived; the younger person would get no more years than the relatively few he has already had, whereas the older person, who has already had more than the younger person, will get several years more.[32]

Alternatively, allocation by age might be not a fundamental moral criterion, but a criterion derived from a broader welfare-egalitarian theory of distributive justice. Veatch and Kamm both would give age a prominent place in the distribution of life-saving medical resources. While to some extent they appear to see age as fundamental, they also see it as an aspect of a broader welfare-egalitarian theory.[33]

If welfare egalitarianism is to support allocation by age, it must be a welfare egalitarianism that seeks to equalize welfare over complete lives rather than at one point in time or over one period of time.[34] Moreover, the focus of this complete-life welfare egalitarianism must be on the total welfare of a complete life, not on average welfare. After all, the average complete-life welfare of a happy 20-year-old could be the same as the average complete-life welfare of a happy 60-year-old. And the average complete-life welfare of a happy 20-year-old could easily be *greater* than the average complete-life welfare of a 60-year-old who has been unhappy all his life.

Even on a total view of welfare over a complete life, age might not be determinative. Arguably, the relevant criterion would be quality-adjusted life years rather than life years; priority should go to those who have had the fewest QALYs, not those who are youngest. A complete-life welfare-egalitarian approach, therefore, would reverse the preference against disabled people that is part of the QALY-maximization approach discussed above; complete-life welfare egalitarianism would substitute instead a preference in *favor* of disabled people.

It would not even matter, under complete-life welfare egalitarianism, whether allocating life-saving resources to the candidate who has had less welfare over the course of her life means that we must deny life-saving resources to *several* other candidates, each of whom has had more welfare over the course of his or her life. And if we assume a version of complete-life welfare egalitarianism unbounded by deontological constraints, we might even be forced to kill several high-welfare people in order to save one low-welfare person.[35]

Thus, the famous imaginary "Transplant" case[36] is actually more of a problem for complete-life welfare egalitarianism than it is for utilitarianism. Most would think it wrong for a utilitarian Dr. Boris Karloff to kill one patient and transplant his organs to five other patients, even if the utilitarian Dr. Karloff could thereby save a net four lives. But suppose Dr. Karloff were instead a welfare egalitarian. Suppose he had a patient who was severely disabled, had suffered greatly all her life, and needed five different life-sustaining organs that had to come (for some reason) from five different people, to avoid immediate death. Or suppose the unfortunate disabled person needed the *same* organ from five different people in succession, because her body rejected each transplanted organ after a brief period of time. An unbounded complete-life welfare egalitarianism would require Dr. Karloff to kill *five* people in order to save the *one* severely disabled patient, as long as each of the five people had enjoyed more welfare over the course of his or her life.

Perhaps such bizarre hypothetical cases are best left aside. Even so, it may still be doubted whether any version of complete-life welfare egalitarianism can justify giving priority to the young instead of to those who have enjoyed the fewest quality-adjusted life years. I confess that I am not best suited to raise these doubts; a similar skepticism could be leveled against my own view that utilitarianism can justify maximizing life expectancy instead of maximizing QALYs. However, utilitarianism can take into account the wider effects of distributive policies, such as their effect on the general disabled community. It is unclear how a thoroughgoing egalitarianism can take such wider effects into account, unless they result in someone being made even worse off than the candidate for treatment who is now worse off.

IMMINENCE OF DEATH

Imminence of death is another egalitarian criterion for the distribution of life-saving medical resources: save first those who would die soonest. Imminence of death is often referred to as medical urgency, though the term "medical urgency" can also have other meanings. I will use these terms interchangeably, unless otherwise noted.

Imminence of death is more prominent than any of the other egalitarian criteria in the distribution of life-saving organ transplants in the United States.[37] Like allocation by age, allocation by imminence of death is often convergent with life-year maximization. If all we know about two candidates for scarce treatment is that one would die tomorrow without treatment, while the other would not die tomorrow, life-year maximization tells us to give the scarce treatment to the more urgent candidate: if we give treatment to the more urgent candidate, two patients will be alive after tomorrow, but if we give treatment to the less urgent candidate, only one patient will be alive.

There can only be a divergence between life-year maximization and allocation by imminence of death if the post-treatment life expectancy of the less urgent candidate is greater than the post-treatment life expectancy of the more urgent candidate. But that alone is not enough. For there to be a divergence between life-year maximization and allocation by imminence of death, we must be confident that

1. Treatment will remain scarce; and
2. The post-treatment life expectancy of the less urgent candidate is greater than the *sum* of (a) the post-treatment life expectancy of the more ur-

gent candidate, *plus* (b) the difference between the life expectancy of the less urgent candidate without treatment and the life expectancy of the more urgent candidate without treatment.[38]

It is sometimes thought that conditions equivalent to these obtain in the allocation of livers among listed candidates for transplant in the United States. The situation is not completely clear, but there may be some inconsistency.[39] Imminence is a very major factor in the allocation of livers, and while life-expectancy factors are also very important, the importance attached to imminence may result in a net loss of life years.

As with age, imminence of death may be a fundamental principle of allocation or, alternatively, part of a welfare-egalitarian theory of distributive justice. Imminence of death does not fit neatly into welfare egalitarianism, however; the fit may be worse than it is for age. We might think that allocation by imminence of death is part of a welfare egalitarianism that seeks to equalize welfare at one point in time—the present point—rather than over complete lives. But the imminence criterion is not logically tied to any particular point in time or segment of time.[40] Theoretically, if we knew that one candidate for treatment would die in five years without treatment and another candidate would die in ten years, the imminence criterion would tell us to favor the candidate who would die in five years—a point rather far into the future.

The most accurate way of expressing the imminence criterion in welfare-egalitarian terms would be to say that at each moment in time, it seeks to equalize (or maximin) welfare over the remaining lives of people who are then alive. As with the age criterion, we must also stipulate that the best measure of remaining welfare is simply remaining life years. And as with the age criterion, this stipulation can be doubted. Arguably, those who will be worse off for the rest of their lives, if denied treatment, are those who would have the fewest remaining QALYs, not those who are closest to death.[41] So, once again, there would be discrimination *in favor* of the disabled.

Many observers believe that the United States and other wealthy countries spend too much of their health-care resources to buy small extensions of life for people who are near death. If applied without limit, a welfare egalitarianism that incorporated the imminence criterion would tell us to spend far more. The implication of such an approach is that resources should be massively redirected to produce tiny extensions of life for people who are now on the point of death, even at the cost of great future increases in the number of deaths and a great shortening of life for people not in immediate danger of death.

WAITING TIME

Allocation by waiting time, or "first come, first served," is less obviously egalitarian than the other allocation criteria discussed in this section. Waiting time *could* be conceived of as an egalitarian criterion. It could be thought that waiting time is a bad, and that we should give preference to the person who has suffered the greatest amount of this bad, that is, the person who has waited the longest. However, allocation by waiting time could also be conceived of as a kind of greater-benefit criterion. It could be thought that in general, the longer one has waited, the harder it is to wait even more: waiting time has increasing marginal disutility. Therefore, the person who has waited the longest would benefit most from avoiding additional waiting time.

With life expectancy, age, and imminence of death, it seemed somewhat credible to say that years of life defined the morally relevant sense in which a candidate would benefit from scarce life-saving treatment, or would be worse off without treatment. Waiting time is not as credible as a measure of benefit or of how badly off someone is. Waiting time is an example of "local justice."[42] It is fairly prominent in the actual distribution of life-saving organ transplants,[43] but not very prominent in theoretical debates. Theorists (such as myself) are likely to discuss it only after we have noticed that it is actually being used.

LIFE EXPECTANCY TAKES ON AGE, IMMINENCE, AND WAITING TIME

How much weight should be given to life expectancy as against the other criteria thus far considered: age, imminence of death, and waiting time? I will here consider three examples that may test our intuitions. I will first consider an example in which there is a large difference between two candidates in life expectancy, and there are also large differences in the egalitarian criteria. I will then consider an example in which there are large differences in the egalitarian criteria, but there is only a small difference in life expectancy. Finally, I will discuss an example, limited to life expectancy and age, in which the differences are arguably equivalent.

Suppose that E and L are two candidates for life-saving medical treatment. E is worse off than L in many ways. E is only 20 years old; L is 55 years old. E has been waiting for treatment for one year, while L has been waiting for treatment only one day. E will die immediately if denied the scarce treatment, whereas L will die in six months if denied the scarce treatment (somehow we know that if we give treatment to E, there will be no treatment available for L at any time in the next six months).

There is also a large difference in post-treatment life expectancy. L would have a post-treatment life expectancy of 10 years, while E, because of a comorbid condition, would have a post-treatment life expectancy of only 1 year. So L would gain 9 1/2 years of life expectancy from treatment (since he would live six months even without treatment), while E would gain only one year. To me, this large difference in benefit completely swamps all other considerations: it would be very wrong to give treatment to E, who is worse off in so many ways, instead of to L, who would gain more years of life expectancy.

Change now the example so that the large differences in the egalitarian criteria remain, but the difference in life expectancy is small. Everything is the same as before, except that L's post-treatment life expectancy is 5 years, while E's post-treatment life expectancy is 4 years. So L would gain only six months more than E from treatment (because he would live for an additional six months even without treatment).

Here I would say that E should get the scarce life-saving resources. I believe this result is consistent with utilitarianism; in particular, it seems likely that a 20-year-old would gain more in life satisfaction from an additional 4 years than a 55-year-old would gain from an additional 4 1/2 years. But while it would seem wrong to me to give L the scarce treatment in this modified example, it would not seem nearly *as* wrong as giving E the scarce treatment in the original example. Even with large differences in egalitarian criteria, a small difference in life expectancy, and utilitarian considerations thrown in on the side of egalitarianism, it does not seem terribly wrong to follow a pure life-expectancy approach.

In my view, life expectancy is the only allocation criterion that does not produce wildly counterintuitive results if it is applied in isolation, with no weight whatsoever given to competing criteria. Admittedly, I can only make this claim if the factors taken into account in determining life expectancy are limited, as suggested above, to medical factors and age.

So far I have considered a case in which the difference in life expectancy is large—perhaps larger than the differences in egalitarian criteria—and also a case in which the difference in life expectancy is smaller than the differences in egalitarian criteria. What about a case in which there are equivalent differences in all the allocation criteria? It is hard to construct such a case, because it is hard to be sure what is an equivalent difference. I will consider only an example in which life expectancy is opposed to age.

Suppose that the two candidates for scarce life-saving treatment are (1) an 18-year-old who would have a post-treatment life expectancy of 2 years and (2) a 54-year-old who would have a post-treatment life expectancy of 6 years. In one way, there are equivalent differences in age and life expectancy: the 54-year-old is three times as old as the 18-year-old, but would gain three times as much in life expectancy. In other ways, however, the difference in age is *bigger* than the difference in life expectancy. The difference in life expectancy is relatively small compared to the maximum possible difference in life expectancy between two candidates. On the other hand, the difference in age is not small compared to the maximum possible difference in age between two candidates—especially if we want to avoid comparisons involving the very early years and very late years. And of course the absolute difference in age (36 years) is far greater than the absolute difference in life expectancy (4 years). So if we think, in this example, that the older candidate should receive treatment, it is fairly clear that we give more weight to life expectancy than to age. But if we think that the younger candidate should receive treatment, it is not as clear that we give more weight to age than to life expectancy.[44]

This example also points up another problem. Suppose we think that the balance tips only slightly toward the 54-year-old who would gain 6 years of life expectancy and away from the 18-year-old who would gain 2 years of life expectancy (that is what I think). It seems, then, that while age does not carry the day for the younger candidate, it does have some intuitive force. But does age have intuitive force for utilitarian reasons (the 18-year-old would benefit more from each additional year) or egalitarian reasons (the 18-year-old is worse off), or both? It is hard to say—for me, at any rate. So if we want to test utilitarianism against egalitarianism, rather than life expectancy against age, we cannot confidently use examples in which the difference in life expectancy is small.

RANDOM ALLOCATION

There are yet other egalitarian approaches to the distribution of life. Random allocation gives everyone an equal chance to receive life-saving treatment, regardless of how much they could benefit from treatment and regardless of how badly off they are. Random allocation has been advocated wholeheartedly by Harris.[45] It has also received favorable mention by Dan Brock[46] and Broome.[47]

Random allocation can be seen as a marginal-egalitarian approach to the distribution of life. Marginal egalitarianism, it will be recalled, tells us to give everyone an equal amount of whatever resources are now available for distribution. In the case of scarce life-saving medical resources, we cannot give everyone an equal amount of what is available for distribution. We can, however, give everyone an equal chance of receiving the scarce resources. Like marginal egalitarianism, random allocation is insensitive to the benefit people would gain from additional resources and also to how badly off people are. Both marginal egalitarianism and random allocation offer us a way to avoid making difficult distinctions between competing candidates.

A consistent policy of random allocation would lead to counterintuitive results. Suppose that the two candidates for life-saving treatment are (1) a 20-year-old with a post-treatment life expectancy of 50 additional years and (2) an 85-year-old with a post-treatment life expectancy of 1 additional year. Surely, we cannot accept a theory that gives the 85-year-old an equal chance of receiving the scarce treatment.

While extreme, this example is very realistic. If we actually tried to implement a random-allocation policy, we certainly would see many cases in which very old people received scarce life-saving treatment that could have gone to much younger candidates with a much longer post-treatment life expectancy.

In support of random allocation, Harris has written that "there is an important sense in which all those who face premature death face the same loss—the same tragedy. Each stands to lose everything—life itself."[48] In one sense, of course, every loss of life is the same. But in another sense, which many would consider more relevant, those who lose more life suffer a greater loss.[49]

Harris has also argued that "a denial of equal opportunities is a slap in the face; it is an existential rejection disproportionate to the value of the good or welfare that the opportunity might have afforded."[50] If reformulated in utilitarian terms, this argument has some force. From the perspective of the candidate for treatment, there is usually a random element in allocation, at least under the life-expectancy approach. The candidate cannot be completely sure, in advance, how scarce treatment will be and how his post-treatment life expectancy will match against the post-treatment life expectancy of other candidates. But if the candidate knows in advance that there is *no* chance of treatment, he may suffer more, waiting for death, than those who believe they have some chance of treatment. On the other hand, the only candidates who are likely to know that they have no chance of treatment, under a life-expectancy approach, are those who would have a very low post-treatment life expectancy. To me, it does not seem right to give these candidates an equal chance.

Brock's Weighted Lottery

Brock has suggested a mixed approach, one that combines life-year maximization with random allocation. Brock notes that a maximizing approach has considerable intuitive force when there is an enormous difference in life expectancy; in such a case, "few people would be willing . . . to give equal chances to receive a scarce organ to [the] two patients."[51] He argues, however, that it does not seem right to allocate scarce life-saving resources based on small differences in life expectancy.[52]

If our moral intuitions have a substantial utilitarian element, we should expect that it will seem more important to maximize life years when there are big differences in life expectancy than when there are only small differences. If two candidates for life-saving treatment differ only slightly in post-treatment life expectancy, the case for allocating resources so as to maximize life years has little moral urgency. On the other hand, to me it does not actually seem wrong to distribute life-saving treatment based on small differences in life expectancy.

Suppose we used life-year maximization when the difference in life expectancy was big and random allocation when the difference was small. We would then have to establish a cutoff point for random allocation, and whatever point we chose would seem arbitrary. Brock suggests the idea of a weighted lottery, which perhaps would obviate problems of arbitrariness.[53] Under a weighted lottery, every candidate for life-saving treatment would have some chance in competition with every other candidate, but those who stood to gain more life years would have a greater chance.[54]

Unlikely events happen. If we used a weighted lottery, some very lucky 85-year-olds would receive treatment in preference to some very unlucky 20-year-olds with a far longer life expectancy. To me that would still seem wrong.

Obviously, intuitions about lotteries differ. Some consider them almost the definition of fair treatment. To me they seem frivolous. They are acceptable for the distribution of minor benefits and burdens, but they are only acceptable for the distribution of major benefits and burdens if there is no better alternative. Life-year maximization, in my view, is a better alternative.

RESOURCE EGALITARIANISM

There are no prominent resource-egalitarian approaches to the distribution of life. The closest in spirit is random allocation, which treats scarce life-saving resources as a special resource and gives everyone an equal chance to receive this resource. A resource egalitarian who adopted random allocation for the distribution of life might stipulate that if someone has once received scarce life-saving resources, he should not get a second chance if he again needs life-saving resources; preference should go to those who have never before been entered in the lottery of life.

As noted in Chapter 5, resource egalitarians are often reluctant to apply their theory in small-scale situations. Nevertheless, we could theoretically attempt a direct application of resource egalitarianism to the distribution of life: we could distribute scarce life-saving resources to those who are or have been poorest.

The case for favoring the poor could be especially strong in a resource-egalitarian theory that seeks to equalize total resources over a complete life. Suppose that one of the candidates has received less than the lifetime minimum income. If she is denied treatment and dies, her premature death will increase resource inequality to a degree that might be thought unacceptable. If, on the other hand, she is selected for treatment, she can continue to earn income, and she may eventually rise above the lifetime minimum.

Suppose now that this poor candidate for life-saving treatment, who has received less than the lifetime minimum income, has no insurance. As explained in Chapter 5, resource egalitarianism cannot, in general, subsidize the medical expenses of the poor. This kind of case, however, is an exception. A resource-egalitarian system that sought to equalize total resources over a complete life could pay for life-saving medical treatment as a means of preventing people from dying before they had received the lifetime minimum income. The cost of life-saving treatment itself, if paid by the government, would bring the total lifetime income of a poor candidate closer to the lifetime minimum.

What if the poorer candidate for life-saving treatment has already exceeded the lifetime minimum income? Then a resource-egalitarian system can no longer subsidize her medical care; such special subsidies would consume resources that could otherwise be used to increase the general income subsidy received by all poor people. A resource-egalitarian theory could still theoretically give preference to the poorer candidate, but the poorer candidate might not be able to take advantage of this preference.

Ironically, another possible resource-egalitarian approach to the distribution of life would be to auction off scarce life-saving resources to the highest bidder. The revenue gained could then be used to increase the general income subsidy for the poor. Under this approach, preference in the distribution of life would effectively be given to the rich, rather than to the poor, but in such as way as to maximize the resource holdings of the poorest class.[55]

AGGREGATION IN THE DISTRIBUTION OF LIFE

Until now I have considered only cases where the choice is to save one person's life or one other person's life. There are also aggregation issues in the distribution of life, corresponding to the aggregation issues discussed in Chapter 10. One issue is whether we should prefer to save two lives instead of one other life, everything else being equal. This might seem an obvious, even foolish question. Who could deny that it is better, all else equal, to save two lives instead of one? In fact, as Veatch notes, this is the area in which the allocation of organ transplants in the United States departs the farthest from utilitarianism.[56] In the allocation of life-saving organ transplants, we indeed must sometimes decide whether to save two lives or instead to save one other life. Some patients need two lungs, while others need only one. Some patients need two different life-saving organs, such as a heart and a lung. Sometimes a liver can be split and distributed to two different patients.[57] In general, UNOS policies do not give priority to saving two lives instead of one other life in such cases.[58]

The innumeracy of UNOS policy seems wrong to me. It also may seem wrong to some egalitarians. As noted in Chapter 5, it is a plausible egalitarian position to say that if we cannot help everyone who is worse off, we should help as many worse-off people as possible.

Another kind of aggregation issue occurs when we must decide whether to grant small life extensions to many people or instead to grant large life extensions to fewer people. Suppose that we can give 10 extra years to one person aged 30 or can instead give 2 extra years to four other people all aged 33. Some, I am sure, would say that even though the life extensions we can give the four people aggregate to less than the life extension we can give the one, we should still help the many rather than the few. (Possibly some who would help the many in this example also feel that utilitarianism is *too* favorable to the many in aggregation cases like those discussed in Chapter 10.)

Aggregation in the distribution of life may be another area where utilitarianism sometimes justifies a departure from a pure life-expectancy approach. In the above example, if the four candidates are denied life extensions of 2 years each, they and their families may suffer psychic harm that sums to more than the psychic harm suffered by the one candidate and his family, in the event he is denied a life extension of 10 years. To put it another way, the psychic harm to self and family of being denied a life extension of 2 years may be more than 1/4 as great

as the psychic harm to self and family of being denied a life extension of 10 years.[59]

Resources and Life

Throughout this chapter, I have used a category—life-saving
resources—that is somewhat artificial. Resources can often be
used either to prolong life or to benefit people in other ways.
Certainly money can be converted to either use. Whether we
consider certain resources to be life-saving resources or non-
life-saving resources may depend on distributive decisions we
have already made, and those decisions can be questioned.

In Chapter 5, I criticized resource egalitarianism for failing to provide highly beneficial life-saving medical care to the
disabled poor, where to do so would reduce the general income
subsidy received by all poor people. I there argued, in effect,
that resource egalitarianism was wrong to use resources for a
non-life-saving purpose (supplementing the income of the
nondisabled poor) rather than for a highly beneficial life-
saving purpose. Also in Chapter 5, I criticized welfare egalitarianism for lavishing enormous sums on the terminally ill
young (if they were considered the worst-off class), some of
which might be used to obtain for them only tiny extensions of
life. I there argued, in effect, that welfare egalitarianism was
wrong to devote some resources to a slightly beneficial life-
saving purpose (obtaining tiny extensions of life at great expense) instead of to the non-life-saving purpose of supplementing the income of the nondisabled poor and of those
disabled poor people who were not among the least-welfare
disabled.

While the category of life-saving resources is somewhat
artificial, the distribution of resources in that category pres-

ents interesting problems. Familiar theories, such as utilitarianism and welfare egalitarianism, branch out in unexpected ways. Considerations that have little prominence in other contexts take on major importance.

Both utilitarianism and egalitarianism have some difficulty with the distribution of life-saving resources. I have repeatedly suggested in this book that the most intuitively appealing aspect of utilitarianism is the way in which it distributes resources to those who can most benefit. In the distribution of life, an apparently straightforward application of the utilitarian greater-benefit criterion seems wrong; it seems wrong to say that we should prefer nondisabled candidates for treatment because they would benefit more from a higher quality of life than disabled candidates would benefit from a lower quality of life. However, the greater-benefit criterion of the life-year maximization approach does not seem wrong; it does not seem wrong to say that we should prefer candidates with a longer life expectancy because they would benefit more from a longer life than candidates with a shorter life expectancy would benefit from a shorter life. No form of egalitarianism can apply this latter greater-benefit criterion. The age-based approach comes closest, but it still fails in cases in which a younger candidate has a far lower life expectancy than an older candidate, because of factors like comorbidity or probable treatment failure. The basic defect of egalitarianism—its insensitivity to relative benefit—carries over from the distribution of resources to the distribution of life.

It may be wondered whether life-year maximization can itself be considered an egalitarian approach. As suggested in the Introduction, there is a very broad sense in which all major contemporary distributive theories are egalitarian; they all can be said to treat people with equal respect. Maximizing theories such as utilitarianism and life-year maximization treat people with equal respect by valuing benefits equally, regardless of who receives them. Utilitarianism values increases in welfare equally, while life-year maximization values increases in life expectancy equally. But there is a big difference between valuing benefits equally and equalizing benefits. The key distinction between maximizing theories and equalizing theories is that a maximizing theory will distribute resources to people who can benefit more, even if those people are already better off. Life-year maximization is a maximizing theory; it is not an egalitarian approach to the distribution of life.

XII
Conclusion:
Philosophy and Policy

Many of us first approach the topic of distributive justice thinking about rich and poor, not disabled and nondisabled. We find that we support redistribution from rich to poor, within nations and between nations. This is a political position, not a philosophical position. Many of us take this position long before considering what its philosophical justification might be.

Utilitarianism, resource egalitarianism, and welfare egalitarianism can all claim to justify redistribution from rich to poor. Utilitarianism can claim to do so on the ground that the poor benefit more from additional money than do the rich; resource egalitarianism can claim to do so on the ground that the poor have fewer resources than the rich; and welfare egalitarianism can claim to do so on the ground that the poor have less welfare than the rich. As there is an apparent convergence among the three theories, how do we decide which, if any, of the theories we would like to endorse?

One approach—the approach taken in this book—is to go beyond thinking of the undifferentiated rich and the undifferentiated poor, and to consider how the three theories deal with issues of disability. When we attend to issues of disability, we can see a greater divergence between utilitarianism and the egalitarian theories. We can consider examples that properly test utilitarianism against its rivals, examples in which it is convincing that people who are better off, in resources or welfare, really would benefit more from additional resources than people who are worse off. A consideration of disability issues even illuminates the way in which the contending theories deal with various classes of poor people. Welfare egalitarianism, it turns out, is not at all favorable to the poor. Resource egalitarianism is very favorable to the nondisabled poor, but it cannot allocate extra resources to the disabled poor.

When we attend to issues of disability, it seems right that resources be distributed to those who can most benefit rather than to those who are in some way worse off. If we accept this conclusion, we may decide to endorse utilitarianism rather than one of the egalitarian theories. We may decide that the fundamental reason we support income redistribution from rich to poor is not because the poor have fewer resources, or because they have less welfare, but because they benefit more from additional money than do the rich.[1] Or, more modestly, we may at least decide that the utilitarian case for income redistribution to the poor partly explains our support for that policy.

How much redistribution to the poor should there be, under a utilitarian system, and in what form? What help, exactly, should a utilitarian government give to the disabled? Should utilitarianism go beyond subsidizing the medical expenses of poor people and establish a system of national health insurance (in those benighted countries that do not already have one)? I have opinions on these matters, some of which may be evident to the reader. In this book, however, I have been more concerned with testing utilitarianism against egalitarianism than with applying utilitarianism to the issues of the day. As illustrated in Chapter 2, many important policy disputes, even in the area of disability, do not draw clear distinctions between utilitarianism and egalitarianism; in many disputes, there are utilitarian arguments on both sides and even egalitarian arguments on both sides.

Nevertheless, it may be well to express some general views on the application of utilitarianism to policy issues. In part, my aim will be to clarify what my theoretical arguments do *not* entail.

In testing utilitarianism against egalitarian theories, I have focused repeatedly on examples in which some people would benefit more from resources, while others are worse off in resources, or in welfare, or in both. This cascade of examples may leave the impression that utilitarian policy analysis consists only of the (possibly difficult) question: "Who would benefit most from the specific resources available for distribution?" In fact, other considerations are also relevant to utilitarian policy analysis. Utilitarians will want to know what effect a given distributive policy will have on the behavior of people. Possibly a distribution of resources to those who most benefit from those specific resources will not maximize welfare overall, because it will change the incentives of people in unfortunate ways. Experience teaches us not to take on faith theoretical predictions of negative incentive effects, but still the issue can be raised.

Also, utilitarianism does not necessarily require a greater-benefit determination every time resources are allocated. For example, laws such as the Americans with Disabilities Act and the Individuals With Disabilities Education Act require sometimes costly accommodations on behalf of some disabled people. In evaluating the overall effect of these laws, we should be sensitive to the cost of accommodations and to the benefits that accrue to disabled people. But it would be a mistake, in my judgment, to say that each time an employer or a school resists accommodation, the extent of the duty to accommodate must depend on whether the benefit of the accommodation exceeds the cost in that particular case. The overall maximization of welfare may not be served by making a greater-benefit decision in each case.

In determining the utilitarian course in policy matters, there is a place for the economic discipline known as cost-benefit analysis. As explained in Chapter 4, cost-benefit analysis gives a different meaning to the term "benefit" than I have given. I have used the term "benefit" in this book to denote an increase in welfare. In cost-benefit analysis, "benefit" is measured in money, not in welfare. Cost-benefit analysis can serve utilitarianism, but it must be applied with caveats. First, the ultimate goal is the maximization of welfare, not the maximization of wealth. If the metric of money is used, it is only because money is easier to count than welfare. Second, the preferences of the poor must be given as much weight as the preferences of the rich, even though the preferences of the poor are not backed up by the same willingness to pay. If, for example, the poor would pay less than the rich to avoid disease, that does not mean it is less important to prevent disease among the poor.

Why Theory?

Suppose the reader has agreed with most of my arguments and is sympathetic to utilitarianism. Is the evaluation of rival theories (at least of the egalitarian variety) now finished? Is the only remaining task to apply utilitarianism in all areas of policy, however difficult that may be? No; such a suggestion would be contrary to the intuitionist approach of this book. We do not only have intuitive responses to philosophers' examples; we also have intuitive responses to actual policy disputes.

Under the intuitionist approach to moral theory, we test competing theories against each other through the use of examples—often examples very far removed from reality. If, in such examples, a theory yields answers contrary to our intuitive judgments, we have reason to reject the theory. If a theory yields answers in accord with our intuitive judgments, we have reason to accept the theory. But since intuition is considered reliable in evaluating bizarre hypothetical examples, should it not be considered at least as reliable in evaluating real policy disputes? If, in a real policy dispute, our previously favored theory yields an answer contrary to our moral intuition, that presumably should be a reason to reject the theory. We should not follow the theory wherever it may lead, heedless of contrary intuition.

Indeed, the avowedly intuitionist approach of this and similar works raises the question whether theory, utilitarian or otherwise, is at all relevant to policy analysis. If a theory is always subject to being discredited, if it is only as good as its performance on the most recent example, then why should we bother with theory at all? Perhaps we should skip the farfetched examples and intricate analysis, and proceed directly to an intuitive evaluation of policy issues. After all, a theory that yielded policy prescriptions contrary to our intuitive judgments would be rejected in any event.

This objection to intuitionist theory has some force. It has special force when examples are used to support a theory, according to the intuitionist approach, and the theory is used to support or reject a policy, but the policy itself is not subjected to much intuitive evaluation. Robert Nozick's book *Anarchy, State, and Utopia*[2] can be seen as an extended polemic against income redistribution to the poor and other welfare-state policies. Nozick's approach, like mine, is intuitionist. Nozick presents many examples in support of his (then-favored) libertarian theory. In addition to conjuring up the specter of the utility monster (discussed in Chapter 2), Nozick implicitly analogizes the redistribution of income to the redistribution of spouses and body parts. At one point, drawing on Dr. Seuss, he asks: "Does Thidwick, the Big-Hearted Moose, have to abide by the vote of all the animals living in his antlers that he not go across the lake to an area in which food is more plentiful?"[3] However, there is no consideration of whether it seems intuitively wrong to allow people to suffer or die for want of income support.[4]

A reader of *Anarchy, State, and Utopia* who supports income redistribution to the poor could say to Nozick: I agree with you about the redistribution of spouses, the redistribution of body parts, the utility monster, and Thidwick the Big-Hearted Moose. On the other hand, a policy of income redistribution to the poor seems intuitively right to me. And since I too follow an intuitionist approach, in determining my position on income redistribution, it surely makes more sense to be guided by my intuitions about income redistribution than my intuitions about Thidwick the Big-Hearted Moose. So if there is any theory that accounts for my intuitions, it is not libertarianism.

A reader of this book could raise similar, if not exactly identical concerns about my advocacy of utilitarianism and its relevance to policy. If the utilitarian course on a particular issue seems wrong, she presumably would reject utilitarianism, at least with regard to that issue, something that is in keeping with the intuitionist approach. And if the utilitarian course seems right, it is unclear how utilitarian theory adds anything to an intuitive policy decision that she would make in any event.

So what is the point of theory if you are an intuitionist? For one thing, theory can filter information. If we find a theory that matches our intuitive judgments in most cases, we may decide that it is generally worthwhile to gather information and undertake analysis appropriate to the theory, in the expectation that we will find the information we obtain relevant to our intuitive evaluation of policy issues.

Also, intuition may sometimes be uncertain.[5] If we find a theory that matches our intuitive judgments in most cases, we may be content to be guided by that theory even when it commands a policy about which we cannot reach a clear intuitive verdict. This assumes, of course, that theory will be more certain than intuition in some cases.

It is also possible for theory to affect intuition. Once we have accepted a theory, we may find that our intuitions on policy become even more consistent with that theory than they were at the start. If this book were to affect readers' views on policy, possibly it would be through this mechanism.

Finally, theory is interesting for its own sake, apart from whatever role it may have in forming our policy judgments. Theorists should display some modesty about the likely benefits of what they do. I hope to do good theory, and I hope to do good in the world, but I am not at all confident that I will do good in the world by doing good theory.

True, once in a while there appears a philosopher like Peter Singer, who motivates large numbers of people to act so as to reduce suffering. But we cannot all be Peter Singer. I do theory mainly because I like theory. And if you, dear reader, have made it to the end of this book, I imagine that you like theory too.

Notes

Chapter 1.
Introduction

1. These are rough descriptions of the utilitarian and egalitarian distributive injunctions. More detail, definition, and classification are given in Chapters 4 and 5.

2. Except, of course, when I am describing Dworkin's own theory.

3. Amartya Sen, *Inequality Reexamined* (Harvard University Press, 1992), pp. 39–56.

4. G. A. Cohen, "On the Currency of Egalitarian Justice," *Ethics* 99, no. 4 (1989): 906–945.

5. Or, in the terminology of Sen and other economists, the space in which the theories operate. Sen, *Inequality Reexamined,* p. 2.

6. Ian Shapiro, *Democracy's Place* (Cornell University Press, 1996), p. 112. "Principle" is Shapiro's term, "function" is mine.

7. See, for example, Ronald Dworkin, *Sovereign Virtue: The Theory and Practice of Equality* (Harvard University Press, 2000), pp. 79–80.

8. See, for example, Sen, *Inequality Reexamined,* pp. 81–84.

9. John McKie, Jeff Richardson, Peter Singer, and Helga Kuhse, *The Allocation of Health Care Resources: An Ethical Evaluation of the 'QALY' Approach* (Ashgate/Dartmouth, 1998), pp. 99–116.

10. On utilitarianism as equal respect, see Will Kymlicka, *Liberalism, Community, and Culture* (Oxford University Press, 1989), p. 26; and R. M. Hare, "Rights, Utility, and Universalization: Reply to J. L. Mackie," in *Utility and Rights,* ed. R. G. Frey (University of Minnesota Press, 1984), p. 107.

I address some related issues, including the old "separateness of persons" chestnut, in Stein, "Utilitarianism and Conflation," *Polity* 35, no. 4 (2003): 479–490.

11. Sen, *Inequality Reexamined.*

Chapter 2.
Intuitionist Theory and Interpersonal Comparisons

1. By intuitionism I mean the common approach to moral theory described in this paragraph, not the ethical pluralism of W. D. Ross.

2. Judith Jarvis Thomson, "A Defense of Abortion," *Philosophy and Public Affairs* 1, no. 1 (1971): 47–66.

3. For a particularly withering description of the intuitionist style, with specific reference to Thomson, see R. M. Hare, *Essays on Political Morality* (Clarendon Press, 1989), p. 126.

4. I take these terms from Elster. Jon Elster, *Local Justice: How Institutions Allocate Scarce Goods and Necessary Burdens* (Russell Sage Foundation, 1992), pp. 84–96.

5. Actually, these things can be sliced in a number of ways, and there is a considerable variety in terminology. See, for example, L. W. Sumner, *Welfare, Happiness, and Ethics* (Oxford University Press, 1996); Robert Goodin, *Utilitarianism as a Public Philosophy* (Cambridge University Press, 1995), pp. 12–16; T. M. Scanlon, "The Moral Basis of Interpersonal Comparisons," in *Interpersonal Comparisons of Well-Being*, ed. Jon Elster and John Roemer (Cambridge University Press, 1991), pp. 17–44; and James Griffin, *Well-Being: Its Meaning, Measurement, and Moral Importance* (Oxford University Press, 1986). As Goodin notes, the distinctions are often overstated. Goodin, pp. 12–13.

6. Although here the second revolutionary probably does not get much pleasure from strawberries with cream; perhaps this joke would be most appropriately marshaled against an objective account of welfare.

7. Robert Nozick, *Anarchy, State, and Utopia* (Basic Books, 1974), p. 41.

8. In Chapter 9, I discuss an example by Scanlon that is done in the right way, though I disagree with the theory he seeks to support through that example.

9. So although my argument about unconvincing stipulated IPCs can be seen as at least a partial response to Nozick's "utility monster," it is not a response to examples offered by opponents of utilitarianism that involve questionable causality rather than questionable interpersonal comparisons. A response to those latter examples might appeal to the "limits of reason," along lines suggested by Hare and Hardin. R. M. Hare, *Moral Thinking: Its*

Levels, Method, and Point (Clarendon Press, 1981); Russell Hardin, *Morality within the Limits of Reason* (University of Chicago Press, 1988).

10. Thomas DeLeire, "The Unintended Consequences of the Americans with Disabilities Act," *Regulation* 23, no. 1 (2000): 21–24.

11. The number of people on the Social Security disability rolls has increased for reasons that are apparently unrelated to the ADA. See Louis Uchitelle, "Laid-Off Workers Swelling the Cost of Disability Pay," *New York Times*, September 2, 2002, Section A, p. 1.

Chapter 3.
Disability and Welfare

1. For a discussion of this surprisingly difficult definitional issue, see Samuel R. Bagenstos, "Subordination, Stigma, and 'Disability,'" *Virginia Law Review* 86 (2000): 397–534, pp. 405–414.

2. 42 U.S.C. sec. 12102(2). This is the core of the ADA's definition of disability. The ADA goes on to say that the definition also extends to those who have a record of such an impairment or are regarded as having such an impairment.

3. G. A. Cohen, "On the Currency of Egalitarian Justice," *Ethics* 99, no. 4 (1989): 906–945, pp. 919, 921; Ronald Dworkin, *Sovereign Virtue: The Theory and Practice of Equality* (Harvard University Press, 2000), p. 297.

4. Michael A. Stein [no relation], "Review Essay: From Crippled to Disabled: The Legal Empowerment of Americans with Disabilities," *Emory Law Journal* 43 (1994): 245–271, p. 266.

5. Joseph P. Shapiro, *No Pity: People with Disabilities Forging a New Civil Rights Movement* (Random House, 1993), p. 14 (polio).

6. Ibid., p. 85 (deafness).

7. Christopher Newell, "The Social Nature of Disability, Disease, and Genetics: A Response to Gilliam, Persson, Holtug, Draper, and Chadwick," *Journal of Medical Ethics* 25, no. 2 (1999): 172–175, p. 174.

8. Marcel P. J. M. Dijkers, "Correlates of Life Satisfaction among Persons with Spinal Cord Injury," *Archives of Physical Medicine and Rehabilitation* 80, no. 8 (August 1999): 867–876, p. 867.

9. See generally Shane Frederick and George Loewenstein, "Hedonic Adaptation," in *Well-being: The Foundations of Hedonic Psychology*, ed. D. Kahneman, E. Diener, and N. Schwarz (Russell Sage Foundation, 1999), 302–329.

10. Dijkers, "Correlates of Life Satisfaction among Persons with Spinal Cord Injury," p. 867 (citing studies).

11. Philip Brickman, Dan Coates, and Ronnie Janoff-Bulman, "Lottery

Winners and Accident Victims: Is Happiness Relative?," *Journal of Personality and Social Psychology* 36, no. 8 (1978): 917–927.

12. Ibid., p. 919.

13. Ibid., p. 921.

14. Frederick and Loewenstein, "Hedonic Adaptation," p. 322 n. 25.

15. Brickman et al., "Lottery Winners," p. 921.

16. Richard Schulz and Susan Decker, "Long-Term Adjustment to Physical Disability: The Role of Social Support, Perceived Control, and Self-Blame," *Journal of Personality and Social Psychology* 48, no. 5 (1985): 1162–1172.

17. Ibid., p. 1170.

18. Ibid., p. 1166.

19. Ibid.

20. Ibid.

21. Ibid.

22. Ibid.

23. Ibid. (original emphasis).

24. Frederick and Loewenstein, "Hedonic Adaptation," pp. 308–309.

25. For a review of studies of progressive neuromuscular diseases, see Hanoch Livneh and Richard Antonak, "Review of Research on Psychosocial Adaptation to Neuromuscular Disorders: I. Cerebral Palsy, Muscular Dystrophy, and Parkinson's Disease," in *Psychosocial Perspectives on Disability*, ed. D. S. Dunn (Select Press, 1994), 201–230; and Richard F. Antonak and Hanoch Livneh, "Psychosocial Adaptation to Disability and Its Investigation among Persons with Multiple Sclerosis," *Social Science and Medicine* 40, no. 8 (1995): 1099–1108.

26. Ruut Veenhoven, "Two State-Trait Discussions on Happiness," *Social Indicators Research* 43, no. 3 (1998): 211–225, p. 216 ("Depression is not identical to [un]happiness. Though most depressed are unhappy, not all unhappy are depressed.").

27. H-T. Koivumaa-Honkanen et al., "Correlates of Life Satisfaction among Psychiatric Patients," *Acta Psychiatrica Scandinavica* 94 (1996): 372–378, p. 376.

28. Ibid., p. 374.

29. Ibid., p. 376.

30. 42 U.S.C. sec. 12102(2).

31. A. Verri, R. A. Cummins, et al., "An Italian-Australian Comparison of Quality of Life among People with Intellectual Disability Living in the Community," *Journal of Intellectual Disability Research* 43, no. 6 (1999): 513–522, p. 516.

32. Ibid., p. 519

33. Robert A. Cummins, "The Second Approximation to an International Standard for Life Satisfaction," *Social Indicators Research* 43, no. 3 (1998): 307–334, p. 326.

34. Ibid., p. 327.

35. See Frederick and Loewenstein, "Hedonic Adaptation."

Chapter 4.
Utilitarianism and Distribution to the Disabled

1. This chapter is based in part on my article "Utilitarianism and the Disabled: Distribution of Resources," *Bioethics* 16, no. 1 (2002): 1–19.

2. For recent general expositions, see William H. Shaw, *Contemporary Ethics: Taking Account of Utilitarianism* (Blackwell, 1999); and Geoffrey Scarre, *Utilitarianism* (Routledge, 1996).

3. In this book, I generally use "benefit" in this sense, unless otherwise noted. The major exception is Chapter 11, where "benefit" also refers to life years gained. Also, I use the terms "utility" and "welfare" interchangeably. This is a common (if perhaps somewhat sloppy) convention among both supporters and opponents of utilitarianism.

4. See Amartya Sen, *On Economic Inequality,* expanded edition (Oxford University Press, 1997), pp. 44–45 [hereinafter cited as Sen, *OEI*]. However, it is not accurate to say that level IPCs are irrelevant to utilitarianism. If utilitarianism is interpreted to require the distribution of life-saving resources to those people who are happiest, utilitarians must make precisely the kind of level IPCs that they can ignore when *non*-life-saving resources are being distributed. In Chapter 11, I discuss the distribution of life from a utilitarian perspective.

5. John Harsanyi, *Essays on Ethics, Social Behavior, and Scientific Explanation* (D. Reidel, 1976), p. 72; Harsanyi, "Rule Utilitarianism, Equality, and Justice," *Social Philosophy and Policy* 2, no. 2 (1985): 115–127, pp. 125–126.

6. Peter Singer, *Practical Ethics,* 2nd edition (Cambridge University Press, 1993), p. 21.

7. Peter Singer, *One World* (Yale University Press, 2002); Singer, *Practical Ethics;* Singer, *Animal Liberation,* rev. edition (Avon Books, 1990).

8. Thomas Pogge, *World Poverty and Human Rights* (Polity Press, 2002); Charles Beitz, *Political Theory and International Relations,* rev. edition (Princeton University Press, 1999).

9. Stein, "Replace Subsidies with a World Food Stamp Programme," *Financial Times,* Letters, February 14, 2004, p. 12.

10. Those who cannot accept this limitation of the subject matter are free to modify and universalize my examples, as appropriate. Where I speak of a rich society, they are free to hypothesize a rich world.

11. One example of a sensible utilitarian compromise may be the provisions of the Americans with Disabilities Act on public transit. When originally enacted, the ADA required that *new* buses and rail systems be wheelchair-accessible. The ADA did not require that municipalities immediately replace or modify older vehicles. 42 U.S.C. sec. 12142.

12. As explained in Chapter 3, I am using a broad definition of disability, under which all illness is disability.

13. Mark S. Stein, "Diminishing Marginal Utility of Income and Progressive Taxation: A Critique of *The Uneasy Case*," *Northern Illinois University Law Review* 12 (1992): 373–397.

14. Thomas Griffith, "Theories of Personal Deductions in the Income Tax," *Hastings Law Journal* 40 (1989): 343–395, pp. 390–391. To be fair, Griffith also notes that the medical deduction can be justified under a Rawlsian approach. Ibid.

15. Sen, *OEI,* p. 195 (Annexe by Sen and Foster).

16. Ibid., pp. 16–17, 111. Many years ago, Professor Sen sent me a kind note after I had sent him one of my papers. This chapter is my churlish response.

17. T. M. Scanlon, "Preference and Urgency," *Journal of Philosophy* 72, no. 19 (November 1975): 655–669, p. 659.

18. Jon Elster, *Local Justice: How Institutions Allocate Scarce Goods and Necessary Burdens* (Russell Sage Foundation, 1992), pp. 89–90.

19. John Roemer, "Egalitarianism against the Veil of Ignorance," *Journal of Philosophy* 99, no. 4 (2002): 167–184.

20. Marc Fleurbaey, "Equality of Resources Revisited," *Ethics* 113, no. 1 (October 2002): 82–105.

21. Jerome E. Bickenbach, *Physical Disability and Social Policy* (University of Toronto Press, 1993), pp. 217–218.

22. Sen, *OEI,* pp. 16–17.

23. Ibid., p. 17.

24. Ibid., p. 111 (original emphasis).

25. G. W. Brown, "Life Events and Affective Disorder: Replications and Limitations," *Psychosomatic Medicine* 55, no. 3 (1993): 248–259; G. W. Brown, Z. Adler, and A. Bifulco, "Life Events, Difficulties, and Recovery from Chronic Depression," *British Journal of Psychiatry* 152 (1988): 487–498.

26. James P. Morgan, Jr., "Bereavement in Older Adults," *Journal of Mental Health Counseling* 16, no. 3 (1994): 318–326. This view was also expressed

to me in conversation by Dr. Steven Prinz, a noted Chicago psychiatrist who is my cousin.

27. For another example of this type, see Singer, *Practical Ethics,* p. 25. I discuss this example in Chapter 5.

28. As discussed in Chapter 9, this example actually stacks the deck against utilitarianism in a number of ways, but these biasing features are counteracted by the enormous difference in benefit.

29. 20 U.S.C. sec. 1400.

30. This may not be a case in which *fewer* resources would be provided to inefficient utility converters (as in Poor Two-Disability Society). However, the example of special education does demonstrate, once again, that inefficient utility converters can be efficient at the margin, so that utilitarianism might support the allocation of substantial additional resources to them.

Chapter 5.
Egalitarianism and Distribution to the Disabled

1. For general discussions of various aspects of egalitarianism, see Larry Temkin, *Inequality* (Oxford University Press, 1993); Douglas Rae et al., *Equalities* (Harvard University Press, 1989); and Amartya Sen, *Inequality Reexamined* (Harvard University Press, 1992).

2. Derek Parfit, "Equality and Priority," in *Ideals of Equality,* ed. A. Mason (Blackwell, 1998), p. 10.

3. Technically, the term "leveling down" also refers to a decision to reduce the welfare (or resources) only of those who are better off, leaving the welfare (or resources) of those who are worse off unaffected. But it is hard to think of even a hypothetical example in which those who are worse off will be completely unaffected, for good or ill, by what we do to those who are better off; it is far more likely that harming those who are better off will either help those who are worse off (in which case it will not be leveling down) or harm those who are worse off.

4. Robert Nozick, *Anarchy, State, and Utopia* (Basic Books, 1974), p. 206; Ian Shapiro, *Democratic Justice* (Yale University Press, 1999), p. 157; Jan Narveson, "On Dworkinian Equality," *Social Philosophy and Policy* 1, no. 1 (1983): 1–23, p. 16.

5. Temkin, *Inequality,* pp. 279–280.

6. See, for example, Judith Jarvis Thomson, *The Realm of Rights* (Harvard University Press, 1990), pp. 135–148.

7. Temkin, *Inequality,* p. 23.

8. Ronald Dworkin, *Sovereign Virtue: The Theory and Practice of Equality* (Harvard University Press, 2000), p. 87.

9. This describes one aspect of Bruce Ackerman's theory. See Ackerman, *Social Justice in the Liberal State* (Yale University Press, 1980), pp. 201–221.

10. See, for example, Harvey S. Rosen, *Public Finance*, 6th edition (Irwin, 2002), pp. 145–146.

11. The reference is to an example from John Rawls, "Social Unity and Primary Goods," in *Utilitarianism and Beyond*, ed. Amartya Sen and Bernard Williams (Cambridge University Press, 1982), pp. 159–185. For similar resource-egalitarian views, see Ackerman, *Social Justice in the Liberal State*, pp. 46–48; and Dworkin, *Sovereign Virtue*, pp. 11–64.

12. See Sen, *Inequality Reexamined*, pp. 39–56.

13. See G. A. Cohen, "On the Currency of Egalitarian Justice," *Ethics* 99, no. 4 (1989): 906–945.

14. Richard Arneson, "Equality and Equal Opportunity for Welfare," *Philosophical Studies* 56 (1989): 77–93. Arneson has more recently modified his position somewhat. Arneson, "Luck Egalitarianism and Prioritarianism," *Ethics* 110, no. 2 (2000): 339–349; Arneson, "Equality of Opportunity for Welfare Defended and Recanted," *Journal of Political Philosophy* 7, no. 4 (1999): 488–497.

15. Robert E. Lane, *The Loss of Happiness in Market Democracies* (Yale University Press, 2000), pp. 59–76.

16. Dworkin, *Sovereign Virtue*, p. 79; Ackerman, *Social Justice in the Liberal State*, p. 269.

17. See the parallel discussion in Chapter 11 of egalitarian approaches to the distribution of life-saving resources.

18. As noted in Chapter 6, many critics of Rawls have thought that the worst-off class should be defined as people who are severely disabled in some way.

19. Someone with a broken heart has a metaphoric disability, not necessarily a real one.

20. Dworkin, *Sovereign Virtue*, p. 60.

21. "It is one of the most moving experiences in classical music to attend a performance by the wonderfully talented Itzhak Perlman. The Israeli, crippled by polio as a child, limps painfully on elbow crutches on to the platform. He slumps gratefully into a chair, stowing his sticks by his side, and reaches for his violin. Then, as if remorseful Fate is trying to atone for his disability, he plays the great works with a sublime and inspired facility." Roger Watkins, "Classical Choice," *Times of London* March 6, 1999.

22. For similar reasons, the resource-egalitarian argument that welfare

egalitarianism allocates too many resources to those with expensive tastes is far less of an argument against utilitarianism.

23. Terminally ill young people who, not needing expensive medical care, must be given cash grants so that they can receive the lifetime minimum income.

24. Resource egalitarianism and welfare egalitarianism might support national health insurance as an alternative to some current systems, but national health insurance would be very far from the ideal in either theory.

25. Rae et al., *Equalities*, p. 50.

26. This distinction is, I think, insufficiently appreciated in Erik Nord's book *Cost-Value Analysis in Health Care: Making Sense of QALYs* (Cambridge University Press, 1999).

27. Peter Singer, *Practical Ethics*, 2nd edition (Cambridge University Press, 1993), p. 25.

28. John Rawls, "Concepts of Distributional Equity: Some Reasons for the Maximin Criterion," *American Economic Review* 64, no. 2 (1974): 141–146, p. 142.

29. Thomas Nagel, *Equality and Partiality* (Oxford University Press, 1991), p. 78.

30. Ibid.

31. Or, since this is the twenty-first century, trim, fit, and satisfied rich people.

32. Two of the contributions to this discussion are Shelly Kagan, *The Limits of Morality* (Oxford University Press, 1989), and Nagel, *Equality and Partiality*.

Chapter 6.
Rawls

1. This chapter is based in part on my article "Rawls on Redistribution to the Disabled," *George Mason Law Review* 6 (1998): 997–1012. For a more Rawls-sympathetic treatment, which nevertheless acknowledges some of the same problems I discuss, see Harry Brighouse, "Can Justice as Fairness Accommodate the Disabled?," *Social Theory and Practice* 27, no. 4 (2001): 537–560.

2. John Rawls, *Justice as Fairness: A Restatement* (Harvard University Press, 2001) [hereinafter *JAF*].

3. Ibid., p. 7.

4. John Rawls, *A Theory of Justice* (Harvard University Press, 1971), p. 12 [hereinafter *TOJ*]. See also *TOJ*, p. 137. I cite to the original edition of

TOJ, rather than the revised edition, because of the historical importance of the original.

5. Rawls, *JAF*, p. 87.

6. Ibid., pp. 18–19.

7. Ibid., pp. 42–43.

8. Ibid., p. 47; Rawls, *Political Liberalism* (Columbia University Press, 1993), p. 297 [hereinafter *PL*].

9. Rawls, *JAF*, p. 43; *PL*, pp. 6–7.

10. Rawls, *JAF*, p. 57.

11. Ibid., pp. 58–59. Essentially the same list is given in *PL*, p. 181.

12. Rawls, *TOJ*, pp. 97–98 (representative individuals "specified by the level of income and wealth"). To similar effect is *JAF*, p. 65.

13. Rawls, *JAF*, p. 65.

14. Rawls, *TOJ*, p. 155.

15. Rawls, *JAF*, p. 95.

16. Ibid., p. 19.

17. Ibid., p. 112.

18. Ibid., p. 57.

19. Rawls, *TOJ*, p. 92.

20. Rawls, *JAF*, p. 61.

21. Amartya Sen, *Inequality Reexamined* (Harvard University Press, 1992), pp. 81–84.

22. Ackerman, *Social Justice in the Liberal State* (Yale University Press, 1980), pp. 267–269; Dennis Mueller, *Public Choice II* (Cambridge University Press, 1989), p. 419; Kenneth J. Arrow, "Some Ordinalist-Utilitarian Notes on Rawls's Theory of Justice," *Journal of Philosophy* 70, no. 9 (1973): 245–263, p. 251; Robert Nozick, *Anarchy, State, and Utopia* (Basic Books, 1974), p. 190.

23. Rawls, *JAF*, pp. 42–43.

24. Indeed, under any definition of the least advantaged class, other than a poverty-based definition, maximin egalitarianism would lead to problems of excessive redistribution to the least advantaged. Only if the least advantaged class is defined as those who are poorest do members of the least advantaged class automatically cease to be least advantaged as soon as there are people who have fewer material resources than they do.

25. Rawls, *PL*, p. 1; *TOJ*, p. 11.

26. Rawls, *TOJ*, p. 136. It is of course a controversial idea that there would be no social cooperation under a system of general egoism.

27. Rawls, *PL*, p. 166.

28. Rawls, *JAF*, p. 87.

29. Rawls, *PL*, p. 279.

30. Stein, "Rawls on Redistribution to the Disabled."

31. Rawls, *JAF*, pp. 171–172.

32. Ibid., p. 174.

33. Ibid.

34. Ibid., p. 173.

35. Norman Daniels, discussed below in Chapter 9, relies on a principle of fair equality of opportunity, but he concedes that he gives that principle a different interpretation than Rawls does.

36. Rawls, *JAF*, p. 44 n. 7.

37. It might also justify a police state, as discussed in Chapter 10.

38. In *PL*, Rawls made a utilitarian-sounding statement on the distribution of medical care, which I once welcomed as showing that he had found wisdom (i.e., utilitarianism) at last. Stein, "Utilitarianism and the Disabled: Distribution of Resources," *Bioethics* 16, no. 1 (2002): 1–19, p. 17, *quoting* Rawls, *PL*, p. 184. However, Rawls moves away from this position in *JAF*.

39. Rawls, *JAF*, p. 170.

40. Rawls, *PL*, pp. 74–75, 305.

41. Eva Feder Kittay, *Love's Labor: Essays on Women, Equality, and Dependency* (Routledge, 1999), pp. 88–90.

42. Rawls, *JAF*, p. 171.

Chapter 7.
Dworkin

1. See, for example, Ronald Dworkin, *Taking Rights Seriously* (Harvard University Press, 1978), pp. 233–238.

2. Ronald Dworkin, "What Is Equality? Part 2: Equality of Resources," *Philosophy and Public Affairs* 10, no. 4 (1981): 283–345 [hereinafter *EOR*]; Ronald Dworkin, "Will Clinton's Plan Be Fair?" *New York Review of Books,* January 13, 1994, pp. 20–25.

Dworkin has republished *EOR*, virtually unchanged, as Chapter 2 of his book *Sovereign Virtue.* He has republished most of "Will Clinton's Plan Be Fair?" as Chapter 8 of *Sovereign Virtue,* under the chapter title "Justice and the High Cost of Health." In this chapter I cite both to *Sovereign Virtue* and to the original articles.

3. Ronald Dworkin, *Sovereign Virtue: The Theory and Practice of Equality* (Harvard University Press, 2000).

4. This chapter is based in part on my article "Ronald Dworkin on Redistribution to the Disabled," *Syracuse Law Review* 51 (2001): 987–1014.

5. Dworkin, *Sovereign Virtue*, p. 68; *EOR*, pp. 286–287.

6. Dworkin, *Sovereign Virtue*, p. 67; *EOR*, p. 285.

7. Dworkin, *Sovereign Virtue*, pp. 77–78; *EOR*, pp. 297–298.

8. Dworkin, *Sovereign Virtue*, p. 478 n. 5; *EOR*, p. 298 n. 6.

9. Dworkin, *Sovereign Virtue*, p. 102; *EOR*, p. 326.

10. Dworkin, *Sovereign Virtue*, pp. 100–101; *EOR*, p. 324.

11. Dworkin, *Sovereign Virtue*, pp. 80–81; *EOR*, p. 301.

12. Dworkin, *Sovereign Virtue*, p. 80; *EOR*, p. 301.

13. Dworkin, *Sovereign Virtue*, pp. 307–319; "Will Clinton's Plan Be Fair?"

14. Dworkin, *Sovereign Virtue*, p. 311; "Will Clinton's Plan Be Fair?," pp. 23–24.

15. Dworkin, *Sovereign Virtue*, pp. 311–317.

16. In *Sovereign Virtue*, Dworkin also uses the hypothetical insurance device to derive proposals on unemployment benefits, welfare benefits such as the former Aid to Families with Dependent Children, and inheritance taxes. Dworkin, *Sovereign Virtue*, pp. 320–350. Many of the points I make here are applicable to all versions of hypothetical insurance, but for the most part I directly address only hypothetical insurance against disability.

17. Dworkin, *Sovereign Virtue*, p. 79; *EOR*, p. 300. Dworkin goes on to say that the welfare-egalitarian approach is not in practice generous because "it leaves the standard for actual compensation to the politics of selfishness broken by sympathy." Ibid.

18. John Rawls, *A Theory of Justice* (Harvard University Press, 1971), pp. 150–183.

19. The nondisabled could, of course, still sell their labor to the disabled.

20. As noted below, I am speaking of risk preferences with respect to welfare, not with respect to wealth.

21. Someone who is risk neutral with respect to wealth buys no insurance, but someone who is risk neutral with respect to welfare often does buy insurance. In order to be sure that a hypothetical insurance buyer will buy no insurance, we must assume that he is a risk seeker with respect to welfare (though not necessarily a maximal risk seeker).

22. Dworkin recognizes a "mild similarity" between utilitarianism and hypothetical insurance (*Sovereign Virtue*, p. 110; *EOR*, p. 335), but he misses the significance of the greater-benefit criterion that both systems share.

23. To use Sen's terminology, I am speaking of risk neutrality in the space of welfare, not in the space of wealth.

24. Rawls, *A Theory of Justice*, p. 165.

25. See, for example, Steven Shavell, "Suit, Settlement, and Trial: A

Theoretical Analysis under Alternative Methods for the Allocation of Legal Costs," *Journal of Legal Studies* 11, no. 1 (1982): 55–81, p. 61.

26. R. Duncan Luce and Howard Raiffa, *Games and Decisions: Introduction and Critical Survey* (John Wiley and Sons, 1957), pp. 22, 32.

27. Dworkin, *Sovereign Virtue*, p. 79; *EOR*, p. 299.

28. This seems to follow from Dworkin's emphatic statement in *Sovereign Virtue*, p. 297, that pain is a disability. In any event, even if the less-disabled would not be considered "disabled" under Dworkin's original formulation of hypothetical insurance, they could still be allocated additional resources under his "prudent insurance" approach to the allocation of health-care resources.

29. Hal Varian, "Dworkin on Equality of Resources," *Economics and Philosophy* 1 (1985): 110–125, pp. 117–18; Will Kymlicka, *Contemporary Political Philosophy: An Introduction* (Oxford University Press, 1990), p. 79.

30. Rawls, *Theory of Justice*, p. 165.

31. Ibid.

32. Ibid.

33. Ibid., pp. 168–173.

34. While Rawls does not say in *Theory of Justice* that parties in the original position must be assumed to be risk averse, he does say (p. 172) that parties should be assumed to choose "as if" they were "peculiarly" risk averse.

35. If parties in the original position assumed they had an equal chance of being any actual person in society, they would necessarily assume that they had a probability of being disabled that was the same as the actual percentage of disabled people in society. The reverse, of course, is not also true.

36. John Harsanyi, "Cardinal Utility in Welfare Economics and in the Theory of Risk-Taking," *Journal of Political Economy* 61, no. 5 (1953): 434–435; Harsanyi, "Cardinal Welfare, Individualistic Ethics, and Interpersonal Comparisons of Utility," *Journal of Political Economy* 63, no. 4 (1955): 309–321; Harsanyi, *Rational Behavior and Bargaining Equilibrium in Games and Social Situations* (Cambridge University Press, 1977), pp. 48–83; William Vickrey, "Measuring Marginal Utility by Reactions to Risk," *Econometrica* 13, no. 4 (1945): 319–333, pp. 328–333; Vickrey, "Utility, Strategy, and Social Decision Rules," *Quarterly Journal of Economics* 74, no. 4 (1960): 507–535, pp. 523–525.

37. Harsanyi's work is the subject of great controversy because of his attempt to aggregate VNM utility functions. For a discussion, see John Weymark, "A Reconsideration of the Harsanyi-Sen Debate on Utilitarianism," in *Interpersonal Comparisons of Well-Being,* ed. Jon Elster and John Roemer (Cambridge University Press, 1991), pp. 255–320.

38. Harsanyi, "Cardinal Utility in Welfare Economics," pp. 434–445.

39. Harsanyi insists that the hypothetical chooser must be risk neutral in aggregating VNM functions, but the individual VNM functions can reflect a risk-averse or risk-seeking attitude. Harsanyi, *Essays on Ethics, Social Behavior, and Scientific Explanation* (D. Reidel, 1976), pp. 73–74.

40. Harsanyi, "Can the Maximin Principle Serve as a Basis for Morality? A Critique of John Rawls's Theory," *American Political Science Review* 69, no. 2 (1975): 594–606, p. 595.

41. Dworkin, *Sovereign Virtue*, p. 109; *EOR*, p. 335.

42. This is actually the reciprocal of a claim made by Dworkin himself. According to Dworkin, utilitarianism owes part of its appeal to its partial coincidence with Dworkin's own theory. Dworkin, *Sovereign Virtue*, p. 110; *EOR*, pp. 335–336. But Dworkin offers nothing more than bald assertion to support his position; I try to offer some arguments in support of mine.

43. To some extent, my argument concerning hypothetical insurance would also apply to the hypothetical-choice utilitarianism of Harsanyi and Vickrey, but I will not pursue that matter here.

44. R. M. Hare, *Moral Thinking: Its Levels, Method, and Point* (Clarendon Press, 1981), pp. 128–129.

45. Dworkin, *Sovereign Virtue*, pp. 76–77; *EOR*, p. 296.

46. Dworkin, *Sovereign Virtue*, p. 478 n. 5; *EOR*, p. 298 n. 6.

47. Presumably, the tax paid by nondisabled people would also be individualized. So the risk-averse nondisabled would pay an enormous tax, which would be used to provide enormous compensation to the risk-averse disabled. Meanwhile, the risk-seeking nondisabled would pay no tax, and the risk-seeking disabled would receive no compensation.

48. Kenneth Arrow, *Social Choice and Individual Values*, 2nd edition (Wiley, 1963), p. 10. A similar point is made by David Wasserman: "Because we regard attitudes toward risk as part of a person's character ... we feel that people are bound by the decisions under uncertainty they actually make. But it is quite a different thing to base compensation for a disability on the insurance that people *would have* bought against it." Wasserman, "Distributive Justice," in *Disability, Difference, Discrimination: Perspectives on Justice in Bioethics and Public Policy*, ed. A. Silvers, D. Wasserman, and M. Mahowald (Rowman & Littlefield, 1998), p. 170.

49. Dworkin, *Sovereign Virtue*, p. 76; *EOR*, p. 296.

50. Dworkin, *Sovereign Virtue*, p. 313; "Will Clinton's Plan Be Fair?," p. 23.

51. Dworkin, *Sovereign Virtue*, p. 492 n. 7; "Will Clinton's Plan Be Fair?," p. 23 n. 13.

52. Dworkin, *Sovereign Virtue*, p. 106; *EOR*, p. 331.

53. Varian, "Dworkin on Equality of Resources," pp. 118–119.

54. Wasserman, "Distributive Justice," pp. 169–170.

55. Ronald Dworkin, *Taking Rights Seriously* (Harvard University Press, 1978), 151.

56. John E. Roemer, "Equality of Talent," *Economics and Philosophy* 1 (1985): 151–187.

57. John E. Roemer, *Theories of Distributive Justice* (Harvard University Press, 1996).

58. Ibid., p. 151.

59. Ibid., p. 153 n. 7.

60. Ibid., p. 151.

61. Stein, "The Distribution of Life-Saving Medical Resources: Equality, Life Expectancy, and Choice behind the Veil," *Social Philosophy and Policy* 19, no. 2 (Summer 2002): 212–245, pp. 231–233; Stein, "Ronald Dworkin on Redistribution to the Disabled"; Stein, "Rawls on Redistribution to the Disabled," *George Mason Law Review* 6 (1998): 997–1012, p. 1011 n. 55.

62. Marc Fleurbaey, "Equality of Resources Revisited," *Ethics* 113, no. 1 (October 2002): 82–105.

63. Ibid., p. 96.

64. Dworkin, *Sovereign Virtue*, p. 67; *EOR*, p. 285.

65. Dworkin, *Sovereign Virtue*, p. 79; *EOR*, p. 300.

66. This, I think, is the upshot of John Roemer's article "Equality of Resources Implies Equality of Welfare," *Quarterly Journal of Economics* 101 (1986): 751–784. Roemer does not appear to model hypothetical insurance in this article (though he does model it elsewhere); rather, he models equality of resources with natural abilities counted as resources.

67. Dworkin, *Sovereign Virtue*, p. 81; *EOR*, p. 302.

68. Dworkin, *Sovereign Virtue*, p. 80; *EOR*, p. 300.

69. The reader may decide whether I demonstrate a similar opportunism in Chapter 11, by articulating a version of utilitarianism that would reject discrimination against the disabled in the distribution of life.

70. Dworkin, *Sovereign Virtue*, p. 80; *EOR*, p. 300.

71. Dworkin, *Sovereign Virtue*, pp. 79–80; *EOR*, p. 300.

72. Dworkin, *Sovereign Virtue*, p. 79; *EOR*, p. 299.

73. Dworkin, *Sovereign Virtue*, p. 80; *EOR*, pp. 300–301.

74. Jan Narveson, "On Dworkinian Equality," *Social Philosophy and Policy* 1, no. 1 (1983): 1–23, p. 16; Ian Shapiro, *Democracy's Place* (Cornell University Press, 1996), pp. 71–72. Note that utilitarian reasons to avoid forcible transplantation, such as concern over fomenting insecurity, are not necessarily available to the egalitarian.

75. Dworkin, *Sovereign Virtue*, p. 73; *EOR*, p. 293.

76. Dworkin, *Sovereign Virtue*, p. 74; *EOR*, p. 293.

77. Dworkin, *Sovereign Virtue*, p. 76; *EOR*, p. 296.

78. Dworkin, *Sovereign Virtue*, p. 76; *EOR*, p. 296.

79. Dworkin, *Sovereign Virtue*, p. 77; *EOR*, p. 297.

80. Narveson, "On Dworkinian Equality," p. 18. This comment is specifically about income-earning ability, but it applies just as well to disability. See also Shapiro, *Democracy's Place*, p. 71, for a similar view.

81. Dworkin, *Sovereign Virtue*, pp. 74–75; *EOR*, p. 294.

82. Dworkin, *Sovereign Virtue*, p. 74; *EOR*, p. 294.

83. An interesting question is whether Dworkin would apply Redistribute Per Hypothetical Gambles to the initial auction itself. Suppose there was a mistake in the distribution of clamshells, so that some immigrants received fewer clamshells than other immigrants. Would Dworkin say that the proper response is not simply to reallocate clamshells so that everyone has an equal share, but instead to ask whether, in a hypothetical insurance market, the average immigrant would have insured against a mistake in the distribution of clamshells?

84. Ronald Dworkin, "Sovereign Virtue Revisited," *Ethics* 113, no. 1 (October 2002): 106–143, p. 132. This is in response to Fleurbaey's argument in "Equality of Resources Revisited."

85. Dworkin, "Sovereign Virtue Revisited," p. 134.

Chapter 8.
Ackerman

1. Bruce Ackerman, *Social Justice in the Liberal State* (Yale University Press, 1980).

2. Ibid., p. 11 (original emphasis).

3. Ibid., p. 31.

4. Ibid., pp. 31–32.

5. Ibid., p. 58.

6. Ibid., p. 46.

7. Ibid., p. 48.

8. Ibid., p. 114.

9. Ibid., p. 116.

10. Ibid., p. 129.

11. Ibid., pp. 130–131.

12. Ibid., pp. 131–132.

13. Ibid., p. 132 (original emphasis).

14. Ibid., p. 267.

15. Ibid., p. 268.

16. Ibid., p. 269 (original emphasis).

17. Ibid., pp. 130–131.

18. Ibid., p. 117.

19. Ibid., p. 118.

20. Ibid., pp. 117–118.

21. Ibid., pp. 129–132, 169.

22. Joseph P. Shapiro, *No Pity: People with Disabilities Forging a New Civil Rights Movement* (Random House, 1993), pp. 14, 85.

23. Ibid., p. 282.

24. Ackerman, *Social Justice,* p. 116, note 5.

25. Ibid., p. 58.

26. Ibid., p. 132 (original emphasis).

27. Ibid., p. 232.

28. Ibid., pp. 237–239.

29. Ibid., p. 246.

30. Ibid., pp. 246–247 (original emphasis).

31. Ibid., p. 247.

32. Ibid., p. 248.

33. Ibid.

34. Ibid., p. 246.

35. Ibid., p. 270.

36. Ibid., p. 247.

37. Ibid., p. 79.

38. Ibid. (original emphasis).

39. Ibid.

40. Ibid., p. 248.

41. Ibid., p. 271 (original emphasis).

42. Ibid., p. 250.

43. Philippe Van Parijs, *Real Freedom for All: What (if Anything) Can Justify Capitalism?* (Oxford University Press, 1995).

44. Ibid., pp. 58–84.

45. Ibid., p. 83.

46. Ibid., p. 77.

47. Ibid., pp. 77–82.

48. Ibid., p. 78 (emphasis added).

49. Ibid.

50. Ibid., p. 83.

51. Ibid., p. 84.

Chapter 9.
Welfarism Weighted or Unweighted?

1. See Amartya Sen, *Inequality Reexamined* (Harvard University Press, 1992), pp. 39–56.

2. Ibid., p. 92.

3. Ibid., p. 144.

4. Ibid., p. 92 (original emphasis).

5. See G. A. Cohen, "On the Currency of Egalitarian Justice," *Ethics* 99, no. 4 (1989): 906–945.

6. Ibid., p. 908.

7. Ibid., p. 911.

8. Ibid.

9. Ibid. (original emphasis).

10. Norman Daniels, *Just Health Care* (Cambridge University Press, 1985); Daniels, *Am I My Parents' Keeper? An Essay on Justice between the Young and the Old* (Oxford University Press, 1988).

11. In *Justice as Fairness*, Rawls moves somewhat closer to Daniels's position, but Rawls's priority for restorative care is not the same as the priority Daniels gives to the worse off.

12. Daniels, *Just Health Care*, p. 57.

13. Ibid.

14. Ibid., p. 41.

15. Ibid., p. 35.

16. Daniels refers to his principle as fair equality of opportunity, but it is different from Rawls's principle of fair opportunity, even after the modifications made by Rawls in *Justice as Fairness*. Accordingly, I use a different term for Daniels's principle.

17. Daniels, *Just Health Care*, p. 35.

18. Daniels, *Parent's Keeper*, p. 40.

19. Ibid., p. 68 (original emphasis).

20. Ibid., pp. 94–95.

21. It might seem that the Prudential Lifespan Account cannot fully counteract LOPP because the former is concerned only with intergenerational distributive issues. But Daniels is actually ambiguous on this score; at one point he claims that the Prudential Lifespan Account can tell us not only whether to transfer resources from one stage of life to another, but also how to direct those resources. Ibid., p. 79. In any event, the Prudential Lifespan Account must inevitably be used to divide resources within generations as well as across generations, because we cannot decide whether one generation

would benefit more from resources than another generation unless we know what the best use of those resources is for each generation.

22. Martha C. Nussbaum, "The Costs of Tragedy: Some Moral Limits of Cost-Benefit Analysis," *Journal of Legal Studies* 29, no. 2 (June 2000): 1005–1036, p. 1021.

23. Ibid., p. 1024.

24. Peter Singer, "The Welfare, Preferences, and Capabilities of Animals: A Response to Martha Nussbaum," http://philrsss.anu.edu.au/tanner/papers/Singer_Response.rtf [accessed November 6, 2003].

25. Nussbaum, "The Costs of Tragedy," pp. 1028–1031.

26. Martha C. Nussbaum, *Women and Human Development: The Capabilities Approach* (Cambridge University Press, 2000).

27. As noted by a sympathetic commentator, the Norwegian sociologist Kari Waerness, Nussbaum "does not give much place to the human conditions of dependency ... Nussbaum's individual is a healthy and strong adult." Waerness, "Comments on Nussbaum," International Development Ethics Assn. *Newsletter,* June, 2001, available at www.development-ethics.org/document.asp?cid=5007&sid=5002&did=1067 [accessed February 19, 2005].

28. Martha C. Nussbaum, "Capabilities and Disabilities: Justice for Mentally Disabled Citizens," *The Religion and Culture Web Forum: Commentary, March, 2003,* http://marty-center.uchicago.edu/webforum/032003/commentary.shtml [accessed June 14, 2003]. This article was drawn from Nussbaum's Tanner Lectures.

29. Richard Arneson, "Property Rights in Persons," *Social Philosophy and Policy* 9, no. 1 (1992): 205–206.

30. Larry Temkin, *Inequality* (Oxford University Press, 1993), p. 245.

31. Paul Weirich, "Utility Tempered with Equality," *Nous* 17, no. 3 (1983): 423–439, p. 424.

32. Liam Murphy, "Institutions and the Demands of Justice," *Philosophy and Public Affairs* 27, no. 4 (1998): 251–291, p. 263, *citing* an unpublished manuscript by Derek Parfit entitled "On Giving Priority to the Worse Off." This piece by Parfit must surely be the most widely cited unpublished manuscript in contemporary political philosophy.

33. Derek Parfit, "Equality and Priority," in *Ideals of Equality,* ed. A. Mason (Blackwell, 1998), p. 12.

34. Ibid.

35. Amartya Sen, *On Economic Inequality*, expanded edition (Oxford University Press, 1997), pp. 20–21, 52–53; John Harsanyi, "Nonlinear Social Welfare Functions: Do Welfare Economists Have a Special Exemption from Bayesian Rationality?," in Harsanyi, *Essays on Ethics, Social Behavior, and Sci-*

entific Explanation (D. Reidel, 1976), pp. 64–85; Yew-Kwang Ng, "Bentham or Bergson? Finite Sensibility, Utility Functions, and Social Welfare Functions," *Review of Economic Studies* 42, no. 4 (1975): 545–569.

36. Arneson, "Luck Egalitarianism and Prioritarianism," *Ethics* 110, no. 2 (2000): 339–349, p. 341 n. 6.

37. Parfit, "Equality and Priority," p. 12.

38. I leave aside other alternatives, though obviously some find them more appealing than either utilitarianism or prioritarianism.

39. R. M. Hare, *Moral Thinking: Its Levels, Method, and Point* (Clarendon Press, 1981). See also R. M. Hare, "Rights, Utility, and Universalization: Reply to J. L. Mackie," in *Utility and Rights,* ed. R. G. Frey (University of Minnesota Press, 1984), p. 107 ("To have concern for someone is to seek his good, or to seek to promote his interests; and to have equal concern for all people is to seek equally their good, or to give equal weight to their interests, which is exactly what utilitarianism requires. To do this is to treat others' interests in the same way as a prudent person treats his own interests, present and future. It is thus inevitable that having equal concern for everybody will lead us, as Mackie puts it, to weigh together the interests of different individuals 'in the way in which a single thoroughly rational egoist would weigh together all his own desires or satisfactions.'"). I discuss some related issues in Stein, "Utilitarianism and Conflation," *Polity* 35, no. 4 (2003): 479–490.

40. Thomas Nagel, *Equality and Partiality* (Oxford University Press, 1991), pp. 12–13, 65–68. Nagel thinks that equal respect and impartiality require an egalitarian bias, but he does not attempt to derive his position from impartiality or equal respect through formal reasoning, as does Hare.

41. John McKie, Jeff Richardson, Peter Singer, and Helga Kuhse, *The Allocation of Health Care Resources: An Ethical Evaluation of the 'QALY' Approach* (Ashgate/Dartmouth, 1998), p. 90.

42. Peter Singer, *Practical Ethics,* 2nd edition (Cambridge University Press, 1993), p. 25.

43. John Rawls, *A Theory of Justice* (Harvard University Press, 1971), p. 26.

44. Henry Sidgwick, *The Methods of Ethics,* 7th edition (Hackett, 1981), pp. 416–417.

45. Thus, returning to Modified Singer Earthquake Case #5 (leg plus little finger versus thumb), someone who believes it is right to help the worse-off victim may be rejecting utilitarianism, but only if he is convinced that the victim who is worse off will not also benefit more from help.

46. T. M. Scanlon, *What We Owe to Each Other* (Harvard University Press, 1998), pp. 226–227.

47. Ibid., p. 227.

48. Ibid.

49. For an example that relies partly on a stipulated interpersonal comparison, see Thomas Nagel, *Mortal Questions* (Cambridge University Press, 1979), pp. 123–124.

50. This is somewhat less of a problem in Scanlon's pain-relief example, because of the way it is constructed.

51. Of course, if we think that those who can benefit *less* from the medical resource should receive a more-than-equal share, we are rejecting both utilitarianism and marginal egalitarianism. If we think that those who can benefit *more* should receive a more-than-equal share, we are rejecting both marginal egalitarianism and at least some prioritarian views.

52. Similarly, in Modified Singer Earthquake Case #2, discussed in Chapter 5, utilitarianism was opposed to welfare egalitarianism, marginal egalitarianism, and a version of resource egalitarianism, but the difference in benefit was also large.

53. William H. Shaw, *Contemporary Ethics: Taking Account of Utilitarianism* (Blackwell, 1999), p. 120.

54. Ng, "Bentham or Bergson?," pp. 546–547.

55. Ibid.

56. Sidgwick himself may be guilty here.

57. James Griffin, *Well-Being: Its Meaning, Measurement, and Moral Importance* (Oxford University Press, 1986), pp. 178–180. The example Griffin gives is (50, 50) versus (101, 0).

58. This distribution, of course, would not be chosen under *either* utilitarianism *or* prioritarianism. See Parfit, "Equality and Priority," p. 10, for a discussion of the "Leveling Down" objection to uncompromising egalitarianism.

59. For those with truly egalitarian intuitions, this is not a problem: they are willing to depart from utilitarianism even in cases, like the original Singer Earthquake Case, where the difference in benefit is large.

Chapter 10.
Intuition about Aggregation

1. See, for example, T. M. Scanlon, *What We Owe to Each Other* (Harvard University Press, 1998), p. 230; and Alastair Norcross, "Comparing Harms: Headaches and Human Lives," *Philosophy and Public Affairs* 26, no. 2 (1997): 135–167.

2. Scanlon, *What We Owe to Each Other,* pp. 229–241; Thomas Nagel, *Equality and Partiality* (Oxford University Press, 1991), pp. 67–68.

3. See, for example, Scanlon, *What We Owe to Each Other*, pp. 233–234.

4. In Chapter 11, I discuss and criticize an aspect of organ transplant distribution that appears to involve the second kind of aggregation: in general, the rules on split-organ and multiple-organ transplants do not give priority to saving two lives instead of one other life.

5. Scanlon, *What We Owe to Each Other*, pp. 239–240.

6. Ibid., p. 239.

7. Dan W. Brock, "Justice and the ADA: Does Prioritizing and Rationing Health Care Discriminate against the Disabled?" *Social Philosophy and Policy* 12, no. 2 (1995): 159–185, pp. 161–162.

8. Scanlon, *What We Owe to Each Other*, p. 235.

9. There may be readers who are convinced. I doubt, however, that any of these readers have ever received extremely painful electric shocks.

10. Ibid.

11. Norcross, "Comparing Harms," pp. 135–136.

12. Richard Tuck, "The Dangers of Natural Rights," *Harvard Journal of Law and Public Policy* 20 (1997): 683–693.

13. If the worst-off class is comprised of those who cannot exercise the vote, such as people with severe intellectual disability or children with terminal disease, sole political power could be held by their legal representatives.

14. Tuck, "The Dangers of Natural Rights," pp. 692–693.

15. Rawls emphasizes that the demands of public reason are moral demands, not legal demands. Rawls, "The Idea of Public Reason Revisited," *University of Chicago Law Review* 64 (Summer 1997): 765–807, p. 769.

16. John Rawls, *Justice as Fairness: A Restatement* (Harvard University Press, 2001), p. 100.

17. James Griffin, *Well-Being: Its Meaning, Measurement, and Moral Importance* (Oxford University Press, 1986), pp. 151–154; William H. Shaw, *Contemporary Ethics: Taking Account of Utilitarianism* (Blackwell, 1999), pp. 13–14; Geoffrey Scarre, *Utilitarianism* (Routledge, 1996), pp. 23–24.

Chapter 11.
Distribution of Life

1. This chapter is based in part on two of my published articles: "The Distribution of Life-Saving Medical Resources: Equality, Life Expectancy, and Choice behind the Veil," *Social Philosophy and Policy* 19, no. 2 (Summer 2002): 212–245; and "Utilitarianism and the Disabled: Distribution of Life," *Social Theory and Practice* 27, no. 4 (2001): 561–578.

2. See Shane Frederick and George Loewenstein, "Hedonic Adaptation," in *Well-being: The Foundations of Hedonic Psychology,* ed. D. Kahneman, E. Diener, and N. Schwarz (Russell Sage Foundation, 1999), 302–329.

3. John McKie, Jeff Richardson, Peter Singer, and Helga Kuhse, *The Allocation of Health Care Resources: An Ethical Evaluation of the 'QALY' Approach* (Ashgate/Dartmouth, 1998) [hereinafter Singer et al., *Allocation*].

4. Another very controversial idea associated with Peter Singer and Helga Kuhse is that parents should be permitted, in limited circumstances, to decide that their severely disabled infants be killed. Peter Singer, *Practical Ethics,* 2nd edition (Cambridge University Press, 1993), pp. 181–191; Helga Kuhse and Peter Singer, *Should the Baby Live?* (Oxford University Press, 1985). I do not discuss the issue of anti-disabled infanticide in this book. First, I do not consider it a core issue of distributive justice. Second, and relatedly, I do not believe that anti-disabled infanticide poses as big a problem for utilitarianism as does discrimination against the disabled in the distribution of life. A very straightforward and seemingly compelling argument can be made, on utilitarian grounds, for discriminating against the disabled in the distribution of life; if someone has to die, shouldn't it be the person who is less happy? The utilitarian argument for infanticide (and even for abortion) is less obvious, as no one has to die. Finally, I do not address the issue of anti-disabled infanticide because it is difficult to do so without also discussing abortion in general and killing in general, issues that are beyond the scope of this book.

5. John Harris, "QALYfying the Value of Life," *Journal of Medical Ethics* 13, no. 3 (1987): 117–123, pp. 119–120.

6. Singer et al., *Allocation*, pp. 25–30.

7. G. De Wit, J. Busschbach, and F. De Charro, "Sensitivity and Perspective in the Valuation of Health Status: Whose Values Count?," *Health Economics* 9, no. 2 (2000): 109–126 (reviewing studies).

8. Torrance reports a utility of 0.39 for "Being blind or deaf or dumb," based on the time tradeoff approach. George Torrance, "Utility Approach to Measuring Health-Related Quality of Life," *Journal of Chronic Diseases* 40, no. 6 (1987): 593–600, p. 595.

9. $((75 - 50) \times 1.0) - ((75 - 35) \times .5) = 5.$

10. $((75 - 50) \times 1.0) - ((75 - 35) \times .75) = -5.$

11. Singer et al. note that public-opinion surveys have found some support for the view that some priority in the distribution of life should be given to "children and young adults—particularly those with dependent children." Singer et al., *Allocation*, p. 118.

12. John Harris, "Double Jeopardy and the Veil of Ignorance—A Reply," *Journal of Medical Ethics* 21, no. 3 (1995): 151–157, p. 156.

13. John McKie, Helga Kuhse, Jeff Richardson, and Peter Singer, "Double Jeopardy, the Equal Value of Lives and the Veil of Ignorance: A Rejoinder to Harris," *Journal of Medical Ethics* 22, no. 4 (August 1996): 204–208, p. 208.

14. One reason this solution is only tentative is because I am concerned that a distinction between the two kinds of utility could itself become paradoxical.

15. John E. Roemer, *Theories of Distributive Justice* (Harvard University Press, 1996), pp. 161–162 (example involving infant mortality).

16. See also Ian Shapiro, *Democratic Justice* (Yale University Press, 1999), p. 207, on the paradoxes of using life expectancy as an allocation criterion.

17. I say "almost complete priority" because one can imagine cases in which the candidate from the "lucky" race has a very low post-treatment life expectancy in any event.

18. Stein, "The Distribution of Life-Saving Medical Resources," pp. 237–240; Sheryl Gay Stolberg, "The Unlisted: Live and Let Die over Transplants," *New York Times*, April 5, 1998, Section 4, p. 3. Another factor that can keep patients off the list is lack of insurance.

19. Lawrence Altman, "The Doctor's World: For Heart Surgeons, Many Careful Steps," *New York Times*, July 10, 2001, Section F, p. 1.

20. UNOS is a private entity that performs quasi-public functions. UNOS administers the Organ Procurement and Transplantation Network (OPTN). The OPTN is also a private entity, but it is authorized by law to oversee numerous aspects of transplant medicine in the United States. 42 U.S.C. secs. 273–274; 42 C.F.R. part 121. In the past it has been generally accurate to say that UNOS *is* the OPTN, but the identity of these two quasi-official bodies may now be diverging.

21. Stein, "The Distribution of Life-Saving Medical Resources," pp. 240–241; OPTN/UNOS, *Organ Distribution,* available at http://www.optn.org/policiesAndBylaws/policies.asp [accessed December 12, 2004].

22. Stein, "The Distribution of Life-Saving Medical Resources," p. 242. Also, the lung allocation rules have recently been changed so as to make priority depend on an explicit calculation of life expectancy. OPTN/UNOS Policy 3.7.6, available at http://www.optn.org/policiesAndBylaws/policies.asp [accessed December 12, 2004].

23. Robert M. Veatch, *Transplantation Ethics* (Georgetown University Press, 2000), pp. 280, 288–289.

24. As suggested in Harris, "Double Jeopardy and the Veil of Ignorance—A Reply," p. 156.

25. Stolberg, "The Unlisted."

26. F. M. Kamm, *Morality, Mortality, Volume I: Death and Whom to Save from It* (Oxford University Press, 1993), p. 237.

27. Ibid., p. 243.

28. Wayne Sumner has advocated something close to such a life-satisfaction conception of welfare. L. W. Sumner, *Welfare, Happiness, and Ethics* (Oxford University Press, 1996).

29. John Broome, "Good, Fairness, and QALYs," in *Philosophy and Medical Welfare*, ed. J. M. Bell and Susan Mendus (Cambridge University Press, 1988), p. 70.

30. For a description and critique, see Trude Arnesen and Erik Nord, "The Value of DALY Life: Problems with Ethics and Validity of Disability Adjusted Life Years," *British Medical Journal* 319 (November 27, 1999): 1423–1425.

31. John Harris, "More and Better Justice," in *Philosophy and Medical Welfare*, ed. Bell and Mendus, p. 92; Michael Lockwood, "Quality of Life and Resource Allocation," in *Philosophy and Medical Welfare*, p. 50.

32. Lockwood, "Quality of Life and Resource Allocation," p. 50.

33. Veatch, *Transplantation Ethics*, pp. 336–351; Kamm, *Morality, Mortality, Volume I*, pp. 234–240.

34. For discussions of equality and time, see Larry Temkin, *Inequality* (Oxford University Press, 1993), pp. 232–244; and Dennis McKerlie, "Equality and Time," *Ethics* 99, no. 3 (April 1989): 475–491. These authors do not focus on the distribution of life.

35. This would not be a case of "leveling down" to equality; we would be harming those who are better off only if we could to some extent help those who are worse off.

36. See, for example, Judith Jarvis Thomson, *The Realm of Rights* (Harvard University Press, 1990), pp. 135–148.

37. Stein, "The Distribution of Life-Saving Medical Resources," pp. 240–241; OPTN/UNOS, *Organ Distribution*, available at http://www.optn.org/policiesAndBylaws/policies.asp [accessed December 12, 2004].

38. Or, equivalently, we must be confident that the difference between the less urgent candidate's life expectancy with treatment and his life expectancy without treatment is greater than the difference between the more urgent candidate's life expectancy with treatment and her life expectancy without treatment.

Suppose we can give life-saving treatment either to A or to B. Candidate A would die without treatment in 1 month, and she would die with treatment in 6 months. Candidate B would die without treatment in 10 months, and he would die with treatment in 14 months. Here, B would have a longer post-treatment life (14 months versus 6 months), but life-year maximization would tell us to give the treatment to A, the more urgent candidate: she would gain 5 additional months of life, while B would gain only 4 additional months of life. Equivalently, the 14-month post-treatment life of B, the less urgent candidate, would be 1 month shorter than the sum of (1) the post-treatment life of A, plus (2) the difference between the remaining life of B without treatment and the remaining life of A without treatment.

39. Stein, "The Distribution of Life-Saving Medical Resources," pp. 243–244.

40. In practice, the imminence criterion is tied to the present moment, as there are always people who are about to die.

41. Veatch, *Transplantation Ethics,* p. 299.

42. Jon Elster, *Local Justice: How Institutions Allocate Scarce Goods and Necessary Burdens* (Russell Sage Foundation, 1992).

43. Stein, "The Distribution of Life-Saving Medical Resources," pp. 240–241; OPTN/UNOS, *Organ Distribution,* available at http://www.optn.org/policiesAndBylaws/policies.asp [accessed December 12, 2004].

44. Near the end of her book on the distribution of life, Kamm states that "one year to a 20-year-old may, morally speaking, be worth three to a 60-year-old." Kamm, *Morality, Mortality, Volume I,* p. 316. For the reasons given in the text, I conclude that in this example, at least, Kamm actually gives life expectancy at least as much weight as age.

45. John Harris, "Justice and Equal Opportunities in Health Care," *Bioethics* 13, no. 5 (1999): 392–404; Harris, "Would Aristotle Have Played Russian Roulette?" *Journal of Medical Ethics* 22, no. 4 (1996): 209–15; Harris, "Double Jeopardy and the Veil of Ignorance—A Reply," pp. 151–157; Harris, "More and Better Justice," pp. 75–96.

46. Dan W. Brock, "Justice and the ADA: Does Prioritizing and Rationing Health Care Discriminate against the Disabled?" *Social Philosophy and Policy* 12, no. 2 (1995): 159–185; Brock, "Ethical Issues in Recipient Selection for Organ Transplantation," in *Organ Substitution Technology: Ethical, Legal, and Public Policy Issues,* ed. Deborah Mathieu (Westview Press, 1988): 86–99.

47. Broome, "Good, Fairness, and QALYs," pp. 57–73; Broome, "Selecting People Randomly," *Ethics* 95, no. 1 (October 1984): 38–55.

48. Harris, "More and Better Justice," p. 93.

49. Broome, "Good, Fairness, and QALYs," pp. 58–59.

50. Harris, "Justice and Equal Opportunities in Health Care," p. 399.

51. Brock, "Justice and the ADA," p. 168. The example Brock gives also involves a difference in quality of life, but I think the difference in life expectancy does all the intuitive work.

52. Ibid., p. 169.

53. Ibid.

54. Brock's weighted lottery might also give a greater chance to candidates who would have a better post-treatment quality of life, but I ignore that issue here and focus on life expectancy.

55. Could such a system also be supported on utilitarian grounds? Probably not. For one thing, the resulting flow of scarce life-saving resources to rich old men would come at a great cost in life years. This consideration, at the very least, makes the utilitarian case for an auction system far less compelling than the resource-egalitarian case for such a system.

56. Veatch, *Transplantation Ethics,* pp. 325–335.

57. Children, especially, can benefit from split-organ transplants. Mark A. Hardy and Elliott R. Goodman, "Transplantation," *JAMA* 271, no. 21 (June 1, 1994): 1716–1717.

58. See UNOS Policies 3.7.7, 3.9.3, available at http://www.optn.org/policiesAndBylaws/policies.asp [accessed December 12, 2004].

59. This effect is also possible in aggregation cases that do not involve the distribution of life, but it would be more limited in such cases.

Chapter 12.
Conclusion

1. More precisely, the poor gain more in welfare, from redistribution, than the rich lose, at least up to a point.

2. Robert Nozick, *Anarchy, State, and Utopia* (Basic Books, 1974).

3. Ibid., p. 269.

4. Mark Stein, "Nozick: A Utilitarian Reformulation," *Northern Illinois University Law Review* 18 (1998): 339–350, p. 345.

5. My discussion here benefits from John Rawls's famous treatment of reflective equilibrium in *A Theory of Justice* (Harvard University Press, 1971), pp. 48–52. However, as my approach is more intuitionist than Rawls's, I present my ideas in a straightforward manner rather than as a commentary on Rawls.

Index